ECONOMICS FOR AGRICULTURALISTS
A BEGINNING TEXT IN AGRICULTURAL ECONOMICS

GRID SERIES IN AGRICULTURAL ECONOMICS

Consulting Editor
JOHN SJO, Kansas State University

Aplin and Casler, *Capital Investment Analysis*
Sjo, *Economics for Agriculturalists*
Smith, *Basic Horticultural Concepts & Practices*

ECONOMICS FOR AGRICULTURALISTS
A BEGINNING TEXT IN AGRICULTURAL ECONOMICS

by

John Sjo
Professor of Agricultural Economics
Kansas State University

©COPYRIGHT GRID, INC. 1976
4666 Indianola Avenue
Columbus, Ohio

ALL RIGHTS RESERVED. No part of this publication may be reproduced, stored in a retrieval system, or transmitted, in any form or by any means, electronic, mechanical, photocopying, recording or otherwise, without prior written permission of the copyright holder.

Printed in the United States.

I.S.B.N. No. 0-88244-072-1
Library of Congress Catalog Card Number 75-26011

Printing: 10 9 8 7 6 5 4 3

To my family
        Irma
        Lisa
        Eric
and to
        Robert
        of my family
        of students

TABLE OF CONTENTS

PART I: INTRODUCTION AND CHANGES IN THE UNITED STATES AGRICULTURE

Chapter   Page

1 **Economics for Agriculturalists**   3
Everyone an Economist; A Study of Human Behavior; Economics Defined; Agricultural Economics; Approaches to Studying Economics; Economic Problems; Limitations; The Plan for the Book

2 **Structure and Changes in United States Agriculture**   9
Definitions; Explanation of the Definitions; The Structure of United States Agriculture; Effects of the Changes in Agriculture

PART II: CONCEPT OF DEMAND

3 **Agriculture Produces for Consumption**   23
Consumer Sovereignty; Consumer Preference; Indifference Curves

4 **Consumer Behavior in the Market**   34
Demand Defined; Demand Schedule; Law of Demand; Change in Demand; Market Demand; Income and Substitution Effect; Income Elasticity; Significance of Income Elasticity of Demand for Food; Price Elasticity of Demand; Effect of Price Elasticity on Total Revenue; Nature of Demand for Agricultural Products; Elasticity of Demand Information as a Basis for Public Policy; In Summary

PART III: CONCEPT OF SUPPLY

5 **Producer Behavior in the Market**   53
Production; Factors of Production; Production Problems; Concept of Production; Some Definitions; Diminishing Returns; Productivity Possibilities; Use of Assumptions

Chapter		Page
6	**The Factor-Product Relationship — How Much to Produce** Stages of Production; Point of Inflection; Profit Maximization; Special Problems and Limitations; In Summary	63
7	**The Cost of Production** Classification of Costs; Computation of Costs; Relation of Costs to the Production Function; Profit Maximization; Changes in Technology; Time and Costs; Economies of Scale; In Summary	77
8	**The Factor-Factor Relationship: How to Combine Inputs** Factor Substitution; Definitions; Profit Maximization Criterion; Profit Maximization for Imperfect Substitutes; Profit Maximization for Constant Substitutes; Profit Maximization for Perfect Complements; Effect of a Change in Input Prices; Expansion of Business Size	87
9	**The Product-Product Relationship—How to Combine Enterprises** Definitions; Types of Product-Product Relationships; Profit Maximization; Profit Maximization Criterion; Business Expansion; In Summary	103
10	**Concept of Supply** Supply Defined; The Law of Supply; Determining a Supply Schedule; Market Supply; Change in Supply; Elasticity of Supply	115

PART IV: MARKETS AND PRICE DETERMINATION

11	**Organization and Structure of Agricultural Markets** Role of Prices; Consumers and Producers Meet in the Market; Market Defined; The Flow of Agricultural Products and Inputs; Agricultural Marketing; Marketing Efficiency; Market Structure; In Summary	123
12	**Price Determination** Pricing Under Perfect Competition; Pricing Under Imperfect Competition; In Summary	133

PART V: AGRICULTURAL BUSINESS MANAGEMENT AND ORGANIZATION

Chapter		Page
13	**The Role of Management in Economic Activity** Management Defined; Management—A Part of Economic Activity; Functions of Management; The Return to Management	143
14	**Types Of Business Organization** Types of Business Organization; Sole Proprietorships; Partnerships; Corporations; Special Types of Business Organization; Business Organization for Agriculture; The Farmer and The Corporation	149

PART VI: WORLD AGRICULTURE

15	**World Agriculture** The Two Worlds; The Role of Agriculture in Economic Growth; Agricultural Resources; Population Growth; Food Production Trends; Man's Alternatives; Trade in Agricultural Products	163

PART VII: AGRICULTURAL PROBLEMS AND POLICIES

16	**Rural Welfare** Quality of Life; Changes in Rural Population; Employment Opportunities; Education; Income; Health Facilities; Housing; Public Services	185
17	**The Economic Control of Agriculture** What is Meant by Economic Control; The Basis For The Problem; What Has Been Happening in Market Decisions; What Has Been Happening to Control of Agricultural Resources; What Has Happened to Farmers' Ability to Use Political Power to Achieve Economic Goals; What Alternatives For Farmers; In Summary	195
18	**Agriculture Today — Farm Income, Prices, Markets, Energy, International Trade, and Taxes** Prices and Income; Marketing Costs; The Futures Market; Energy; International Trade; Taxes	201

PREFACE

Teaching principles of agricultural economics since 1967, I gradually developed a set of objectives for the course. A principles course must be simultaneously a basic introduction to economics for those majoring in agricultural economics and an application of economics to agriculture for nonmajors. It must be both a building block and a one-time, general education course. It must be presented so a student links previous experiences to the economic ideas taught. Rural youth have strong convictions about agriculture's place in the economy and strong commitments to agriculture. That makes them skeptical of consumers, middlemen, foreign trade, farmers' depending on other sectors of the economy or government, and the academic discipline of economics and its teachers. On the other hand, urban youth who choose to study agriculture have had little experience in economics; and almost none in agriculture. An economics teacher, more than other agricultural teachers, needs to appreciate and understand the convictions and commitments of both groups of students. Otherwise he could unwillingly make economics a traumatic experience rather than the beginning of a new understanding, a new viewpoint, and a new appreciation of agriculture.

In this text I start where the high school graduates are, to link with their previous experiences and education, to be sensitive to their values, and to build from that point. To do that, *Economics for Agriculturalists* is problem oriented. Basic economic concepts are presented and related to agricultural problems. The interdependence of the subsectors of agriculture is emphasized: among farming, agribusiness, and government; between agriculture and other sectors of the economy; and among individuals within agriculture. The significance and role of consumers to agriculture are presented. Special recognition is given to the concept that farmers are a part of a worldwide community and that world agricultural problems are vital to today's farmer.

If students who use this book can say they gained a better understanding of the economic relationships in agriculture, the book's goal will be satisfied.

Over the years many people encouraged and urged me to write an introductory agricultural economics text for aspiring agriculturalists. Several deserve special acknowledgment.

Nils Anderson, senior editor, Grid, Inc., encouraged, guided, and helped during the entire process of producing the book.

Economics for Agriculturalists was written in shorter time because Paul L. Kelley, Head, Department of Economics, and Carroll V. Hess,

Dean, College of Agriculture, both of Kansas State University, supported the project by releasing me from teaching responsibilities the spring semester, 1974. I benefitted from the experience of John Riley, Kansas State, who tested the first draft in the classroom.

Professor Robert W. Taylor's detailed, constructively critical review was most helpful in improving the accuracy and quality of the text. His gentle and sympathetic way of making suggestions was encouraging and stimulating.

The vitality, optimism, and inquisitiveness of hundreds of students I have had in the principles class have stimulated and rewarded me. There is a bit of each one of them in this book—and more than a bit of some, Robert Munson, for example. As a student and later a student teaching assistant, he encouraged me to write the book, then conscientiously reviewed the hand-written draft.

I am indebted to Arlo Biere for years of stimulating and interesting conversation and debate; for encouragement to strive for excellence, for faith in teaching; and for assuming my teaching responsibilities on his own initiative while I started the text. That committed me to finish it. During the writing his suggestions, ideas, and evaluations assisted in developing the logic and organization of the text.

Irma Sjo, wife, partner, and confidant, earned the most special recognition—for her faith that I could write the book and for assistance in preparing it. She was the first editor and reviewer. She corrected spelling and grammar, typed and retyped the manuscript, and proofed the final draft. Most importantly she and our children, Eric and Lisa, made a home that encouraged and supported writing.

Without the help of everyone mentioned and many others, *Economics for Agriculturalists* would not have been written. Even with their help the book may still contain errors and weakness. For them I alone am responsible.

> John Sjo
> Professor of Agricultural Economics
> Kansas State University
> January 1, 1976

PART I

INTRODUCTION AND CHANGES IN UNITED STATES AGRICULTURE

ECONOMICS FOR AGRICULTURALISTS   1

EVERYONE AN ECONOMIST

Every day each of us is confronted with economic choices. Each of us must choose which goods, services, and activities mean most to us. We have limitations to our time and resources available for acquiring the goods, services, and activities we want. How we decide to use the scarce resources to fulfill our unlimited wants is the process of economizing. From the time we receive our first nickels and dimes for treats we must decide which treat to buy with the coins. And beginning in childhood, we must choose among opportunities—whether to go with Dad to the pasture or with Mother to the store. Making such a choice is an economizing decision. As we grow older the economizing decisions become more complex—attending college or taking a job; buying a tractor or adding to the cowherd; modernizing the milking barn or buying a living room carpet. All of us continually practice the art of economizing, but not all of us study or understand economics.

Agriculturalists, farmers, agribusinessmen, and public administrators are faced with economizing problems every day. Studying the application of economic principles to agriculture is no assurance of success in economic decision making but should give one a better understanding of the economizing process and lead to better decisions.

Because each of us must economize many times daily, our practice of economics is much greater than our understanding of economic theories. Daily we use the ideas and terms of economics: demand, supply, wealth, prices, competition. But the everyday usage (often quite different from the scientific meaning of the terms) leads to confusion and misunderstanding, which can be corrected only by carefully defining economic concepts and terms so that all of us will use them in the same way.

A STUDY OF HUMAN BEHAVIOR

Economics is a social science. Other social sciences include sociology, political science, parts of psychology, and anthropology. All are academic disciplines in which different kinds of human behavior are described and studied. Social scientists study both individual and group human behavior.

Each type of human behavior is influenced by the other types. Economic behavior is influenced by our political behavior. Rationing energy, a political decision, has great economic consequences. The social customs of people, such as diet preferences, greatly influence economic decisions in farming. Although this text primarily explains economic concepts as applied to agriculture, the reader must remember that economics cannot be studied without an understanding and appreciation of the other social sciences.

Economics is a study of these kinds of human behavior:
1. How people make a living
2. How people produce goods and services
3. How people exchange goods and services
4. How people acquire wealth

ECONOMICS DEFINED

To define economics we must consider four separate parts:
1. Unlimited wants of people
2. Limited resources
3. Allocation of resources
4. Designated time period

Combining the four parts into a single statement provides a working definition of economics. *Economics is a study of how people, individually and in groups, allocate scarce resources among competing wants to maximize satisfaction over time for each and for the group.*

AGRICULTURAL ECONOMICS

Agricultural economics is an applied social science in which the principles and analytical methods of economics are used to seek solutions to the economic problems in agriculture. Broadly, two types of economic problems confront agriculturalists: Agricultural economists must determine the needs and wants of consumers for agricultural products; and they must deal with the problems of production and distribution of agricultural products. Traditionally agricultural economists have been most concerned with the second type. Today, however, the economy is becoming more consumer oriented, leading agricultural economists to seek a better understanding of consumers' wants.

AGRICULTURAL ECONOMICS AND OTHER STUDIES

The agricultural student seeking to understand the economics of agriculture should be aware that economics cannot be applied to agriculture independent of and separate from the knowledge gained in other courses. Effective use of any specialized knowledge depends upon the user's ability to integrate that knowledge with all other knowledge acquired. For example, the gains from effective marketing may be lost through ineffective feeding methods on a livestock farm. Figure 1-1 shows the relationship of agricultural economics to other areas of knowledge.

ECONOMICS FOR AGRICULTURALISTS   5

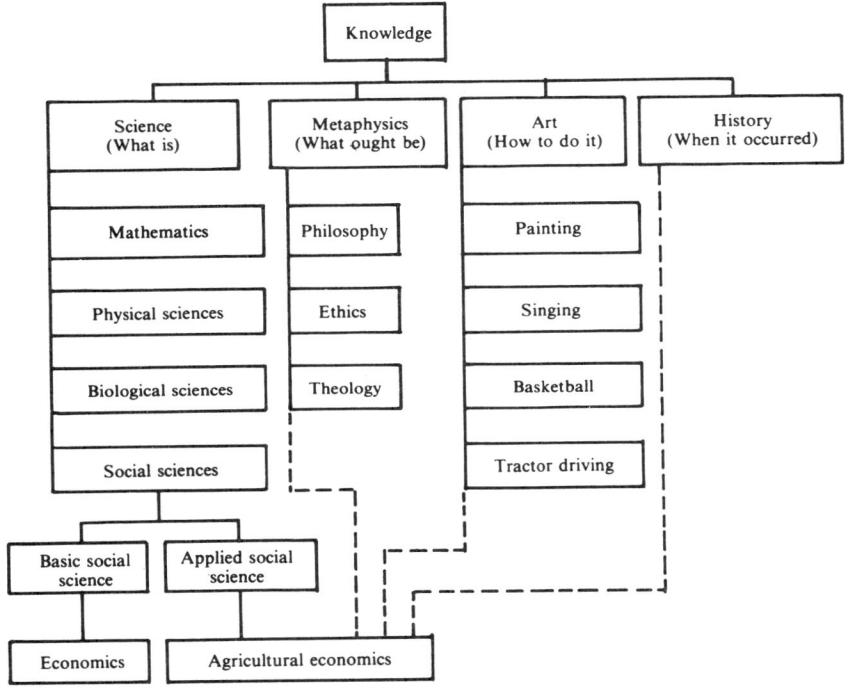

Figure 1-1. Agricultural Economics is Related to Other Areas of Knowledge.

APPROACHES TO STUDYING ECONOMICS

THEORETICAL—APPLIED

An academic discipline is based on a body of fundamental knowledge referred to as theory. Sometimes pure theory is studied; other times, theory is applied to solving specific problems. In agricultural economics we must understand theoretical concepts before we can effectively use theory to solve problems. In this text the emphasis is on using theory to solve problems, but first the theories will be presented. As a student you should guard against falling into the trap of believing applied economics is more practical than theoretical economics. Application is relevant to a specific problem only so long as the problem lasts. Your understanding the theory underlying the application, which remains with you after a specific problem is gone, can be applied again and again when similar problems arise. Applied science has shorter usefulness than theoretical science. Because the height of your professional productiveness is probably twenty years in the future, the economic theory you understand today may be more practical then than the applied economics you find more useful today. Theory gives the basis for solving problems. A student of agricultural economics should judge the value of his studies by how well they prepare him for solving problems.

Theory is a general body of knowledge that describes a certain phenomenon. Theories are built up through observation (inductive learning) and logical reasoning (deductive learning). Theory permits one to abstract from reality, so that one variable can be studied by itself. The real test of a theory is how well it describes reality and how useful it is in solving real world problems. Specifically, theories simplify complex relationships, provide basis for problem identification, for classification, and for problem solving.

MICRO—MACRO

Two major areas of study have emerged within economics: microeconomics and macroeconomics. Economists are concerned with the economic activities of individuals and of groups. *In microeconomics we study the activities of individual producers and consumers and the market they make up.* Macroeconomics is concerned with an aggregation of economic units or with the whole economy. *Macroeconomics deals largely with problems of national income, employment, savings, investment, and inflation.* Agricultural economists deal mostly with organizing individual business firms for optimal resource use. Consequently, teaching has emphasized microeconomics. But now that the various sectors of the economy have become more interdependent, such economic problems as unemployment, inflation, and investment levels have a greater impact on the farmer and the agribusinessman. Today's agricultural student needs to understand not only how to organize a business for optimum returns but how changes in the whole economy affect his economic decisions.

CONSUMPTION—PRODUCTION

Another two-way split of economics is between the consumers and the producers. The two are irrevocably linked and interdependent. The producer turns out a product or service to meet the needs of the consumer. The consumer depends upon the producer for the goods and services to satisfy his needs and wants. In economics, considering each separately has been useful because the behavior of each determines the characteristics of each side of the market—demand by the consumers, supply by the producers.

Agricultural economists, until recent years, have emphasized the economics of production because they were working with the problems of individual farmers, each of whom found it difficult to recognize the significance of the consumer upon his business. In recent years the consumer has often raised his voice to state his preferences, and farmers are becoming more aware of him.

POSITIVE—NORMATIVE

Economists have long disagreed among themselves on the relative merits of the positive and normative approaches to economics. In the positive approach the economist reports what he finds without trying to determine whether the findings are good or bad. The positive economist only determines the alternatives, without trying to identify what is best. In the positive approach the economist avoids value judgments. In the normative approach the economist may make judgments about observed economic facts.

Observing that farm incomes are lower than nonfarm incomes is positive economics. Concluding that farm incomes based on that observation are lower than they should be is normative economics.

ECONOMIC PROBLEMS

Every society, whether primitive or advanced, whether educated or uneducated, whether individualistic or centrally controlled, must deal with four basic economic problems:
1. What and how much to produce
2. How to produce the products
3. How to distribute the products
4. How to distribute the benefits from production

LIMITATIONS

All studies have their own limitations. Expectations beyond these limits result in disappointments by those engaged in the studies. In studying economics, students should recognize that our limited understanding of individual human behavior limits our understanding of economics. Often economists' effectiveness is limited by their inability to measure economic variables accurately. For example, how does one measure satisfaction? In most sciences laboratory experimentation is the usual method of studying identified variables. When studying human behavior the social scientist cannot bring his subjects into the laboratory. Also, it has been found that observed behavior is often different from true behavior (that of the subject if left unobserved).

ASSUMPTIONS

To simplify complex situations and relationships, scientists often make assumptions. For example, physicists assume a "vacuum" for much of their work. An economist assumes that the objective of a business is to make profits. The purpose of assumptions is to reduce the number of variables to be studied, thus making it easier to determine relationships among the factors being observed. Because social scientists seldom can use laboratory experimentation for their studies, they make greater use of assumptions than do biological and physical scientists.

THE PLAN FOR THE BOOK

With that brief explanation of economics, we are ready to begin our study of economic ideas and their application to agricultural problems.

This text is divided into eight parts. The first four parts, **Chapters 1 through 12,** introduce the basic microeconomic principles and show how they are used to explain the economics of consumption and of production as related to agriculture. Part V, Chapters 13 and 14, is a survey of the role of management and alternative types of business organization used in the agricultural sector of the economy. Part VI, Chapter 15, on international agriculture provides a broader perspective for students. Part VII, **Chapters 16 through 18** deals with the national economic problems of agriculture. Topics included are farm prices, farm income, marketing costs, futures marketing, energy, international trade, and taxes.

That organization permits me first to introduce economic concepts, then to show their application to agricultural situations, and finally to consider the most pressing economic problems in today's agriculture.

SUGGESTED READINGS

Doll, John P., Rhodes, V. James, and West, Jerry G. *Economics of Agricultural Production, Markets, and Policy.* Richard D. Irwin, Inc., 1970, Chapter 1.

Leftwich, Richard H. *The Price System and Resource Allocation*, 3rd Edition. Holt, Rinehart, and Winston, 1966, Chapters 1 and 2.

Peterson, Willis L. *Principles of Economics: Macro*, Revised edition. Richard D. Irwin, Inc., 1974, Chapter 1.

Peterson, Willis L. *Principles of Economics: Micro*, Revised edition. Richard D. Irwin, Inc., 1974, Chapter 1.

Samuelson, Paul A. *Economics, An Introductory Analysis*, 9th Edition. McGraw-Hill, 1973, Chapters 1 and 2.

Smith, Warren L. *Macroeconomics.* Richard D. Irwin, Inc., 1970, Chapter 1.

STRUCTURE AND CHANGES IN UNITED STATES AGRICULTURE   2

In this chapter we define and explain agriculture, farming, and agribusiness. We show the significance of each and the interrelationships among them and with the whole economy. Terms so familiar to us would seem to need little explanation. But as is often the case, everyday terms have a way of meaning different things to different people. When reading agricultural economic texts, different authors use the terms differently. You will also find the terms applied differently in curriculum and research organization from the textbook definitions. The confusion arises partly because of changes in agriculture that have occurred over the last hundred years.

In 1870 the United States was just moving into the era of commercial agriculture. At that time most farms were small self-sufficient units that produced little for sale. Agriculture was what happened on farms. There was little nonfarm agricultural business. Few business principles were used by farmers in operating their farms, and agriculture was considered an economic activity distinctly separate and different from business. All that has changed. Farmers today are businessmen. Nonfarm businesses are engaged in what were once agricultural activities, for example, processing food, mixing livestock feeds, operating commercial feedlots. The term "agribusiness" was coined to describe the combining of agricultural and business activities, but after several years of usage we still have not found a fully acceptable and agreed-upon meaning.

DEFINITIONS

In this text we use the following definitions in discussing the structure of agriculture.

Agriculture is the whole complex of producing, processing, and distributing plant and animal raw materials, supplying farm inputs, and providing public services to farmers.

The agricultural industry as we have defined it has three parts: the farm subsector, the agribusiness subsector, and the public service subsector. Each is defined in the following paragraphs.

Farming is the on-farm part of agriculture and includes producing plant and animal raw materials for food, fiber, and industrial uses.

Agribusiness is the off-farm part of agriculture and includes the processing and distributing of plant and animal raw materials and supplying inputs to farmers.

Public service is the federal, state, and local government activities that are related to farming and agribusiness and includes education, research, information, regulation, inspection, and control.

EXPLANATION OF THE DEFINITIONS

This textbook uses a definition of agriculture consistent with its original meaning. Originally agriculture referred to the aggregate of all the functions performed on all farms. The whole of farming was called agriculture. Farms were the individual units within agriculture. The small self-sufficient individual farms produced nearly all the farm products needed for the farm family consumption and as inputs for further farm production (horses for power, oats and hay for horse feed, posts, seeds, etc.), processed nearly all farm products (churning butter, butchering, preserving fruits and vegetables, etc.), stored the farm products on the farm, and distributed most of the farm products to the ultimate consumer, the farm family itself. The farm was the basic agricultural unit and was the center of most agricultural activity.

That centuries-old concept has been greatly affected by dramatic changes in the structure of agriculture. In the last several decades nearly all farm functions of processing, distributing, and supplying have been removed from the farm. The farm remains primarily the producer of raw materials. As these changes occurred, the term agriculture was sometimes used to identify the aggregate of farms, sometimes to identify the original functions of agriculture whether now performed by farm or nonfarm units. This book uses the latter meaning—agriculture is the whole complex of individual units producing, processing, and distributing farm products and supplying farm inputs whether farm or nonfarm located. Almost all these activities are accomplished by individual private units, but in the last century a governmental involvement in agriculture, which we identify here as a part of agriculture, has gradually been added.

We have defined farming, once the dominant function of agriculture and the principal economic activity of the nation, as the on-farm part of agriculture. Today farming is limited almost exclusively to producing raw materials—food, fiber, feeds, oil seeds, etc.—most of which go to nonfarm businesses to be processed, stored, and distributed. Farm families largely meet their own consumption and farm input needs by purchasing from nonfarm firms.

As the functions of processing, storing, distributing, and supplying were moved to nonfarm businesses, neither the term "agriculture" nor "farm" seemed suitably descriptive of these new businesses. Simultaneously farmers were adopting modern business practices and in many ways had more in common with urban businesses than with self-sufficient farms of the past. In search of a term describing both the farm and nonfarm agricultural-related businesses, agriculturalists gradually began to use "agribusiness." However, it has not found wide acceptance, particularly when used to include farm businesses. As used today, most agriculturalists include only the nonfarm processors, distributors, and suppliers when they use the term agribusiness. Most Land Grant College curriculum and courses use agribusiness to cover only the nonfarm activities. Farm businesses continue to be known as farms. "Agriculture" is most commonly used to include both farm and nonfarm businesses and the public services related to agriculture.

STRUCTURE AND CHANGES IN UNITED STATES AGRICULTURE 11

The purpose of definitions is to state clearly and concisely the widely accepted meaning of terms. In our judgment the term agribusiness today as used by agriculturalists should be limited to the nonfarm sector of agriculture.

Since many nonfarm firms service a wide range of clientele, only part of their business activity is agriculturally related. A good example would be Sears, Roebuck and Company, a business that provides inputs directly to farmers, but also sells to nonfarm businesses and other consumers. A large portion of the petro-chemical industry's production is sold to farms; some goes to processors and farm suppliers, but much goes to industries and consumers far removed from farming. The same is true of machinery, automotive, banking, insurance, and many other industries. Should those businesses be classified as agribusinesses—fully, partly, or not at all? In this text we consider only that portion of their output sold directly to farm businesses as agribusiness.

Keys used in this text to determine if a business is engaged in agribusiness are: Is it selling inputs to farmers and is it serving as a link between the farm producer and final consumer?

The third sector of agriculture is federal, state, and local government activities associated with agriculture. Most government activities came into existence after the Department of Agriculture was established in 1862. We shall consider this as a part of agriculture.

THE STRUCTURE OF UNITED STATES AGRICULTURE

Definitions developed in this chapter let us use the following structural model to describe the agricultural industry:

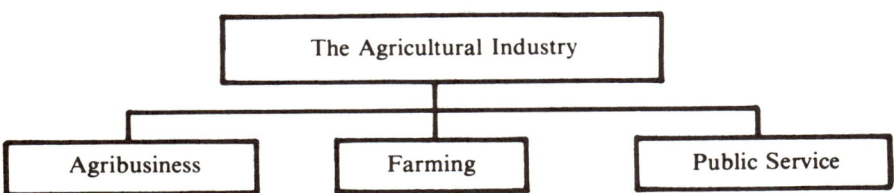

This simplified illustration of the agricultural sector and its subsectors is further developed in Figure 2-1 to show interrelationships and interdependence among the three subsectors and between agriculture and the rest of the economy.

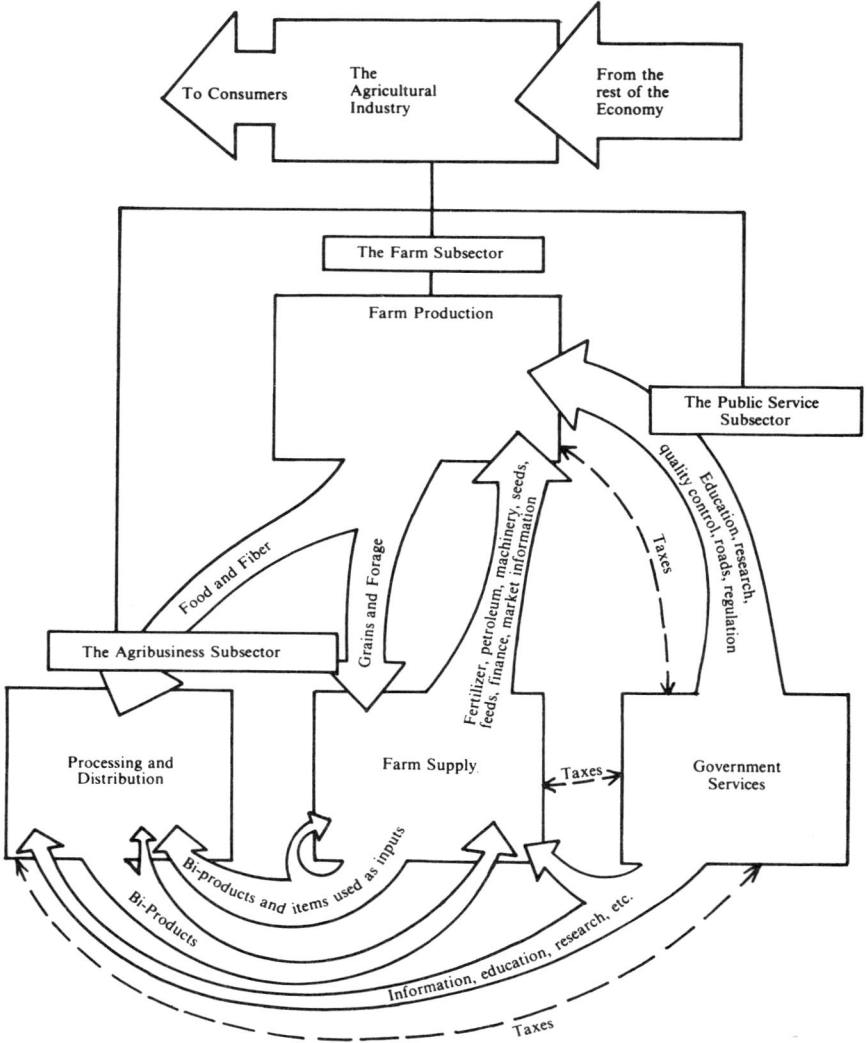

Figure 2-1. The Structure of the United States Agricultural Industry.

AGRICULTURAL INDUSTRY

The total agricultural industry is one of the largest and most important sectors of the United States economy. It is a complex industry that affects all economic activity. Its subsector, farming, is the producer of raw materials that must be processed, stored, and distributed to consumers. All those activities provide employment and generate additional economic activity.

STRUCTURE AND CHANGES IN UNITED STATES AGRICULTURE

It is difficult to determine the total size of agriculture and to identify its total contribution to the nation's economic activity. In Table 2-1 we have shown estimates of the contribution of agriculture to the national income and of the number of people employed in agriculture. Agriculture generates about one fifth of the national income, and about one of three employed persons finds a job in agriculture. Within agriculture we find that the agribusiness subsector provides about four fifths of all the agricultural jobs and contributes about 85 percent of the 162 billion dollar agricultural income. Processing and distribution of food and fiber are the largest part of the agribusiness complex. Only a small portion of agriculture, either in jobs or income, is in public services.

Table 2-1. The Contribution of the Agricultural Industry to the National Economy, 1970.

The subsectors	Employment		National Income	
	Millions Employed	Percent of Nat'l. Total	Billions of Dollars	Percent of Nat'l. Total
Farming	4.5	5.3	17.0	2.1
Agribusiness	20.0	23.5	141.00	17.6
Processing Distributing	(12.5)	(14.7)	(100.0)	(12.5)
Supply	(7.5)	(8.8)	(41.0)	(5.1)
Public service	.3	.3	4.0	.5
Total agriculture	24.8	29.1	162.0	20.2
United States total	85.0	100.0	800.8	100.0

Source: *Agricultural Statistics and Statistical Abstract of the United States.*
Roy, Ewell P., *Exploring Agribusiness*, Interstate, 1967.

THE CHANGING STRUCTURE OF AGRICULTURE

Inventions and scientific discoveries of the nineteenth century provided the basis for the transformation of traditional farming methods and organization. The cotton gin and the reaper were among the first inventions that reduced labor requirements in farm production. The internal combustion engine as a source of power further reduced labor requirements and all but eliminated animal power on farms. Improved varieties and breeds of plants and animals increased yields and thus improved labor productivity. Development of factory processing and preserving techniques further reduced labor requirements; those and similar developments made possible the commercialization of farming. The early years of the twentieth century completed the full transition.

The basic farm changes are:

1. The substitution of machinery and mechanical and electrical power for human and animal power. Table 2-2 illustrates the substitution of machinery for labor. As investment in machinery increased more rapidly than investment in all capital assets, farm labor decreased.

Table 2-2. Changes in Total Farm Resource Use on United States Farms, 1920-1971.

	Years			
	1920	1940	1960	1971
Total assets in billions	$80.3	$52.9	$203.1	$317.2
Capital assets in billions	n.a.	$19.4	$ 68.3	$104.8
Machinery in billions	n.a.	$ 3.1	$ 18.1	$ 35.0
Machinery as % of total assets	n.a.	5.1	8.8	11.0
Machinery as % of capital assets	n.a.	16.0	$ 26.5	33.4
Number (millions) of people employed on farms	13.4	10.9	7.1	4.4

Source: *Statistical Abstract of the United States, Agricultural Statistics.*

2. Substituting machines for men and animals increased labor productivity. Table 2-3 shows that a single farmer fed 8.3 others in 1920, 52.4 in 1972.

Table 2-3. Changes in Farm Labor Productivity, 1920 to 1972.

	Years			
	1920	1940	1960	1972
Persons Fed by One Farmer	8.3	10.7	25.8	52.4

Source: *Agricultural Statistics* and *Statistical Abstract of the United States.*

3. Increased labor productivity has resulted in farmers being able to operate larger farms and consequently causing a decline in the number of farms and the number of people living on farms (Table 2-4). Other measures of size of farm are total assets used, production expenditures made by farmers, and gross farm income. Each increased rapidly during the last fifty years (Table 2-5).

Table 2-4. Changes in the Average Size of Farms, Number of Farms and Number of People Living on Farms, 1920 to 1972.

	Years			
	1920	1940	1960	1972
Average Size of Farm (acres)	148	174	297	381
Number of Farms (millions)	6.4	6.1	3.9	2.8
Number of People on Farms (millions)	31.9	30.5	15.6	9.6
Percent of Population on Farms	30.1	23.2	8.7	4.6

Source: *Agricultural Statistics* and *Statistical Abstract of the United States.*

STRUCTURE AND CHANGES IN UNITED STATES AGRICULTURE 15

Table 2-5. Changes in the Total Assets Used on Farms and Total Production Expenses, 1920 to 1972.

	Years			
	1920	1940	1960	1972
Total Assets Used on Farms (billions)	$80.3	$52.9	$203.1	$317.2
Total Production Expenses (billions)	$ 9.1	$ 6.7	$ 26.4	$ 49.2
Total Gross Farm Income (billions)	$15.9	$11.0	$ 38.0	$ 69.0

Source: *Agricultural Statistics* and *Statistical Abstract of the United States.*

4. Farms have become large and complex business organizations specializing in the production of raw materials. The raw materials are sold to agribusiness firms to continue the production process into consumer-ready products, as detailed in Chapter 11. Farms have become just one phase of the total agricultural production process.

5. Many production resources are produced in nonfarm businesses, for example, tractors, electricity, insecticides, fertilizer, gasoline, etc.

AGRIBUSINESS—PROCESSING AND DISTRIBUTION

The processing and distribution of farm products became the most important contributions to the agricultural sector of the economy in the first half of this century. Before 1900, there were processing and distributing of cotton, wool and flax fibers, and tobacco. Off-farm food processing, wholesaling, and retailing were just beginning. In 1910, 171,000 people were employed in food processing, and by 1970 the figure had increased tenfold.

In 1910 many were already employed to process fibers and tobacco since labor requirements were high for both industries. Since then the great amount of automated equipment has made possible a reduction in the labor force required.

Table 2-6 summarizes the development of agribusiness activities.

Table 2-6. Number of People Employed in Selected Agricultural Processing and Distribution Industries, 1910 to 1970.

Type of Industry	Number Employed			
	1910	1930	1950	1970
Food Processing	171,000	380,000	1,523,000	1,796,000
Food Retailing	n.a.	239,000	1,231,000	1,737,000
Textiles Milling	737,000	1,095,000	1,292,000	965,000
Tobacco Manufacturing	168,000	124,000	103,000	79,000

Source: *Statistical Abstract of the United States.*

AGRIBUSINESS—SUPPLYING

A large portion of the suppliers of inputs to farmers also produce inputs for many other industries. Two such suppliers are the manufacturers of farm machinery and fertilizers. Both, like most other farm supply industries, were just getting started at the turn of the century. Their growth and development has occurred in the span of a single lifetime. Using the number of people employed as a measure of growth, the rapid increase of each since 1910 is shown in Table 2-7.

Table 2-7. Number of People Employed in Selected Agricultural Supply Industries, 1910 to 1970.

Type of Industry	Number Employed			
	1910	1930	1950	1970
Farm Machinery Manufacture	n.a.	19,000	180,000	129,000
Fertilizer Manufacture	10,000	20,000	35,000	58,000

Source: *Statistical Abstract of the United States.*

PUBLIC SERVICE

The key year in establishing the government as a participant in agriculture was 1862 when the Department of Agriculture, the Land Grant College system, and the distribution of public land under the Homestead Act were established. In the following decades governmental activity in agriculture increased with the passage of the Hatch Act in 1887 establishing agricultural experiment stations, the Smith-Lever Act of 1914 establishing the agricultural extension service, and the Smith-Hughes Act of 1916 establishing the vocational agriculture program.

The public service subsector has gradually become a more significant portion of agriculture as shown by the number of people employed by the United States Department of Agriculture and the size of its budget.

Table 2-8. Number of People Employed by the United States Department of Agriculture and Size of Its Budget.

	Years			
	1913	1930	1950	1970
Number Employed	15,420	26,050	84,097	116,012
Budget (millions)	$20.5	$177.3	$2,784.0	$6,201.0

Source: *Statistical Abstract of the United States.*

EFFECTS OF THE CHANGES IN AGRICULTURE

The basic structural change in agriculture made possible by applying technology has been the shifting from a farm-centered agriculture to a farm—nonfarm agricultural industry. That basic change has been felt throughout the economy with varying effects on different parts of agriculture.

ON THE FAMILY FARM

Fundamental to the United States economy has been the independent one family farm unit. No other industry has been based on a business unit so closely identified with the family. Over the years, because of its economic and social success, the family farm dominated agriculture has been considered the best type of organization, not only for agriculture but also for the nation.

When we talk about the family farm we are speaking of a farm unit where the principal source of labor and management is a single family unit. That type of farm business has been able to adjust from self-sufficient, labor intensive farming of a century ago to the interdependent, capital intensive farming of today. Each farm has greatly increased in acres, in capital investment, and in volume of output, but the family has survived as the basis for the farm business.

Until recently most economic analyses have shown the one-man farm as the most economical business unit. There appeared to be no real cost advantages in larger units. Farms did not seem well suited to factory type organization where operations could be delegated to hired labor. Biological processes, soil, weather, and other natural factors influence the growth of farm plants and animals. Factory production, on the other hand, tends to deal with inanimate production. Because of that heavy dependence upon natural forces, farming seemed to prosper best when the farm operator was in closest contact with all operations. There seemed to be no substitute for the farmer being his own principal source of labor. Even with technological developments reducing the effects of the natural hazards, the family farm has shown a remarkable ability to compete with nonfamily type farms.

Table 2-9. Changes in the Number of Large[a]Farms, 1929, 1959, and 1964.

	Years		
	1929	1959	1964
Total Number of Small Farms	6,280,125	4,002,421	3,430,286
Percent Small Farms of Total	99.8%	97.5%	96.0%
Total Number of Large Farms	7,875	102,099	141,914
Percent Large Farms of Total	.2%	2.5%	4%

[a]Farms with more than $30,000 value of products sold, 1929; more than $48,600 in 1959; and more than $48,450 in 1964.

Source: Krause, Kenneth, and Kyle, Leonard, *Economic Factors Underlying the Incidence of Large Farming Units: The Current Situation and Probable Trends*, American Journal of Agricultural Economics, Vo. 52, No. 5, Dec., 1970, Table 1, Page 749. Agricultural Statistics.

In a recent study Krause and Kyle, two agricultural economists, determined that the percentage of large farms was increasing. (Table 2-9). If "large" farms are primarily nonfamily type farms and "small" farms are primarily family farms, we can see the present trend is away from family farms. Although the portion of total that are "large" farms is small, their number is growing rapidly. Because of their size they represent a bigger percentage of total farm output than they do in numbers.

Some of the advantages of larger farms include:

1. Large scale farming permits special economies, particularly in large scale buying and selling. A large volume producer can get premiums on his sales and discounts on his purchases.
2. Small farms are at a disadvantage in acquiring investment capital.
3. Small farmers are at a managerial disadvantage. The large farm may be able to acquire a full-time, better trained, and experienced manager than the family farm laborer-manager.

A young man entering farming today cannot hold on without qualifying the belief that the family farm is inherently superior to the large farm. The success of either type will finally be determined by the quality of managerial input.

ON COMMERCIALIZATION AND INDUSTRIALIZATION OF FARMING

We have already made the point that commercial farm operations have replaced largely self-sufficient units. A commercial farm is one that produces a product primarily for sale. Nearly all farms today do that.

Industrialization occurred much earlier in manufacturing than in agriculture. Industrialization occurs when production factors are provided by separate individuals or groups. In a farm business one family has traditionally been the source of the land, capital, labor, and management. One individual was simultaneously owner, operator, and laborer on his farm. An industrialized farm is one in which a group of investors may acquire the land, equipment, and other capital inputs, and hire a professional full-time manager who is authorized to employ laborers.

In some types of farm operations there has been a significant move to that type of business. Sugar and pineapple production in Hawaii, horticultural crops in California, and commercial feedlots of the Plains are examples.

ON INTEGRATION OF AGRICULTURAL FIRMS

Vertical integration, as used in business, refers to bringing more than one production and marketing function under a single unit of management. For example, the feed mixing plant that engages in a broiler feeding operation has integrated. Most farms originally were almost completely vertically integrated operations. A self-sufficient farm produces raw food and fibers that are processed and finally consumed on the farm.

STRUCTURE AND CHANGES IN UNITED STATES AGRICULTURE   19

Most of the inputs used in production are also produced at that farm. One of the first impacts of the technological advances in farming was to make specialization on farms more profitable than the integrated and diversified operation. Farmers responding to the advantage of specialization shifted to production of fewer farm raw materials on each farm to be sent to non-farm firms for processing and distributing.

The first processor and supplier firms were also quite specialized operations. As they developed, grew, and finally dominated the linkage between farmers and consumers and the supply market, they looked to vertical integration as a way to solve some of their problems. Food retailers were confronted with consumers who wanted high quality, uniform products in large volume. To assure that, the retailers acquired processing plants with a guaranteed flow of uniform quality raw products from farms. Contracts between the farmers and retailers often guaranteed the volume and the quality of raw product delivered for processing. Thus present integration has been primarily by agribusiness firms down to the farm level, rather than farmers bringing processing, wholesaling, and retailing under their control.

There are, of course, farmers who integrate. For example, a vegetable grower who opens a roadside market has vertically integrated. Vertical integration has been used most in producing broiler chickens, eggs, turkeys, citrus fruits, and vegetables. Other lines of production—beef cattle, lambs, hogs, and milk—also are often carried out by integrated firms.

Horizontal integration is another type. Rather than carrying out more than one phase of production, processing, or distribution under a single unit of management for a single product, a horizontally integrated firm adds more than one product for a particular phase. For example, a cattle feeder who adds hog feeding has integrated horizontally, as has the meat retailer who adds milk and eggs to his store's offerings.

There has been a steady movement toward both types of integration in recent years.

ON URBANIZATION OF THE UNITED STATES

Technology in agriculture released vast human resources for other lines of production. Scarcely a hundred years ago most human resources were required to provide food and fiber. Each farm producer could produce little above his needs; therefore a large portion of the labor force was tied to the farm. Technology, as we showed in Table 2-3, has greatly increased farm labor productivity. Over the last century we have been able to release a large part of the farm labor force to produce other goods and services. That and the growing nonfarm agricultural businesses provided employment opportunities in cities. The surplus farm labor began gradually to seek employment in urban centers and in the 1930s, 1940s, and 1950s became almost a mass movement. Table 2-10 shows the farm-to-town population shift.

Table 2-10. The Farm-to-town Population Shift in the United States, 1910 to 1970.

Years	Number (thousands) and Percentage by Place of Residence					
	Farm		Town		Total	
	Number	Percent of total	Number	Percent of total	Number	Percent of total
1970	9,712	4.8	194,553	95.2	204,265	100.0
1960	15,635	8.7	164,372	91.3	180,007	100.0
1950	23,048	15.3	128,084	84.7	151,132	100.0
1940	30,547	23.2	101,273	76.8	131,820	100.0
1930	30,169	24.6	92,328	75.4	122,497	100.0
1920	31,614	29.9	74,097	70.1	105,711	100.0
1910	32,077	34.9	59,895	65.1	91,972	100.0

Source: *Agricultural Statistics.*

In one year, 1956 to 1957, farm population declined 1,056,000 persons, from 18,712,000 to 17,656,000. Another year the decline was 946,000, from 14,313,000 in 1962 to 13,367,000 in 1963. The farm-to-town shift continues. In 1970 farm population decreased by about 300,000 persons.

An aspect of urbanization often overlooked is the influence of urban centers on the remaining farm population. It is becoming increasingly difficult to distinguish between town and farm families. Rapid transportation, radio and television, electricity, and consolidated schools have all contributed to erasing town and farm differences.

SUGGESTED READINGS

Davis, John H., and Goldberg, Ray A. *The Concept of Agribusiness.* Alpine Press, Inc., 1957.

Economic Research Service, United States Department of Agriculture. *Agricultural Markets in Change*, Agricultural Economic Report No. 95, 1966.

Krause, Kenneth R., and Kyle, Leonard R. *Economic Factors Underlying the Incidence of Large Farming Units: The Current Situation and Probable Trends.* American Journal of Agricultural Economics, Vol. 52, No. 5, December, 1970.

Roy, Ewell. *Exploring Agribusiness.* The Interstate Printers and Publishers, Inc., 1965.

Ruttan, Vernon W. et al, editor. *Agricultural Policy in an Affluent Society.* W. W. Norton & Company, 1969, Part One.

Thomas, Gerald W. *Progress and Change in the Agricultural Industry.* William C. Brown Book Company, 1969.

PART II

CONCEPT OF DEMAND

AGRICULTURE PRODUCES FOR CONSUMPTION 3

Agriculture includes two broad types of economic activities: production of goods and services and their consumption. Goods cannot be consumed until they have been produced, but produced goods not wanted by consumers are wasted. The two activities are interdependent, and it is difficult to determine which to treat first in a text. Usually the study of agricultural economics starts with the economics of production because of the strong ties of agricultural students to farming and because consumption cannot occur until the product has been produced. In this book the economics of consumption will be considered first for reasons given in the following paragraphs.

CONSUMER SOVEREIGNTY

In a market economy, such as in the United States, the consumer has been called "king" of the economy. Perhaps it would be more accurate to say the consumer of farm products is "queen" of the market since studies have shown women to be the main food shoppers. As market decision makers, they greatly influence the degree of success of different lines of farm production; in setting the consumption patterns of their families, they determine how much will be spent on food and then on what types of food—red meat or poultry, lettuce or cabbage, oranges or grapefruit. The agricultural producer—farmer, processor, or retailer—wanting to maximize his economic well-being will seek to produce those products most demanded by the consumer. By buying a product the consumer casts a "vote" for the production of that product. The vote, along with the votes of other consumers, determines the demand for the product. The wise producer continually watches demand and allocates resources to producing goods most demanded. In our market system the consumer is usually free to express his or her preferences. Sometimes producers are able to influence consumers by advertising or limiting the quantity supplied. If that happens the consumer is not fully sovereign; however eventually the producer must satisfy the consumer.

CONSUMER PREFERENCE

What the consumers want—called consumer preference—does not remain the same over time, nor are the wants of each consumer the same. In fact, no two consumers have identical preferences. Both may want bread in their diet, but one may want white bread and the other pumpernickel; and as situations change, each may change the quantity of bread wanted. Because consumer preferences are continually changing, it is difficult for the agricultural producer to know these preferences and how to respond to them.

Preference is based on wants. People have certain food needs to sustain life, but each of us has likes and dislikes (wants) that affect preferences. Yet wanting a product does not make a person a buyer. There must also be the ability to buy, that is, having money to make the purchase. Unrealized food needs and wants do not make markets for farmers.

MEASURING CONSUMER PREFERENCES

Consumers prefer to purchase a particular product over any other because they expect to get more satisfaction from that product for the money spent, than from any other. But it is difficult to determine just how much satisfaction they get or to compare the satisfactions one person derives from consuming a particular good with that another person derives. It is equally difficult to compare the satisfaction one person derives from consuming each of two or more products.

Economists attempting to measure satisfaction developed the concept of utility. *Utility is the measure of personal satisfaction derived from owning and using goods and services for some period of time.*

DIMINISHING MARGINAL UTILITY

Each unit of good or service has its own unique utility. For example, if a man is very thirsty, the first glass of cold water gives him great satisfaction (utility). From the second, third, fourth, or more glasses of water drunk, he derives successively a smaller amount of utility, as his thirst is satisfied. The utility must be determined for each individual unit consumed in the sequence consumed—for example, the utility gained from each of those glasses of water. This determination introduces an economic idea that underlies all economic problem solving (analysis)—the marginal unit. The concept of *the marginal unit, the last or the additional unit*, is illustrated in Figure 3-1. If I drink only one glass of water (Case 1), that glass is the marginal glass—the last or additional one. If I drink two glasses, (Case 2), glass 1 is no longer the marginal unit; number 2, by replacing it, is the additional glass of water and thus the new marginal unit. If I drink a third and then a fourth glass, each in sequence becomes the marginal unit. It is this marginal change—either addition, as illustrated, or subtraction—that is basic to economic decision making.

The observation that the utility gained from each additional unit is less than that from the previous unit is fundamental to economics and is known as diminishing marginal utility.

Diminishing marginal utility is apparent when as additional goods and services are consumed, the utility derived from each successive unit declines.

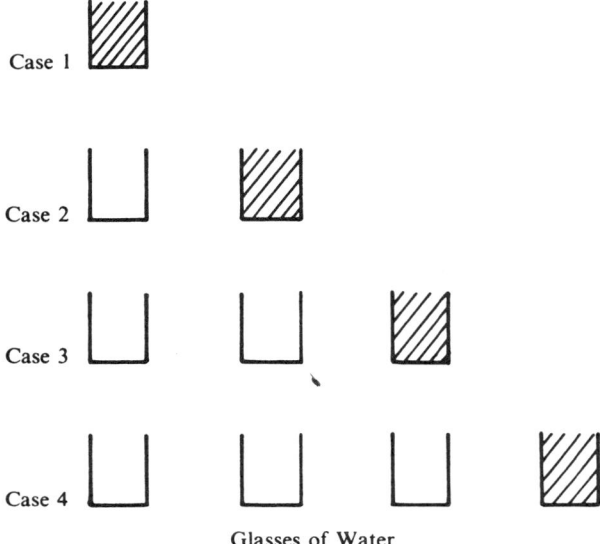

Figure 3-1. The Concept of the Marginal Unit
(marginal unit is shaded)

Table 3-1. Total and Marginal Utility Derived From Drinking Glasses of Water.

Glasses of Water Drunk	Total Utility Derived	Marginal Utility
0	0	--
1	8	8
2	13	5
3	16	3
4	17	1
5	16	-1

The concepts of marginal utility and diminishing marginal utility—and the relationship between units consumed and utility gained—are illustrated in Table 3-1 and Figure 3-2. Drinking water gives the drinker satisfaction—called utility. Let us assume that drinking one glass gives him 8 units of utility, two glasses a total of 13 units, and three glasses 16 units. Each additional glass of water adds to the total utility. The added amount, marginal utility, can be determined as follows:

Marginal Utility	=	Change in total utility / Change in units consumed
8	=	(8 - 0) / (1 - 0)
5	=	(13 - 8) / (2 - 1)
3	=	(16 - 13) / (3 - 2)
1	=	(17 - 16) / (4 - 3)
-1	=	(16 - 17) / (5 - 4)

It should be noted that it is possible for a person to consume so much that disutility occurs. For example, after one drinks so much water he may be unable to drink more without having discomfort. Thus, the fifth glass would cause total utility to decline, (from 17 to 16), resulting in a –1 marginal utility.

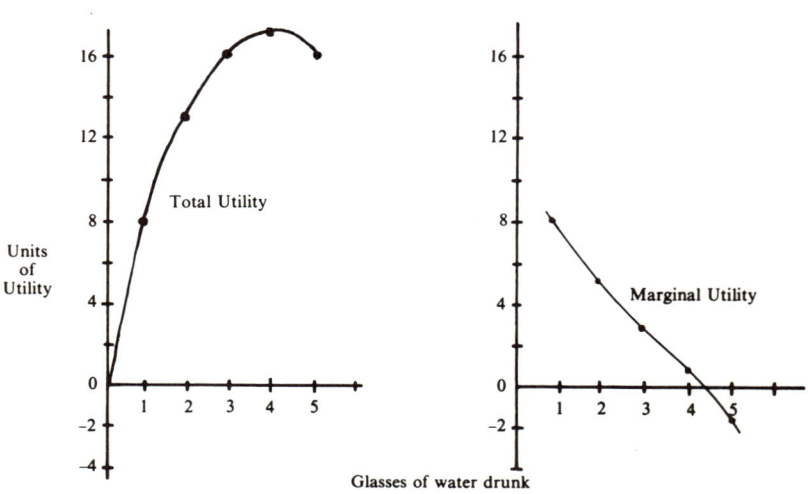

Figure 3-2. Utility Gained from Drinking Water (using data in Table 3-1).

AGRICULTURE PRODUCES FOR CONSUMPTION

As our food wants are partially met, those wants become less intense; thus, each additional unit yields less utility, and diminishing marginal utility occurs. It also occurs because we like to eat a variety of foods. A steak accompanied by a baked potato, lettuce, and French bread is enjoyed more than steak alone. Consumers prefer to spend their income on more than one consumption item because doing so increases their satisfaction. However, if only one product is consumed, a consumer would buy it as long as the utility derived from owning and using it is greater than the utility derived from the money it costs. We make purchases only when we expect the resulting satisfaction to be greater than that gained from keeping the money.

MAXIMIZING UTILITY

In making consumption choices the consumer seeks more, not less, satisfaction. The consumer's objective, to maximize satisfaction, is achieved when he finds the combination of goods and services that give the greatest utility from the income available for expenditure. Because of income limitations, the consumer cannot buy all the goods wanted. He must determine how to use his limited income to purchase, from a large number of goods and services, those adding the most utility. That can be done by using each unit of income where it adds the most utility. Different goods and services give various amounts of utility, but also each has a different price. The consumer must consider jointly the marginal utility gained from and the market price of a unit of the good.

Basic ideas can be expressed symbolically in a mathematical formula. For example, if our water drinker also enjoys milk, we would find a separate utility curve and price for milk. If the consumer knows how much money is available to spend, 10¢, and knows his marginal utility for each and the price of each, he can maximize his satisfaction by fulfilling this formula.

$$\frac{\text{MU of a glass of milk}}{\text{Price of a glass of milk}} = \frac{\text{MU of a glass of water}}{\text{Price of a glass of water}}$$

Let us say the MU per glass of milk = 5
MU per glass of water = 10
Price per glass of milk = 10¢
Price per glass of water = 10¢.

Then $\quad \dfrac{5}{.10} \neq \dfrac{10}{.10}$

and the consumer would likely spend his dime for water because he would add more utility, 10 units as opposed to 5 units if spent on milk. Because of diminishing marginal utility, the consumer would get less than 10 units of utility from the next dime spent on water. Eventually he would get just 5 units of utility from the added unit of water. Then:

$$\frac{5}{.10} = \frac{5}{.10}$$

and he would have maximized utility. If he bought another glass of water, MU of water = 4, he would then switch to buying milk until the MU was equal to 4. This method of utility maximization can be applied to any number of goods and services:

$$\frac{MUY_1}{PY_1} = \frac{MUY_2}{PY_2} = \ldots = \frac{MUY_n}{PY_n}$$

RESOURCES AND PRODUCTS

Since we will use the terms product (and its synonyms—output, goods and services) and resource (and its synonyms—input and factor) continuously as we progress through the book, we need to distinguish between the two. In economic activity we produce and consume. Those items used in production—land, labor, machinery, gasoline, seed, animals, etc.—are resources. Those items resulting from production are the products—meat, wheat, hay, clothing, etc. Products having a physical form (as in the example) are goods. Products not having a physical form—a mechanic's labor, a haircut, a lawyer's advice, delivery of gasoline, etc.—are services. Note what is a product for one producer (wheat produced by a farmer) may become a resource to another producer (a miller who mills wheat into flour). Economists often use Y to represent products and X to represent resources. In this text we will do that. When producing several products we will identify them as Y_1, Y_2, Y_3 ... Y_n (where n represents any number). When using several resources we will identify them as X_1, X_2, X_3 ... X_n.

INDIFFERENCE CURVES

Economists have developed an analytical method to compare the relative satisfaction derived from two products when only a given level of money is available to buy both. This method is indifference curve analysis. It is a complex method, but one important to students planning to continue their economic studies.

An indifference curve represents the consumer's preference between two goods. Returning to our milk-water illustration, let us assume the drinker has 20 glasses of water with the opportunity to trade them for glasses of milk. How many glasses of water would he be willing to give up to gain 1 glass of milk? Let us say he would give up 5 glasses of water. Then he would be equally staisfied (indifferent) with 20 glasses of water and no milk or with 15 glasses of water and 1 glass of milk; as illustrated in Figure 3-3. At points A and B he is equally happy, or equally so at C, D, and E, but to give up the successive glasses of water he would have to get a larger and larger number of glasses of milk for each trade:

AGRICULTURE PRODUCES FOR CONSUMPTION

First trade	5 for 1
Second trade	5 for 3
Third trade	5 for 4
Fourth trade	5 for 6

We have now established that he would be equally satisfied with:

	Glasses of Water	Glasses of Milk
A	20	0
B	15	1
C	10	4
D	5	8
E	0	14

By connecting points A, B, C, D, and E (Figure 3-3, I_1) we can construct an indifference curve. We could have started on a higher (or lower) indifference curve, say with more than 20 glasses of water (or fewer than 20), and developed indifference curves such as shown by I_2 and I_3. We have made no attempt here to determine what would cause the drinker to select one combination over another because we lacked information on the price of each commodity and the total money he has to spend (budget constraint).

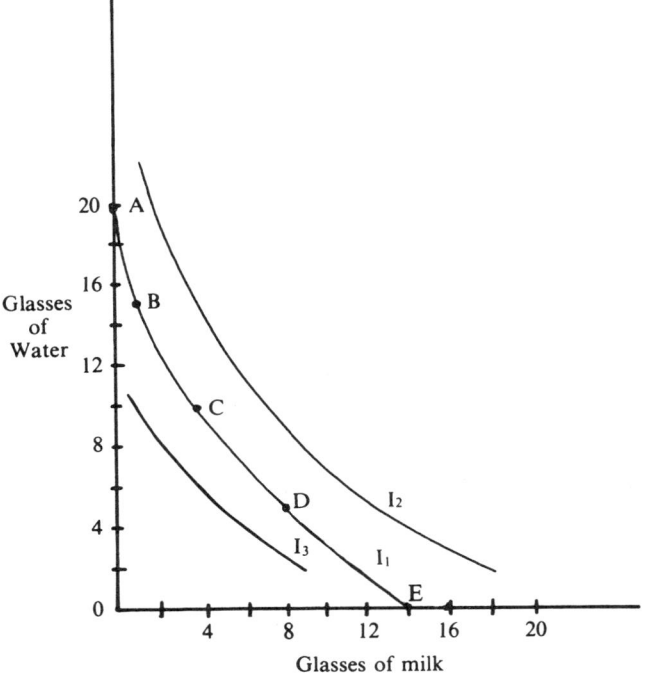

Figure 3-3. Indifference Curves.

If a glass of milk is 20¢ and water 10¢, and he had $2.50 to spend, he could buy 25 glasses of water, 12½ glasses of milk, or some combination of the two.

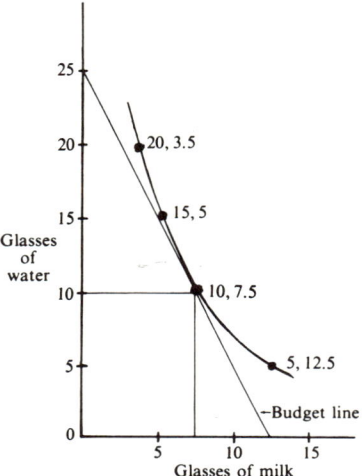

Figure 3-4. Indifference Curve and Budget Line Used to Determine the Optimum Combination of Two Goods.

The budget line, Figure 3-4, represents all possible combinations of water and milk that can be bought with $2.50 when the price of water is 10¢ and milk 20¢. The budget line would be tangent to an indifference curve at point A, 10 glasses of water at 10¢ and 7½ glasses of milk at 20¢ each. Spending $1.00 on water and $1.50 on milk would maximize utility. At that point 5 glasses of water gives exactly the same satisfaction as 2½ glasses of milk. Going from 15 of water and 5 of milk to 10 and 7.5 required a 5 for 2½ trade. A glass of milk gave twice the utility of a glass of water. The price of milk was twice the price of water. At that point

$$\frac{\Delta \text{ water}}{\Delta \text{ milk}} = \frac{P \text{ milk}}{P \text{ water}} \left(\frac{5}{2\frac{1}{2}} = \frac{.20}{.10} \right).$$

IN SUMMARY

The consumer influences the economic success of agricultural producers by making food-buying decisions based on the family's preferences. Each consumer, acting individually, casts a "vote" for the product chosen. Votes are a message to the producers to produce that product. The profit-oriented producer, in responding to the consumers' message, a large number of votes represented by the large number of purchases, shifts resources to produce the product. We observe in a market economy that the market is consumer oriented, and the whole production system is geared to meeting consumer preferences.

SUGGESTED READINGS

Burk, Marguerite C. *Consumption Economics: A Multidisciplinary Approach.* John Wiley and Sons, Inc., 1968.

Clower, Robert W., and Due, John F. *Microeconomics.* Richard D. Irwin, Inc., 1972, Chapters 2, 3, 4, and 5.

Leftwich, Richard H. *The Price System and Resource Allocation*, 3rd Edition. Holt, Rinehart, and Winston, 1966, Chapters 3, 4, 5, and 6.

Peterson, Willis L. *Principles of Economics: Micro*, Revised edition. Richard D. Irwin, Inc., 1974, Chapter 2.

Samuelson, Paul A. *Economics an Introductory Analysis*, 9th Edition. McGraw-Hill Book Company, 1973, Chapter 4.

Snodgrass, Milton M. and Wallace, Luther T., *Agriculture, Economics, and Growth*, Second Edition. Appleton-Century-Crofts, 1970, Chapters 11 and 15.

CONSUMER BEHAVIOR IN THE MARKET   4

Every market is made up of two groups, the consumers (demand) and the producers (supply); their behavior determines prices. In Chapter 3 we consider the behavior of the consumer in the market. In this chapter we shall explore how this behavior affects the market and explain the economic concept of demand, as well as the nature of consumer demand for agricultural products.

DEMAND DEFINED

Consumer demand arises from the wants of people, is constrained by their income limitations, and with supply, determines how resources are to be used.

Demand is often confused with the quantity of a good or service bought. An understanding of the economic meaning of demand will greatly increase the understanding of our market system. Remember demand for beef is not the same as the quantity of beef eaten; the demand for tractors is not the number of tractors bought by farmers. Demand is a relation between the number bought and the price of the good—a concept that can be stated as follows:

Demand is a schedule of the quantities of a good or service the consumer is willing and able to buy at a given time and place at different price levels.

Note that the definition is specific on several points. The consumer must not only need and want (be willing) to buy the good or service but also must be able (have the money) to do so. His "willingness" and "ability to do so" must be for one particular time at a specified place. Demand is not a comparison of willingness and ability to buy for different times or places.

DEMAND SCHEDULE

The definition of demand can be illustrated by constructing a schedule (Table 4-1) of prices and quantities of a good or service a consumer is willing and able to buy. Most of us are quite willing and able to buy milk. The price we have to pay influences how much we are willing and able to buy. Each of us has his own "demand schedule"—an economist's way of recognizing the individuality of consumer wants. In Table 4-1 we have listed the number of quarts of milk a particular consumer would buy at different prices at a specified time, to establish his demand schedule.

Table 4-1. A Consumer's Demand Schedule for Milk.

Price (per quart of milk)	Quantity Bought (quarts of milk)
.50	6
.40	10
.30	15
.20	23
.10	40

By plotting quantities purchased against price we can show the demand schedule as a demand curve, which helps us visualize the price-quantity relationship.

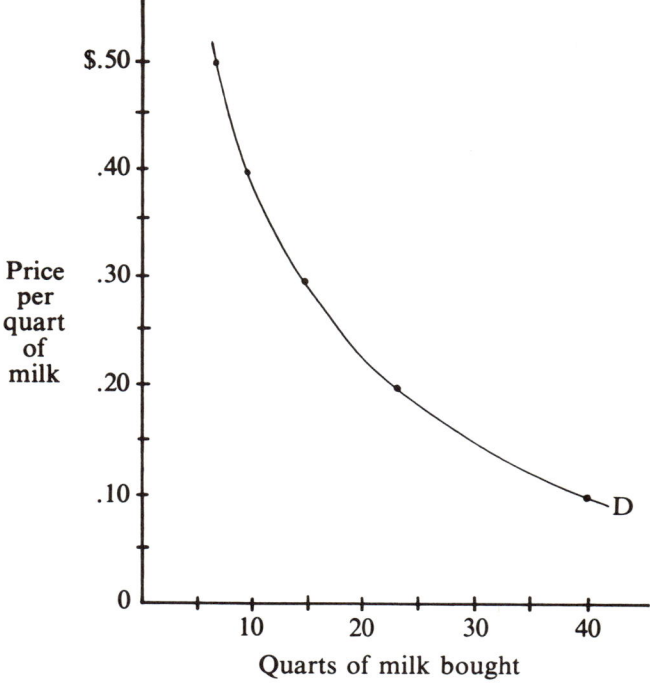

Figure 4-1. A Consumer's Demand Schedule for Milk.

LAW OF DEMAND

Whether we consider the table or graph, it is obvious that the quantity of milk a consumer is willing and able to buy increases as price declines. The observation that a negative or inverse relationship exists between

CONSUMER BEHAVIOR IN THE MARKET 35

price and quantity is basic to the study of economic behavior and has become known as the law of demand:

Consumers will buy a larger quantity as price is reduced.

All of us have heard "the law of supply and demand determines prices." But in economics there is no one law of supply and demand; there is a separate law of demand and a separate law of supply. Later, after we have studied supply, we shall show how demand, the schedule of the quantities and prices of a good or service consumers are willing or able to buy, is combined with supply to determine prices.

Table 4-2. A Change in Demand.

Price of Milk	Quantity of Milk (quarts)	Change in demand for milk D_1 Increase (quarts)	D_2 Decrease (quarts)
.50	6	12	1
.40	10	20	3
.30	15	28	8
.20	23	40	12
.10	40	68	23

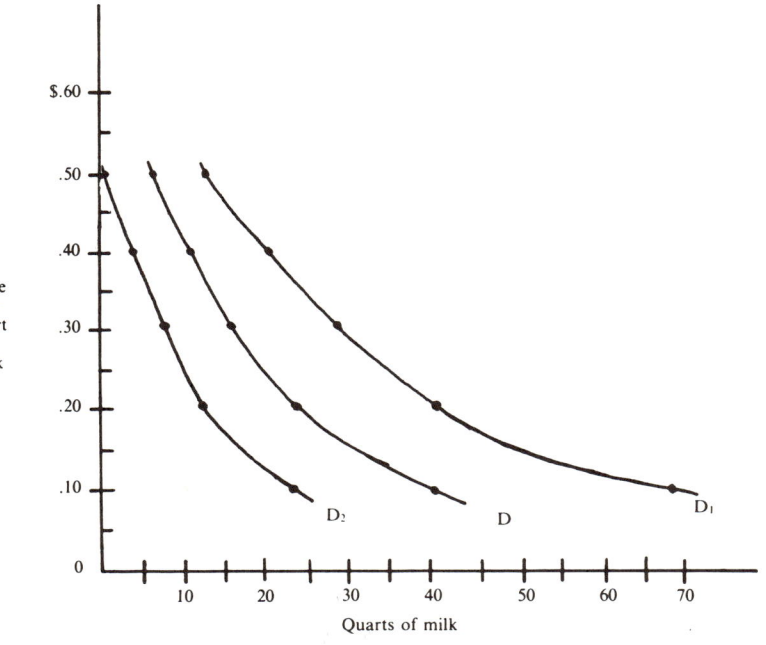

Figure 4-2. A Change in Demand.

CHANGE IN DEMAND

A movement from one point to another on the demand schedule does not represent a change in demand. The whole schedule is demand; one point on the schedule is not demand. Therefore, any one of the price-quantity relationships on the schedule represents the same demand as that at any other point. To show a change in demand we must shift to another demand schedule. In Table 4-2 and Figure 4-2 two changes in demand are shown: an increase, a shift to the right resulting in a higher demand schedule (D_1); and a decrease, a shift to the left, resulting in a lower demand schedule (D_2).

A consumer may change his demand for a product because there is a change in his wants, disposable income, or family situation; because a substitute product becomes available; because the weather changes or holidays occur; or because of prices of other products, his propensity to save, or producer influences change.

A consumer's wants are continually changing. Tastes and desires change with age or education, or the consumer just becomes tired of an old product and looks for a new one.

Demand is closely associated with level of income available for expenditure. As our income increases we may buy more steaks and less hamburger at given prices. Demand for steaks increases, demand for hamburger decreases, as income increases.

A family with growing children has an increasing demand for shoes. As the children mature and leave home the family's demand for shoes decreases.

New products developed as good substitutes for an existing one affect demand. An example is oleomargarine developed as a butter substitute. Vegetable protein substitutes for meat products currently are being developed; this may change demand for meat. A similar influence is the change in the price of substitute products. A decrease in the price of chicken lessens the demand for beef and pork.

Climatic variations and holidays often shift demand. A wet, cold winter certainly increases demand for overshoes. Easter and Mother's Day creates an entirely new demand schedule for flowers.

Although we emphasize consumer sovereignty in the market, many believe today that promotion and advertising influences the consumer so much that he is less than sovereign. The purpose of advertising is to change demand—increase it. To the degree that advertising is effective, it does change demand.

Each consuming unit, usually called a household, has the alternative of saving income instead of making consumption expenditures. The desire to save differs from family to family and for any one family from time to time. The desire to save is known as the *propensity to save*. The propensity to save and any changes in it affects demand. A strong propensity to save will decrease demand. Farm families who are highly integrated into the farm business are continually confronted with having to choose between consumption and saving for business investment.

MARKET DEMAND

Thus far we have considered only the demand of the individual for goods and services. Many individuals, each with his or her own demand schedule, are willing and able to buy a product. The total of all the individual demand schedules for the product represents the market demand for that good or service.

A producer trying to decide among different lines of production is vitally interested in the market demand for each product he is considering. The individual demand schedule provides little help, but the summation of all individual schedules gives an indication of how well the product may sell.

Thus, we see that for each good or service, every buyer has an individual demand schedule for that good. A single aggregate (market) demand schedule reflects all buyers.

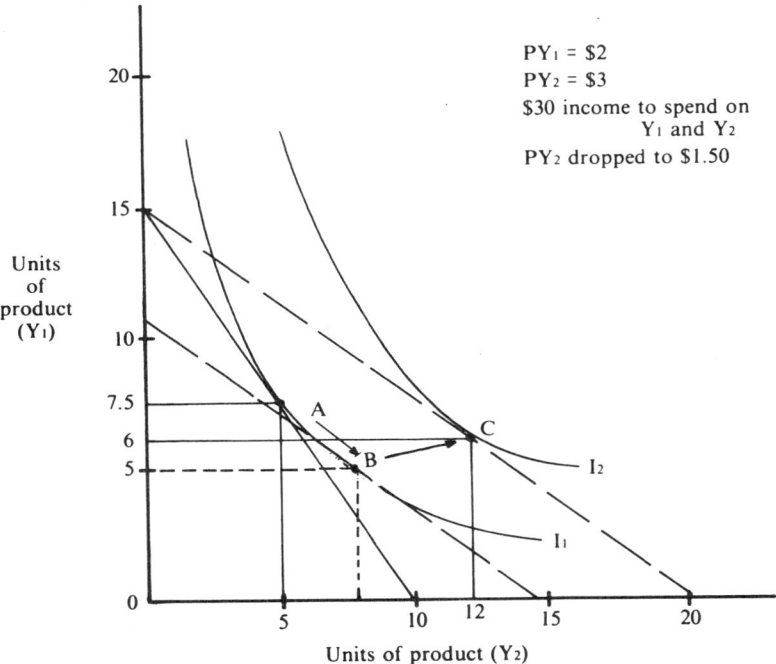

Figure 4.3. The Income and Substitution Effect.

INCOME AND SUBSTITUTION EFFECT

As shown by the law of demand consumers will buy a larger quantity of a product as its price is reduced. Such a negative relationship arises from two influences: the income effect and the substitution effect.

The income effect results from the influence a price decrease has on the consumer's purchasing power. A reduced price has the same impact as an increase in income—more of the product can be purchased. Returning to our indifference curve example in Chapter 3, a price reduction would enable a consumer to move to a higher indifference curve within his income. A higher price has, of course, the opposite effect; the consumer can no longer buy as much as before with a given income.

Lowering the price of a product changes the price relationship among the products. The consumer is stimulated to buy more of the cheaper product and less of the unchanged ones which are now relatively more expensive. Substituting less expensive products for the more expensive ones is called the substitution effect.

Figure 4-3 prepared using the indifference curve analysis, illustrates both the income and the substitution effect. If the consumer has $30 to spend on Y_1, and Y_2, with PY_1 = $2 and PY_2 = $3, he could buy 15 units if he spent it all on Y_1; 10 units if all was spent on Y_2.

A straight line connecting the two points gives all possible combinations of Y_1 and Y_2 that could be bought with $30. At point A, where the budget line is equal to the substitution rate between Y_1 and Y_2, the consumer could buy 7.5 units of Y_1 and 5 of Y_2. If the price of Y_2 dropped to $1.50, the consumer would buy more of the cheaper product, Y_2, and less of the more expensive one, Y_1, thus substituting Y_2 for Y_1; point B represents the consumer's new combination of Y_1 and Y_2 he could buy after the change in price: 5 units of Y_1 and 9 units of Y_2. The consumer would also discover that the fall in PY_2 would increase his purchasing power; he could buy a greater combined amount of Y_1 and Y_2 with his money. Thirty dollars would not buy 20 units of Y_2, rather than 10 units, if all were spent on Y_2. The new budget line would connect Y_1 = 15 and Y_2 = 20. At point C, where the indifference curve and the budget line would be equal, he could buy 12 units of Y_2 and 6 of Y_1 with the $30. Thus, we see that lowering PY_2 to $1.50 resulted in a substitution of Y_2 (the product with the lowered price) for Y_1 (the product with the unchanged price) and an increase in purchasing power (shifting from I_1 to I_2).

INCOME ELASTICITY OF DEMAND

We listed disposable income as one of the factors that affect the demand for goods and services. Three general observations about the effect of income on demand for food are:

1. The poorer a family, the higher will be the portion of its income spent on food.

2. As income changed, food consumption will change in the same direction.

3. As income changes, the purchased food items change.

Economists have developed procedures for measuring the relationship between demand and income. *The measure of a change in consumption of a good resulting from a change in income is called income elasticity of demand.* It is expressed as the percent change in quantity demanded resulting from a one percent change in income.

Table 4-3. Computing Income Elasticity of Demand.

Disposable Family Income	Family Expenditure on Product Y	Computation	Income Elasticity
I_1 $750	Q_1 $300		
I_2 $1,500	Q_2 $750	$\dfrac{300 - 750}{300 + 750}$ $\dfrac{750 - 1,500}{750 + 1,500}$	1.285
I_3 $3,000	Q_3 $1,500	$\dfrac{750 - 1,500}{750 + 1,500}$ $\dfrac{1,500 - 3,000}{1,500 + 3,000}$	1.000
I_4 $6,000	Q_4 $2,250	$\dfrac{1,500 - 2,250}{1,500 + 2,250}$ $\dfrac{3,000 - 6,000}{3,000 + 6,000}$	0.600
I_5 $12,000	Q_5 $2,250	$\dfrac{2,250 - 2,250}{2,250 + 2,250}$ $\dfrac{6,000 - 12,000}{6,000 + 12,000}$	0.000
I_6 $24,000	Q_6 $2,025	$\dfrac{2,250 - 2,025}{2,250 + 2,025}$ $\dfrac{12,000 - 24,000}{12,000 + 24,000}$	−0.157

$$E_I = \dfrac{\dfrac{Q_1 - Q_2}{Q_1 + Q_2}}{\dfrac{I_1 - I_2}{I_1 + I_2}}$$

Income elasticity of demand can be computed by:

$$\text{Income elasticity of demand} = \frac{\% \text{ change in consumption (\$)}}{\% \text{ change in income (\$)}}$$

or

$$E_I = \frac{\dfrac{Q_1 - Q_2}{Q_1 + Q_2}}{\dfrac{I_1 - I_2}{I_1 + I_2}}.$$

We can illustrate the computation of income elasticity of demand (E_I) by studying the example in Table 4-3.

When family income increased from $750 to $1,500, expenditures for product Y increased from $300 to $750; or, for each 1 percent increase in income, there was a 1.285 percent increase in consumption. When consumption increases more rapidly than expenditures, the income elasticity is said to be elastic. The second income increase, $1,500 to $3,000, resulted in a smaller percentage increase in consumption; a 1 percent income increase brought forth a 1 percent consumption increase, or the income elasticity was unitary. In the next case, $3,000 to $6,000, a 1 percent income increase resulted in .6 percent increase in consumption, or the income elasticity was inelastic. In each instance consumption and income moved in the same direction. When their consumption increases as income increases, goods and services are *superior*.

Note, Table 4-3, that the $6,000-to-$12,000 income increase did not change consumption. With $6,000 income, the consumer was able to satisfy all needs and wants, so a further income increase did not stimulate him to buy more products. Further income increases in fact resulted in a decrease in consumption of the product because income was now sufficient to buy preferred substitutes that were too expensive to buy at lower incomes. The consumer's income elasticity was now negative. A negative income elasticity identifies a good or service as being *inferior*. For example, starches (potatoes, rice, cassava) are comparatively inexpensive foods and therefore are likely to be basic diet items among the very poor. When income permits, people substitute preferred (superior) foods for those less preferred (inferior) ones.

Income elasticity of demand varies with the level of income, usually being most elastic for low incomes and least for high. The elasticity is related to the type of product; the more preferred a product is, the greater will be the elasticity. For a farm product elasticity is low at the farm level, but it increases as services are added; for example, the elasticity increases as wheat is turned into flour, into a cake mix, into a baked cake. Also affecting income elasticity is the availability and price of competing products. For example, because chicken and turkey are similar foods, the price of each affects the income elasticity of demand for the other.

SIGNIFICANCE OF INCOME ELASTICITY OF DEMAND FOR FOOD

We have pointed out that income elasticity of demand for food is greatest among low income families. Therefore, one way to increase demand for farm products is to increase the disposable income among the very poor, who will spend a larger portion of their increased income on food than will high income families receiving an equal increase.

Income elasticity can be thought of as consumer response to changes in income. Food is essential so we buy it first, but after meeting our food wants, we begin satisfying less pressing wants. Therefore, income elasticity for food (farm products) decreases as incomes increase.

PRICE ELASTICITY OF DEMAND

A careful study of the price-quantity relationship (our definition of demand) reveals certain characteristics. We have seen that for superior goods, the relationship between prices and quantity purchased is always negative and that for every individual consumer and for every product that relationship is unique. That means the demand schedule in Figure 4-1 represents demand for only one consumer for one product and that a schedule for anyone else will be different.

Price elasticity of demand is the measure of a percentage change in quantity demanded relative to a percentage change in price.

For example, it is the percentage increase in quantity resulting from a one percent decrease in price; it can be determined by using the following:

$$\text{Price elasticity of demand} = \frac{\% \text{ change in quantity}}{\% \text{ change in price}}$$

or

$$E_d = \frac{\dfrac{Q_1 - Q_2}{Q_1 + Q_2}}{\dfrac{P_1 - P_2}{P_1 + P_2}}$$

Table 4-4. Computing Price Elasticity of Demand.

	Price of the Product ($)	Quantity Purchased (units)	Computation	Coefficient of Price Elasticity
P_1	.70	Q_1 20		
P_2	.583	Q_2 30	$\dfrac{20 - 30}{20 + 30}$ $\dfrac{.70 - .583}{.70 + .583}$	2.222 elastic
P_3	.50	Q_3 35	$\dfrac{30 - 35}{30 + 35}$ $\dfrac{.583 - .50}{.583 + .50}$	1.00 unitary
P_4	.40	Q_4 38	$\dfrac{35 - 38}{35 + 38}$ $\dfrac{.50 - .40}{.50 + .40}$	0.3698 inelastic
P_5	.30	Q_5 38	$\dfrac{38 - 38}{38 + 38}$ $\dfrac{.40 - .30}{.40 + .30}$	0

The coefficient of price elasticity is a negative number. That tells us that a given decrease in price results in an increase in the quantity demanded and that the demand curve slopes downward. Although the coefficient is always negative, we often drop the negative sign in discussing elasticity, making statements such as: The elasticity of demand for food is less than 1.0 (rather than more than −1.0). Even when the negative sign is omitted, it is always understood to be there.

The data in Table 4-4 illustrates three types of price elasticity: elastic, unitary, inelastic. Demand is elastic when the coefficient of price elasticity is greater than 1, which means that a small percentage change in price induces the consumer to make a relatively larger percentage change in the quantity demanded. Or we may say the consumer is very responsive to prices.

Usually a consumer responds more to prices for luxury goods. For example, most of us will increase our percentage purchases of filet mignon much more than of weiners if the price of each is cut in half. Figure 4-4 illustrates an elastic demand: A 16.9 percent decrease in price (.70¢ to .583¢) caused a 50 percent increase in quantity (20 to 30 units) demanded.

CONSUMER BEHAVIOR IN THE MARKET   43

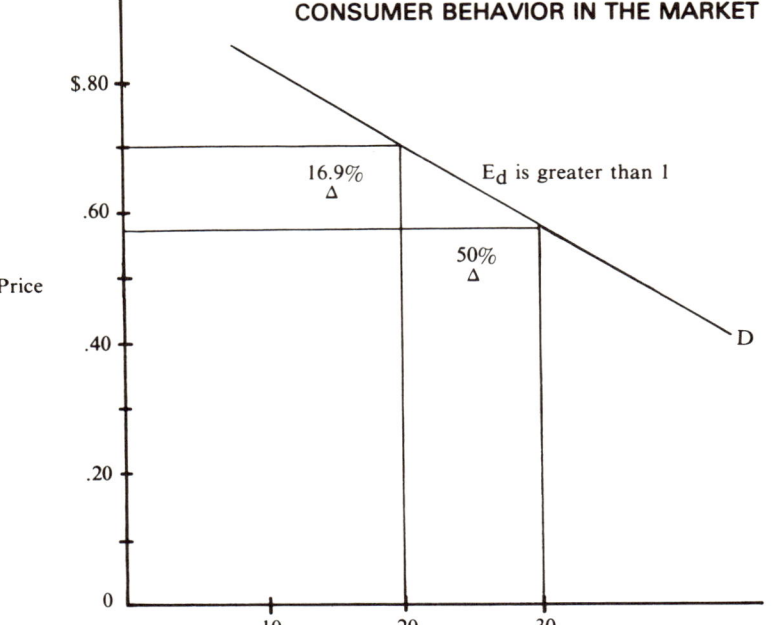

Figure 4-4. Elastic Price Elasticity of Demand (see Table 4-4).

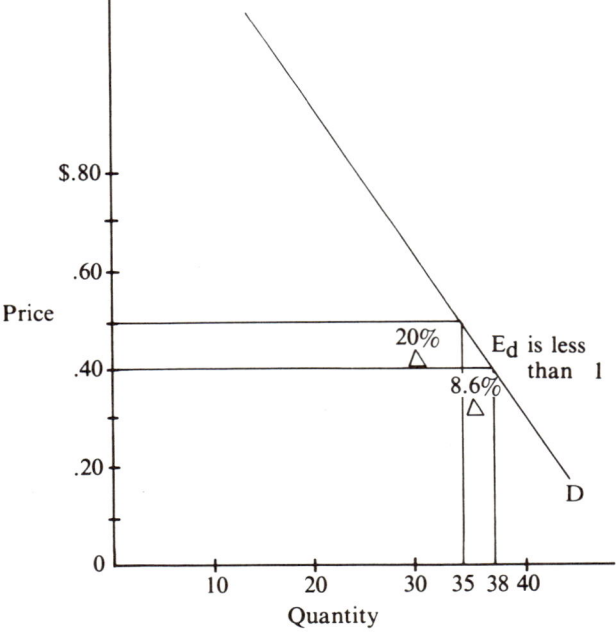

Figure 4-5. Inelastic Price Elasticity of Demand (see Table 4-4).

Demand is inelastic when the coefficient of price elasticity is less than 1, in which case the consumer is not very responsive to price changes. Because most food items are necessities, they have an inelastic demand. Hence, a price change in them does not cause a consumer to make a great change in the quantity bought. Figure 4-5 illustrates inelastic demand: A 20 percent price decrease (50¢ to 40¢) increased purchases by 8.6 percent (35 to 38 units).

If the price elasticity coefficient is exactly one (E_d = 1), percentage change in quantity is the same as that in price. We then have unitary elasticity, which is the breaking point between the elastic and inelastic demand situation.

There are two special cases of elasticity of demand: the perfectly inelastic and the perfectly elastic demand. For a few goods—salt is often used as an example—the consumer wants a given amount, so essentially disregards price. Price has little effect on the quantity taken, as shown in Table 4-4, when P_5 = 30 and Q_5 = 38. When E_d = 0 we have a perfectly inelastic demand and the demand curve is a vertical line (Figure 4-6).

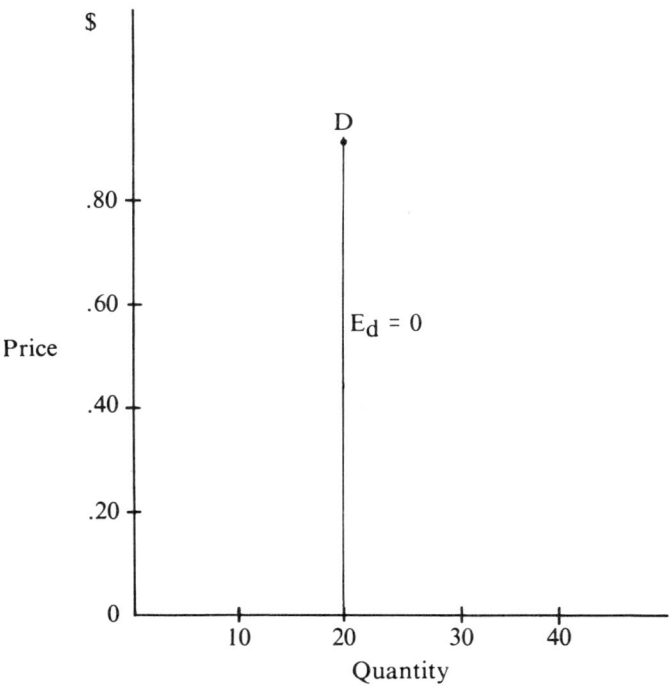

Figure 4-6. Perfectly Inelastic Price Elasticity of Demand.
(see Table 4-4).

In the second special case, the perfectly elastic demand curve, (Figure 4-7), the consumer is willing to purchase any quantity of the good at a given price, but none at any higher price. Because the consumer is willing and able to buy any quantity offered at that price, the seller will not offer any at a lower price. The resulting demand curve is horizontal. Many farmers individually face that kind of market demand schedule. For example, a wheat farmer may deliver to the elevator as many bushels of wheat as he can on any day, receiving that day's price for all of it. In such an instance, we say the seller is a price taker.

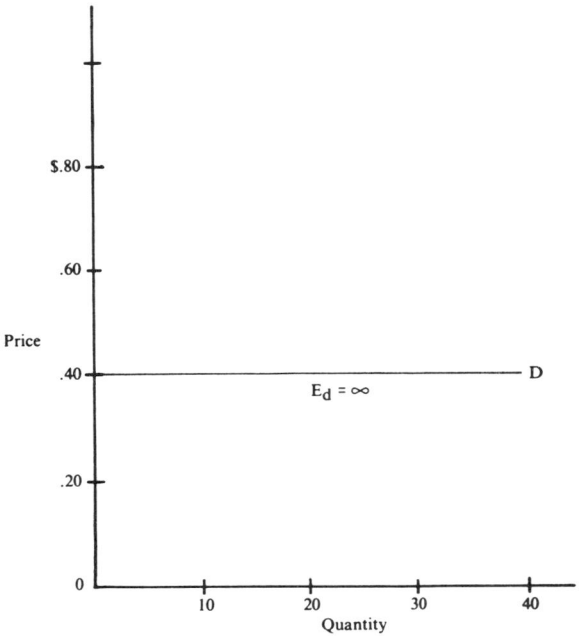

Figure 4-7. Perfectly Elastic Price Elasticity of Demand.

THE EFFECT OF PRICE ELASTICITY ON TOTAL REVENUE

If we know the price elasticity of demand for a product, we can better understand the consequences of a price change on total revenue going to the producers of that product. If a price falls producers get a lower price and consequently a lower total revenue for a given amount of product sold. However, the impact of the lower price is at least partially offset by the increased quantity that may be sold at the lower price. Hence, the resulting total revenue going to the producers may remain unchanged, increase, or decrease, depending on elasticity of demand. If there is unitary elasticity, total revenue remains unchanged because the identical percentage changes in price and quantity offset one another. If there is an elastic demand, total revenue will increase because the larger percentage increase in quantity will more than offset the lower price. If demand is inelastic, total revenue falls when prices are lowered. The increase in quantity sold at the lower prices is insufficient to offset the loss resulting from lowered prices, as illustrated in Table 4-5.

Table 4-5. Computing Total Revenue for Elastic, Unitary, and Inelastic Demand.

	Price of the Product	Quantity Purchased (units)	Computation TR = P x Q	Total Revenue
P_1	$.70	Q_1 20	.70 x 20	$14.00
P_2	.60	Q_2 30	.60 x 30	18.00 elastic
P_3	.50	Q_3 36	.50 x 36	18.00 unitary
P_4	.40	Q_4 38	.40 x 38	15.20 inelastic

NATURE OF DEMAND FOR AGRICULTURAL PRODUCTS

Most agricultural products, particularly food, are considered to be necessities. Necessities tend to have:

1. An income elasticity of demand that is relatively elastic at low income levels and less elastic at higher income levels.
2. A price elasticity of demand that is relatively inelastic.
3. A higher price and income elasticity at the retail than at the producer level.
4. A high degree of variation among products for both price and income elasticity.

The U.S. consumer's income elasticity of demand for food is inelastic, about .3, which means that a 1 percent increase in income results in .3 percent increase in expenditures on food. Income elasticity of demand varies among food items. In Table 4-6 we have shown selected foods in three elasticity categories. In fact less is spent for some foods, those with a negative income elasticity, (column 1, Table 4-6), as incomes increase. (If incomes were lowered the foods would probably have a positive coefficient). The other two columns illustrate types of commodities with positive coefficients at two levels of responsiveness; increases in consumer incomes would result in larger percentage expenditure increases for commodities in the right-hand column.

Table 4-6. Relative Income Elasticity of Demand for Selected Foods Compared, United States, 1965.

Response of Consumers to a One Percent Increase in Income for Selected Foods		
Negative or No Response	Lowest Positive Response	Highest Positive Response
Chicken	Apples	Canned pineapple
Corn meal	Bananas	Carrots
Corn syrup	Beef	Fresh milk
Dried fruits	Breakfast cereals	Frozen fruits
Dry vegetables	Butter	Frozen vegetables
Eggs	Canned corn	Ice cream
Evaporated milk	Canned peaches	Lamb
Fish	Canned peas	Lettuce
Fresh beans	Canned tomatoes	Turkey
Lard	Cheese	Veal
Margarine	Coffee	
Rice	Fresh tomatoes	
Sugar	Onions	
Sweet potatoes	Oranges	
Wheat flour	Pork	
	Potatoes	
	Salad dressing	
	Shortening	
	Soup	

Source: George, P.S., and King, G. A., *Consumer Demand for Food Commodities in the United States With Projections for 1980*, Giannini Foundation Number 26, California Agricultural Experiment Station, University of California, Davis, 1971.

Table 4-7. Relative Price Elasticity of Demand for Selected Foods Compared at Retail Level.

Percent Responsiveness of Consumers to a One Percent Change in the Price of Selected Foods		
Inelastic		Elastic
Least Response $E_d = 0$ to $-.49$	Medium Response $E_d = -.50$ to -1.0	Greatest Response $E_d =$ less than -1.0
Cereals	Beef	Chicken
Dry beans	Butter	Lamb
Eggs	Cheese	Turkey
Fluid milk	Fish	Veal
Lard	Fruit	
Potatoes	Ice cream	
Sugar	Margarine	
Vegetables	Pork	
	Shortening	

Source: Brandow, George E., *Interrelations Among Demands for Farm Products and Implications for Control of Market Supply*, Bulletin 680, Pennsylvania Agricultural Experiment Station, 1961.

Table 4-7 shows three levels of price elasticity of demand. In the first column are listed food items for which consumers already buy about all they want; price is not so much a limiting factor as to the amount bought as in the other two columns; thus a lower price does not stimulate sales so much. For foods listed in the middle column the consumer is more price conscious and so will buy considerably more if prices are reduced. Those listed in the last column have an elastic price demand—a one percent price decline will increase the quantity sold by more than one percent; that means the consumer is very responsive to price changes.

ELASTICITY OF DEMAND INFORMATION AS A BASIS OF PUBLIC POLICY

Because income elasticity is greatest when incomes are lowest, increases in the incomes of low income people will increase demand for food more than will comparable income increases for higher income people. If we have a national objective to increase expenditures for food (that is, increased sale of farm products), then family assistance in the form of cash payments to the very poor will be consistent with our objective.

If we look at the world food market, we quickly observe that lack of purchasing power restricts the amount of food consumed in most countries. Increasing per capita income in the low income countries would increase demand for farm products. As incomes in low income countries rise, we could expect them to import food to meet part of their increased demand. Thus, it would be to the interest of United States farmers for the United States to assist those nations in their development.

Learning that farm products have an inelastic *price elasticity* of demand is useful in understanding some of the farm income problems. When demand is inelastic, as we have demonstrated, the quantity demanded changes less than price. For example, when price decreased ten percent, quantity demanded rose five percent. The resulting income to the aggregate of all producers falls. Thus, it is impossible for the aggregate of producers of a product for which the demand is inelastic to improve their income by increasing production. An increase in output will cause a proportionally larger price drop, resulting in, if the producers are farmers, a decrease in total income on all farms. However, the individual farmer could increase his income by increasing production.

The inelasticity of price demand for food underlies the government policy of production controls to improve farm incomes. Because people need some minimum level of food, reducing production only slightly will cause a proportionally larger price increase and higher incomes for the producer of the controlled product. Farm marketing cooperatives use their knowledge of elasticity of demand for the product to make decisions about how many units to market to give the highest income to the producers.

IN SUMMARY

Consumer behavior in the market is fundamental to all economic activity. To meet the needs and wants of people is the purpose of all production, which, to be profitable, must satisfy either directly or indirectly, those using the product. Producers, including those in agriculture, who increase their understanding of consumer behavior will make better production and marketing decisions.

SUGGESTED READINGS

Brandow, George E. *Interrelations Among Demands for Farm Products and Implications for Control of Market Supply*, Bulletin 680. Pennsylvania Agricultural Experiment Station, Pennsylvania State University, 1971.

George, P. S., and King, G. A. *Consumer Demand for Food Commodities in the United States With Projections for 1980*, Giannini Foundation Monograph Number 26. California Agricultural Experiment Station, University of California, Davis, 1971.

Leftwich, Richard H. *The Price System and Resource Allocation*, 3rd Edition. Holt, Rinehart, and Winston, 1966, Chapters 3, 4, 5, and 6.

McConnell, Campbell R. *Economics: Principles, Problems, and Policies*, 5th Edition. McGraw-Hill Book Company, 1972, Chapters 24 and 25.

Samuelson, Paul A. *Economics an Introductory Analysis*, 9th Edition, McGraw-Hill Book Company, 1973, Chapter 22.

Shepherd, George S. *Agricultural Price Analysis*. Iowa State University Press, 1947, Chapter 4.

Trapp, James, and Sjo, John. *Kansas Farm Products on the International Market*, Bulletin 560. Kansas Agricultural Experiment Station, Kansas State University, 1972.

PART III

CONCEPT OF SUPPLY

PRODUCER BEHAVIOR IN THE MARKET   5

In Chapter 3, we pointed out that every society consists of two groups, consumers and producers. Each of us is simultaneously both, so we should not be led into thinking of the two groups as ever-warring antagonists. The fate of each depends upon the other. The consumer will not eat if the farmer does not produce; the farmer will not produce if the consumer does not eat. In a primitive society each, except the very young and very old, consumes most of what he or she can produce. As societies became more complex, people began to specialize their production. Almost no producer meets all his consumption needs; rather, he produces surpluses of those things he can produce best, and he trades the surpluses for goods he wants and needs but does not produce by himself. Thus, a market economy develops; it is essential today for our well-being.

As a producer, each of us is trying to satisfy our needs and wants either directly or indirectly; directly, if we produce what we consume; indirectly, if we trade what we produce for what we consume. But in either instance our production is determined by either our own or someone else's consumption needs. As a consumer, we each try to maximize our utility. As a producer, we each try to maximize our net returns (profits) by discovering the products that are most profitable to produce—usually those wanted most by the consumer. Thus, the most successful producers, those making the most profit, are those best able to adjust to the consumer's wants and needs. The producer in a developed economy produces for a market. The purpose of Chapters 5, 6, 7, and 8 will be to explore the effect of producer behavior on the market.

PRODUCTION

Production is the transformation of two or more resources (factors of production) into one or more products. Combining seed, fertilizer, labor, equipment, and land to produce wheat is an example of production.

FACTORS OF PRODUCTION

In the production process, resources used can be classified into four factors of production: land, labor, capital, and management.

Land provides the space and the natural resources for production. *Land is the natural resource untouched by human effort. It is the total of the earth and water, the plants and animals, and the minerals that existed in nature.* Today that pure concept of land has been nearly lost; almost all land has been altered through human effort. Thus, the portion of the earth's surface you farm is partly land, but also partly those things added by your effort—terraces, fences, fertilizers, wells.

Labor is the human effort, physical or mental, expended in the production process. In the earliest times, man was primarily a gatherer of food. Almost all human effort was used to gather berries, nuts, and seeds, which were eaten at the moment gathered. That was the simplest of all production situations; only two factors of production were used—labor and land.

Capital is land and labor combined and saved for further production. In a simple example, capital results when a person breaks a limb from a tree and uses it to dig roots. The limb was land; the effort to break it was labor. Instead of consuming the limb it was saved to dig the roots, which were eaten. The broken limb became capital. Although today's tractor is a far cry from the limb, both fit our definition for capital. To fit today's complex capital situation, we need to refine the definition: *Capital is goods and services saved from consumption, used by or as a part of the human agent in further production, including investment in improving the human resource.* Today land has had so many capital improvements that it is difficult to separate the two. Even labor today has some characteristics of capital. Getting an education is an act of saving and improving labor for later production.

Management, because it is quite different from the three other factors and because it is much more difficult to handle in economic analysis, is often excluded from the list of factors of production. *Management is the organization and operation of affairs to achieve a predetermined objective.* An abstract concept dealing with human behavior, it is difficult to identify and to measure. (In Chapter 14 we will give a detailed discussion of management.)

PRODUCTION PROBLEMS

The producer is confronted with three basic types of problems: how much to produce, how to use resources for production, and what to produce.

CONCEPT OF PRODUCTION

Thus far we have said production is the human activity of converting resources to forms that better meet human needs and wants. It is the conversion of resources into consumable goods and services. The quantity of goods and services produced varies with the quantity of resources used. Thus, we can express the relationship in the following way:

Goods and services   result from   combining resources.

Using Y to symbolize goods and services and X to symbolize resources (see Chapter 3) we could write the production concept as a simple mathematical expression, called a production function.

$$Y = f(X)$$

This is read: Y (output) is a function of X (the resources used). Output is measured in units of total physical product (TPP) produced from the units of resources (X). The total physical product varies with the quantity of resources used in production. Table 5-1 illustrates the production function for one extremely simple production situation.

Table 5-1. The Production Function: $Y = f(X_1/X_2 \ldots X_n)$.

Units of X_1 Used	TPP Units of Y Produced
0	0
1	3
2	8
3	11
4	12
5	11

Here consider just one firm producing only one product, using just one variable resource, with all other resources constant. The production function fitting our illustration is a modification of our general function

$$Y = f(X)$$
$$\text{to}$$
$$Y = f(X_1/X_2 \ldots X_n)$$

where X_1 is a specific resource used in various amounts with a set of fixed resources $X_2 \ldots X_n$. A farmer often has that situation. For example, a dairy farmer must decide, for each cow, how much protein supplement to feed in combination with grain and hay. The production of the cow can be affected by changing the amount of protein fed with a given amount of grain and hay.

Input-output information from Table 5-1 was used to construct a graph (Figure 5-1) showing the input-output relationship.

Through repeated studies scientists have observed some consistent characteristics among input-output relationships. When only one input is varied (X_1) while all others are held constant ($X_2 \ldots X_n$), TPP (total physical product) will at first increase rapidly, then increase less rapidly, and finally decrease. Because production economics rests on that observation, it is essential to explore it in greater depth.

SOME DEFINITIONS

To proceed with our study of the economics of production we must first define terms that will be used repeatedly. Unless each uses the same

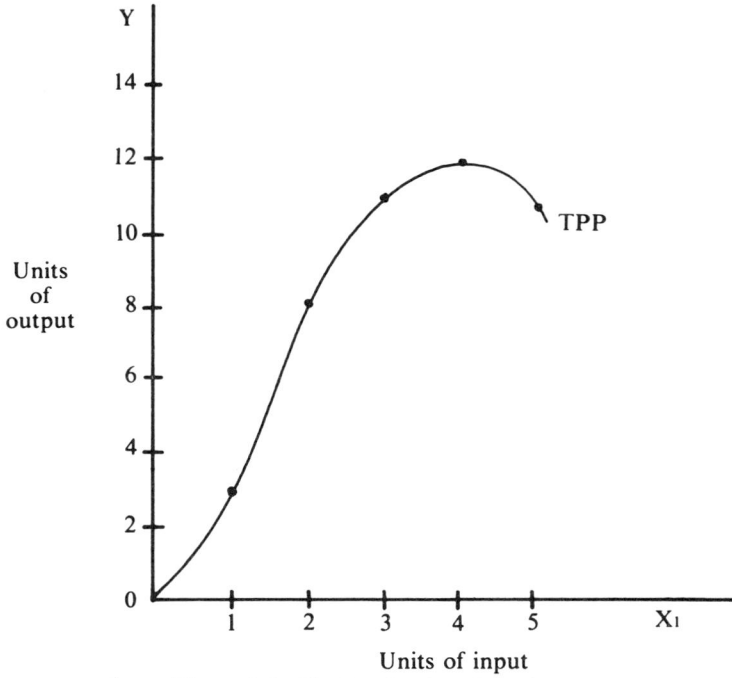

Figure 5-1. The Production Function.

definitions there can be no uniform understanding of production economics concepts.

A production function represents the input-output relationship (that is, the algebraic formula, the table, the graph).

A variable resource is a resource that varies as production changes.

A fixed resource is a resource that does not vary as production changes.

Marginal physical product (MPP) is the product added by using an additional unit of the variable resource. It is computed by dividing the additional output by the additional input necessary to produce the added product:

$$MPP = \frac{\Delta Y}{\Delta X}.$$

Average physical product (APP) is the amount of output per unit of variable input. It is computed by dividing the total physical product by the number of units of variable input used:

$$APP = \frac{Y}{X}$$

or

$$APP = \frac{TPP}{X}.$$

DIMINISHING RETURNS

Were there no diminishing returns, we would be relieved of studying economics; or, if economics existed at all, the subject would be entirely different. Economics arises from scarcity of resources available to satisfy needs and wants.

If there were no diminishing returns, there would be no limit to the amount of apples that could be grown on an acre of land. Theoretically, the nation's demand for apples could be met by planting more and more trees and putting more and more fertilizer on that one acre. We know that is impossible because of diminishing returns—a phenomenon that has become so established as a basis for economic studies, we call it the *law of diminishing returns*.

The law of diminishing returns: When successive equal units of a variable resource are added to a given quantity of a fixed resource, at some point the addition to total output will decline.

Note that in Table 5-2 we have added successive equal units of X_1 say nitrogen fertilizer, to a set of fixed resources, $X_2 \ldots X_n$, say one acre of land including everything else needed. The production of Y, say wheat, changed with each unit of X_1 used. One unit of X_1 gave us an output of 3 units of Y, 2 units, 8 units of Y, or an addition to the TPP of 5 units. Total physical product first increased at an increasing rate 0 to 3 to 8, but with the third unit of X_1, the total only increased to 11; or the addition to the total was less for the third than for the second unit of X_1. The MPP column shows the addition to the total for each successive unit of variable resource used. It is possible (as in the illustration) to use so much of the variable resource that total production is reduced. Too much nitrogen, in other words, will harm yields.

Table 5-2. Diminishing Returns.

Variable Resource X_1	Fixed Resource $X_2 \ldots X_n$	TPP Y	Addition to TPP $MPP = \frac{\Delta Y}{\Delta X_1}$	Output per Unit of X_1 $APP = \frac{Y}{X}$
0	1	0	—	—
1	1	3	3/1 = 3	3/1 = 3
2	1	8	5/1 = 5	8/2 = 4
3	1	11	3/1 = 3	11/3 = 3 2/3
4	1	12	1/1 = 1	12/4 = 3
5	1	10	−2/1 = −2	10/5 = 2

By graphing the information in Table 5-2 we can show the relationship among TPP, MPP, and APP more clearly (Figure 5-2). Though the relationships will hold in all cases, we should keep in mind that the hypothetical data were selected to illustrate the relationship as clearly as possible. If we were to collect real data, we would find variations due to such things as insect damage and soil differences. Then all points might not fall in a pattern that gives a nice smooth curve; the curve would still have the characteristic ∫ shape.

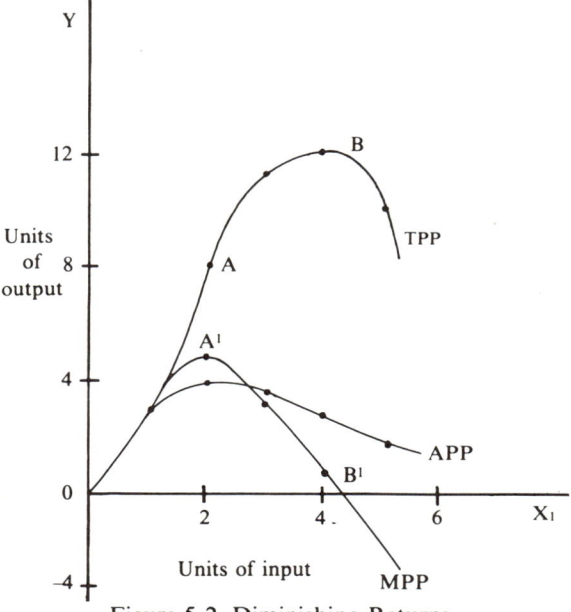

Figure 5-2. Diminishing Returns.

Certain relationships will always exist between TPP and MPP. Look at Table 5-2 and Figure 5-2. TPP from $X_1 = 0$ to $X_1 = 2$ increased at an increasing rate, and MPP was increasing. After the second unit of X_1, the addition to TPP declined so that after point A, TPP increased at a slower rate. The MPP reached its peak, point A', at the same point that TPP began its slower rate of increase. Between A and B, TPP continued to increase; and MPP, between A' and B', continued to decline but was always a positive amount. With each successive equal unit of X_1, less was added to output. Between the fourth and fifth units of X_1, the additional input did not increase output. When TPP was greatest, at point B, MPP = 0 at point B'. If enough X_1 was used to cause TPP to decline, the MPP would be negative.

Also the relationships of APP to MPP and TPP should be noted. APP always increased as long as it was less than the MPP because the marginal output pulled the average up. Each student is an expert in this concept as applied to grades. Instantly, a student knows that the grade he receives on the last test will improve his average as long as the grade is greater than the average. APP will be greatest, point C, when APP = MPP and will always be greater than zero so long as there is any output. (These relationships will be discussed further in Chapter 6.)

PRODUCER BEHAVIOR IN THE MARKET

PRODUCTIVITY POSSIBILITIES

The rate at which output increases from using additional equal units of a variable input may increase, decrease, or remain constant. For any resource–product relationship all three will occur, depending upon level of output. In Figure 5-2 we found the rate increasing from O to A, constant at A, and decreasing from A to B.

Productivity has a special meaning and cannot be considered the same as production. Production is the total output. Productivity is the relationship between output and the inputs used (Y/X) and is an efficiency measure: when per unit output increases, productivity increases.

INCREASING PRODUCTIVITY

As successive equal units of a variable resource are added to a given quantity of a fixed resource, total physical product increases at an increasing rate, or the marginal physical product increases. (See Table 5-3 and Figure 5-3.)

DECREASING PRODUCTIVITY

As successive equal units of a variable resource are added to a given quantity of a fixed resource, total physical product increases at a decreasing rate or the marginal physical product decreases. (See Table 5-3 and Figure 5-3.)

CONSTANT PRODUCTIVITY

As successive equal units of a variable resource are added to a given quantity of a fixed resource, total physical product increases at a constant rate or the marginal physical product remains constant. (See Table 5-3 and Figure 5-3.)

Table 5-3. Increasing, Decreasing, and Constant Productivity.

Increasing			Decreasing			Constant		
Units of X_1	TPP	MPP	Units of X_1	TPP	MPP	Units of X_1	TPP	MPP
0	0	0	0	0	0	0	0	0
1	1	1	1	5	5	1	3	3
2	3	2	2	9	4	2	6	3
3	6	3	3	12	3	3	9	3
4	10	4	4	14	2	4	12	3
5	15	5	5	15	1	5	15	3

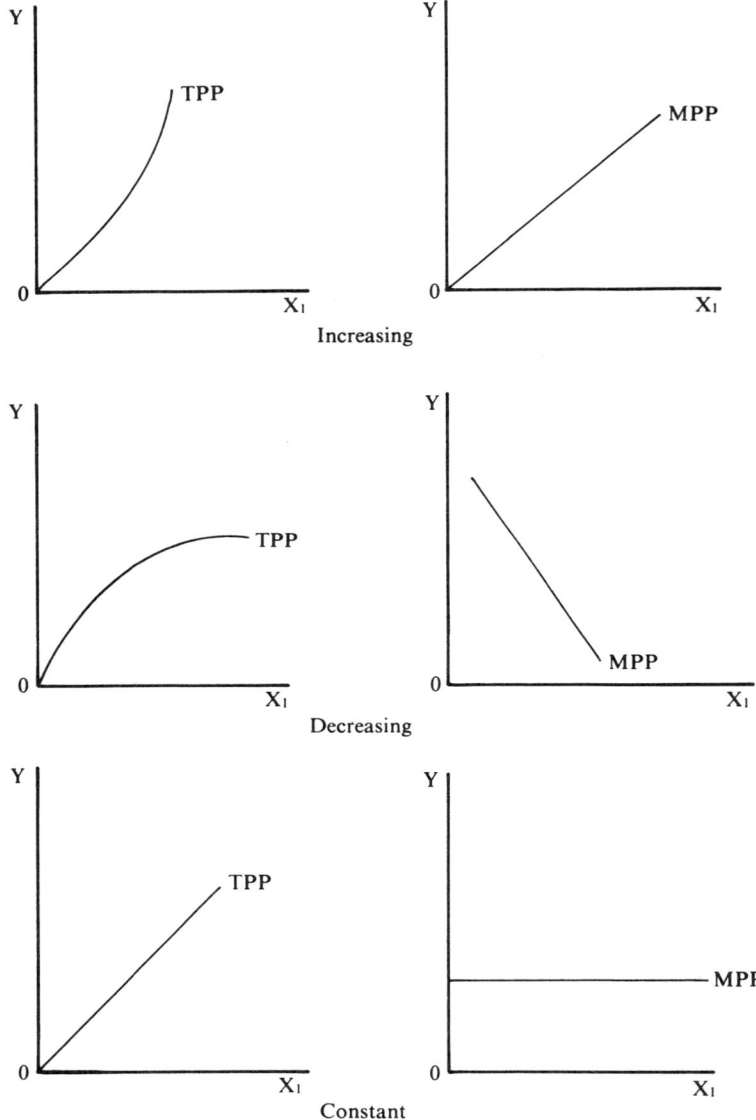

Figure 5-3. Increasing, Decreasing, and Constant Productivity.

USE OF ASSUMPTIONS

Scientists usually try to isolate the thing they are studying from outside influences. Many can come close to doing that in a laboratory. There, biologists can use growth chambers to control the factors. Chemists can carefully measure elements and compounds used in their experiments. In Chapter 1, however, we showed that economists, unlike other scientists, cannot easily use laboratory experimental techniques. When conditions cannot be controlled, we must make assumptions. For example, until physicists can create a vacuum, they assume a vacuum. Economists, because they cannot control human conditions under which production occurs, make a number of assumptions.

Scientists use assumptions to simplify complex situations, to assist them in abstracting from real situations, and to enable studying one variable at a time.

The assumptions we will use in studying the economics of production include:

1. The producer wishes to maximize profits.
2. There is a single business (farm) producing only one product.
3. There is a single infinitely divisible input, and no limit on the availability of that resource.
4. There is no uncertainty.
5. There is no change in technology or institutions.

SUGGESTED READINGS

Doll, John P., Rhodes, V. James, and West, Jerry G. *Economics of Agricultural Production, Markets, and Policy*. Richard D. Irwin, Inc., 1968, Chapter 3.

Heady, Earl O. *Economics of Agricultural Production and Resource Use*. Prentice-Hall, 1952.

Samuelson, Paul A. *Economics an Introductory Analysis*, 9th Edition. McGraw-Hill Book Company, 1973, Chapter 27.

Vincent, Warren H. Editor, *Economics and Management in Agriculture*. Prentice-Hall, 1962, Chapter 3.

CONCEPT OF SUPPLY: THE FACTOR-PRODUCT RELATIONSHIP— HOW MUCH TO PRODUCE   6

To understand the supply side of the market we shall first consider how an individual business can determine how much to produce to maximize profits. In a market economy each producer continuously adjusts his production to give the highest profits. The production process and the decision making underlying it constitute a dynamic, ever-changing situation. No one production organization will remain best (most profitable) for long. As soon as there is change in technical efficiency of the resources or in price relationships, a new organization is needed. The objective in this chapter is to show how a producer can determine the most profitable level of output. Production will take place under the conditions specified by the assumptions listed in Chapter 5. To determine the best level of output, the productivity of the resource and the prices of the inputs and the product must be known.

STAGES OF PRODUCTION

Economists have found in studying the production function, that it can be broken into three separate parts, each with its own characteristics. Being able to consider the three segments separately simplifies determining the most profitable point on the production function. Identifying the three—Stage I, Stage II, and Stage III—rests on diminishing returns and the resulting relationships among TPP, MPP, and APP (presented in Chapter 5).

Stage I which occurs when very little of the variable resource is used, is strongly influenced by the increasing productivity of the variable resource and continues beyond the point of diminishing returns because of that strong influence (while it occurs). Stage I is that portion of the production function having an increasing average physical product and a marginal physical product greater than the average physical product.

The greatest technical efficiency—the highest per unit output (Y/X)—occurs when the average physical product is highest (Point B, Figure 6-1). That occurs at the end of Stage I of production. The greatest addition to total output (TPP) from one unit of the variable input occurs when the marginal physical product is highest (Point A, Figure 6-1). It is easy to conclude that the best level of production may be at either point A or B (Figure 6-1). Neither is, and much of this chapter will be devoted to showing that profits are greater in Stage II of production than any place in Stage I.

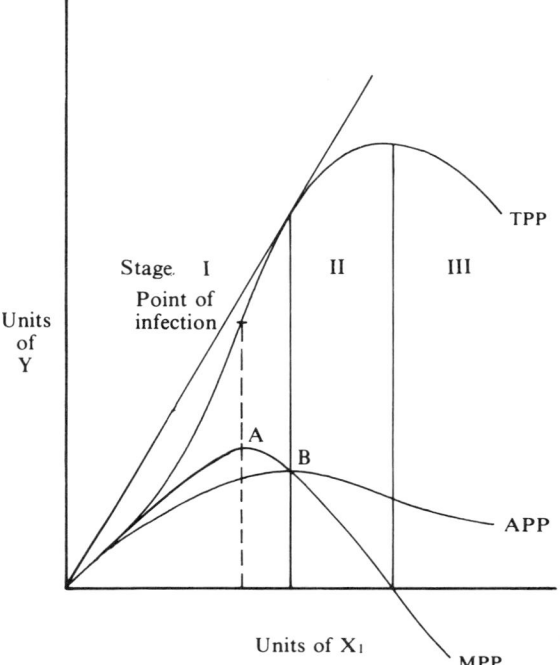

Figure 6-1. The Stages of Production.

In Stage I the MPP is greater than APP; MPP reaches its maximum, and TPP increases at an increasing rate.

Stage II is that portion of the production function when MPP is less than APP, (but greater than zero), and TPP is still increasing. Stage II ends when additional input results in a decrease in output. Stage III begins at that point (TPP is greatest and MPP = O). Profits can never be maximized in Stage III because the use of additional inputs causes a decrease in output.

The following criteria can be used to determine the stages of production:

Stage I: from point of X_1 = 0 to the point at which MPP = APP and APP is greatest.

Stage II: from point at which MPP = APP to the point at which MPP = 0 and TPP is greatest.

Stage III: from the point at which MPP = 0.

Remember, profits cannot be maximized in Stages I and III. A producer interested in maximizing profits must produce in Stage II. For that reason Stages I and III are known as irrational stages of production and Stage II as a rational stage.

POINT OF INFLECTION

As long as MPP is increasing, TPP will increase at an increasing rate. When MPP peaks and begins to decrease, TPP will continue to increase but at a decreasing rate; that is, each additional unit of input used will add less to total output. The point at which TPP changes from increasing at an increasing rate to increasing at a decreasing rate is the point of inflection. That occurs at the point of diminishing marginal productivity (MPP is greatest).

PROFIT MAXIMIZATION

Let us now show how profits can be maximized for the individual business producing only one product with a single variable resource. Algebraically, we can express it as:

$$Y = f(X_1/X_2 \ldots X_n).$$

It will always pay to use more of the variable resource, X_1, as long as the increased output, Y, from the added X_1 is worth more than the cost of the added X_1 used to produce it. That is a marginal concept. We are considering the cost of added inputs and the value of added output. We can express the criteria for profit maximization as follows:

$$\frac{\text{Change in output}}{\text{Change in input}} = \frac{\text{Price of input}}{\text{Price of output}}$$

or

$$\frac{\Delta Y}{\Delta X_1} = \frac{PX_1}{PY}.$$

To determine the most profitable level of output, we must know the productivity of the input, the price of the input, and the price of the output. Only after we have this information can we solve our problem.

The profit maximization formula can be stated more simply if we multiply each side by the PY, then,

$$MVP = PX_1.$$

MVP is read, marginal value product. The MVP is computed as follows: MPP · PY.

Whenever MVP is greater than PX_1 more X_1 should be used because the value of the added output will more than pay for the X_1 used to produce it. There is a net addition by the amount MVP exceeds PX_1 to profits. Keep using more X_1 until there is no addition to profits, or MVP = PX_1. Conversely, if MVP is less than PX_1 there will be a net reduction in profits and less X_1 should be used.

To illustrate profit maximization for the factor-product situation we have used hypothetical data to construct Table 6-1 and Figures 6-2, 6-3, and 6-4.

Table 6-1. Profit Maximization for $Y = f(X_1/X_2 \ldots X_n)$ when $PX_1 = \$6.00$ and $PY = \$1.00$.

	Units of Input X_1	Units of TPP Y	Units of APP (Y/X_1)	Units of MPP $(\Delta Y / \Delta X)$	Average Value Product AVP (APP·PY)	Marginal Value Product MVP (MPP·PY)	PX_1	Total Value Product TVP (Y·PY)	Total Cost TC $(X_1 \cdot PX)$	Profit (TVP-TC)
	1	3	3	3	$3.00	$3.00	$6.00	$3.00	$6.00	$-3.00
	2	12	6	9	6.00	9.00	6.00	12.00	12.00	0.00
Stage I	3	24	8	12	8.00	12.00	6.00	24.00	18.00	6.00
	4	38	9.5	14	9.50	14.00	6.00	38.00	24.00	14.00
	5	53	10.6	15	10.60	15.00	6.00	53.00	30.00	23.00
	6	67	11.2	14	11.20	14.00	6.00	67.00	36.00	31.00
	7	78	11.0	11	11.00	11.00	6.00	78.00	42.00	36.00
	8	86	10.8	8	10.80	8.00	6.00	86.00	48.00	38.00
Stage II	9	92	10.2	6	10.20	6.00	6.00	92.00	54.00	38.00
	10	96	9.6	4	9.60	4.00	6.00	96.00	60.00	36.00
	11	98	8.9	2	8.90	2.00	6.00	98.00	66.00	32.00
Stage III	12	94	7.8	-4	7.80	-4.00	6.00	94.00	72.00	22.00

▤ Increasing Marginal Productivity

▨ Decreasing Marginal Productivity

☐ Negative Marginal Productivity

▰ Diminishing Marginal Returns

▥ Profit Maximization MVP = PX_1

Table 6-1 illustrates the physical relationships between inputs (X_1) and output (Y) and how to determine the optimum level of production.

Increasing and decreasing productivity: note MPP first increases, 3, 9, 12, 14, 15, through 5 units of X_1. After the fifth unit MPP begins to decrease. Diminishing returns are apparent after the fifth unit of X_1.

Stages of production: Stage I of production ends and Stage II begins after the seventh unit of X_1, when MPP = APP (11 = 11) and APP is highest (11). Stage II ends and Stage III begins after the eleventh unit of input, when MPP = 0 and TPP is greatest, 98.

Optimum level of production: Profits are maximized with the ninth unit of input, when MVP = PX_1. By checking the profit column, we can confirm that this is the point at which profits, $38.00, are highest.

The data in Table 6-1 are shown graphically in Figures 6-2, 6-3, and 6-4. Figure 6-2 shows the physical relationships. Special attention should be given to the incremental increases of the TPP and MPP curves. The step increases (shaded areas) show the increase in TPP resulting from each successive unit of input used.

FACTOR-PRODUCT RELATIONSHIP—HOW MUCH TO PRODUCE

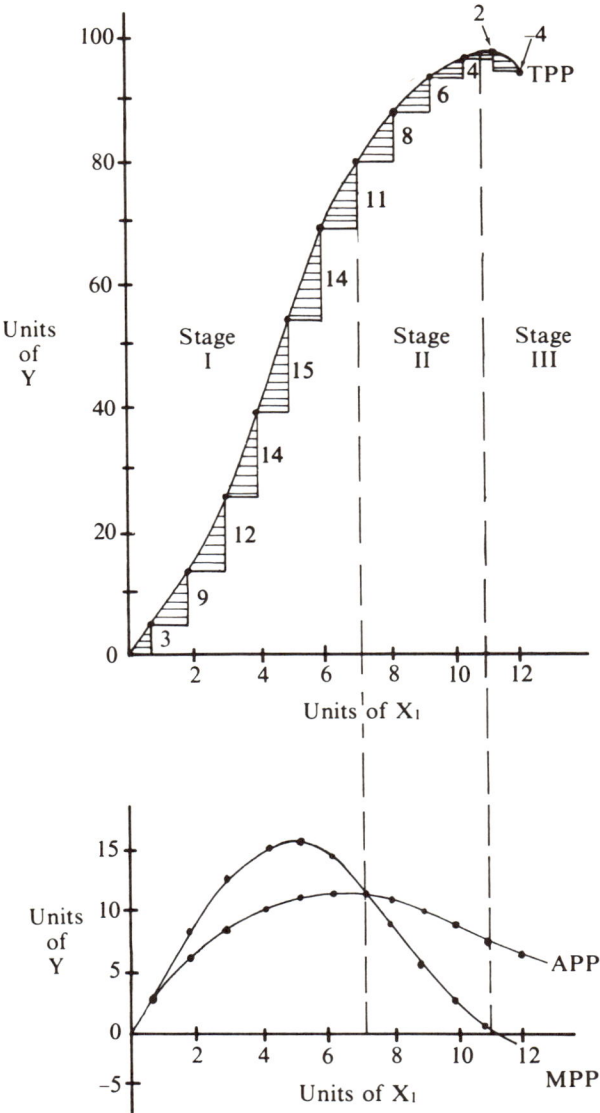

Figure 6-2. Production Function: $Y = f(X_1/X_2 \ldots X_n)$.

In Figure 6-3 we plotted the TVP, MVP, and AVP curves. Note that taking the physical product times its price did not alter the relationships seen in Figure 6-2.

The formula for profit maximization, MVP = PX_1, is the criterion or

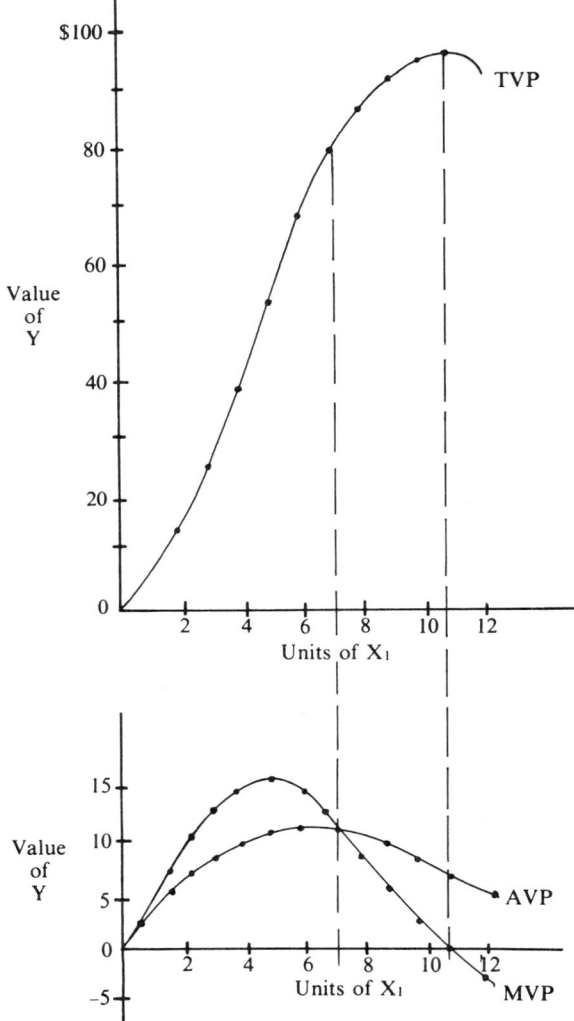

Figure 6-3. Total Value Product, Marginal Value Product, Average Value Product.

guide we shall use in determining the best level of production, defined not as the level of production that gives the greatest profit for a single unit of input, but that which gives the greatest total profit. Remember, each increment of input can be used only once; there can be only one fifth increment. Let us carefully study Figure 6-4. When you understand that stopping with the highest profits from one unit of input (the fifth unit) will not result in the greatest total profits, then you will have overcome one of the major hurdles confronting the beginning economics student. Total profits are the sum of the profits resulting from using each unit of resource.

(Profit = TVP-TC)

To apply the accounting profit formula to Figure 6-4, we must show how TVP and TC is the sum of all the increments: TVP is the sum of all the area (a through i) under the MVP curve; TC is the sum of all the area under the PX_1 line (a through i); and profit is the sum of all the area (a through i) between the PX_1 line and the MVP curve. Thus, we find profits maximized at MVP = PX_1. After that point the cost of using another unit (PX_1) will exceed the value of the product (MVP) produced. The total profits are the sum of the profits (MVP-PX_1) for each unit of X_1 used, a + b + ... +i. The fifth unit of X_1 adds more to profits than any other unit, but we can only get the fifth, e, addition to profits by first having a, b, c, and d. Because e adds the most, it is easy to conclude that no more X_1 should be used. But stopping there would result in foregoing profits from f, g, h, and i, all of which have higher returns than their cost of production ($6). The producer wishing to maximize profits must take advantage of all profit opportunities.

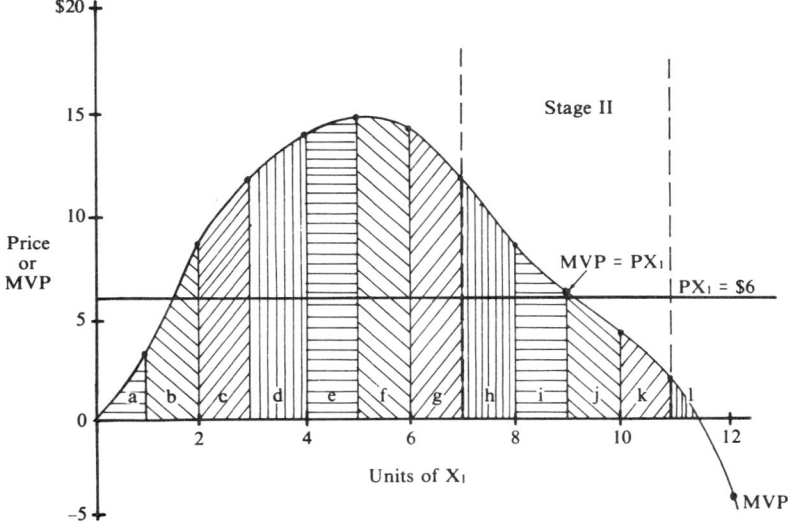

Figure 6-4. Profit Maximization: MVP = PX_1.

SPECIAL PROBLEMS AND LIMITATIONS

To present the factor-product relationship we made several assumptions. Also, to present the relationship as simply as possible, we ignored some special situations, some of which we now will consider.

THE SUFFICIENT CONDITIONS

Profits are maximized when MVP = PX_1. But Figure 6-4 shows MVP = PX_1 at a point between 1 and 2 units of input as well as at the seventh unit, which was most profitable. Why? Visually surveying the diagram, it can be seen that all profits would have been given up if production had stopped between 1 and 2 units of input. Though MVP = PX_1 is a necessary condition for profit maximization, it must occur when there are diminishing marginal returns. As long as the MPP is greater than the APP, the APP will increase. Without knowing the prices of Y or X_1, we can conclude that profits will increase (or losses decrease) while APP is increasing. If the producer is to produce at all, he should always produce in Stage II of production, the only stage in which profits can be maximized.

STAGES OF PRODUCTION AND PRODUCTION DECISIONS

The decisions on "how much input to use" and "how much product to produce" are not separate and different decisions. They are the same. Agriculturalists advising producers on how much input to use (or how much product to produce) have very different advising problems, depending on the stage of production. If a producer is in Stage III, a recommendation is fairly straightforward—use less input or produce less product. If the producer is in Stage I, the recommendation would be to use more of the input or produce more product. We do not even need to know prices to make such recommendations. In Stage II, however, we can make no recommendations about input use or level of production until we know both the MPP and the prices of X_1 and Y. For any of you planning to be extension agents or vocational agriculture teachers, that fact will have a real practical application. For example, if your farmer clients are using no fertilizer but using it would increase profits, you can make a general recommendation to all farmers—use fertilizer; use more fertilizer. Everyone following your advice will have good results. But as soon as some farmers use enough fertilizer to be in Stage II, your rule of thumb recommendation—to use more fertilizer—could get you into trouble. Those farmers whose increased use would put them beyond MVP = PX_1 would have lower profits. Only for farmers in Stage I are general or rule of thumb (fifty pounds of nitrogen per acre) recommendations useful. Each farmer's resource use problems are unique when they are in Stage II. A farm adviser must teach farmers how to figure their MVP and determine PX_1 so they can individually make their resource-use decisions.

CHANGE IN PRICES

Both PX_1 and PY are necessary to determine MVP = PX_1. Any change in the price of either the product or the input will give a new optimum resource level. If the PY goes up, it pays to use more X_1; if the PY falls, the amount of X_1 used must be cut back. If the PX_1 falls, use more X_1; if PX_1 increases, use less. (See Figures 6-5 and 6-6.)

FACTOR-PRODUCT RELATIONSHIP—HOW MUCH TO PRODUCE

When PX_1 = A, profits can be maximized by using OA units of X_1 (Figure 6-5). If PX_1 increases to B, profits will be maximized by reducing the use of X_1 to OB. Or if the PX_1 = D, then increase use of X_1 to OD. Note that at any PX_1 over C, PX exceeds the MVP at all points and no profits are possible.

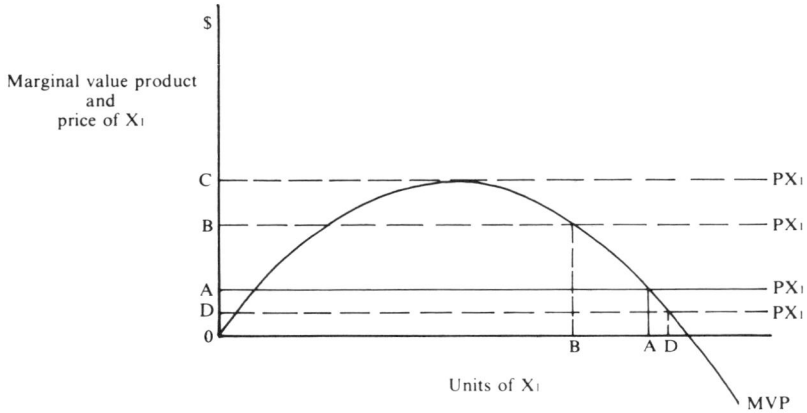

Figure 6-5. Effect of a Change in Price of the Input on Level of Input use.

With a given PY there will be $MVP_1 = PX_1$ using OA of X_1 (Figure 6-6). If the PY increases, the MVP will be higher, MVP_2; profits will be maximized when more X_1 is used, AB units of X_1. If the PY falls, the MVP_3 will be lower and less X_1, OC, should be used.

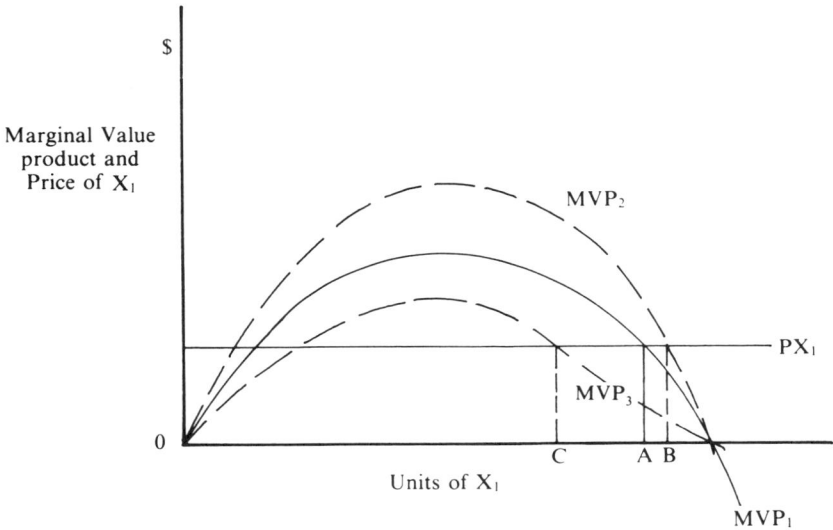

Figure 6-6. Effect of a Change in Price of the Product on Level of Input Use.

INDIVISIBILITY OF INPUTS

We assumed that the inputs are infinitely divisible to enable us to determine exactly the optimum resource use. Even with inputs (such as fertilizer) that can be applied in any amount, in practice they are usually applied in some unit (for example, one pound, two pound, or three pound increments). We can compute the TPP only at points for those units (Figure 6-7). Observe how the TPP curve (the points connected) changed as the size increment was increased. The smaller the increment, the greater will be the accuracy, but we can only guess at the results between the points until a smaller increment is used.

In that MPP = $\frac{\Delta Y}{\Delta X_1}$ we will find that the MPP between each point remains unchanged; thus, it really is the average of a whole series of unknown MPPs based on infinitely divisible units of X_1. Many farm inputs are not readily divisible. A tractor or combine, a cow or a sow, a well or a terrace, come in one unit increments of some size and cannot be further divided.

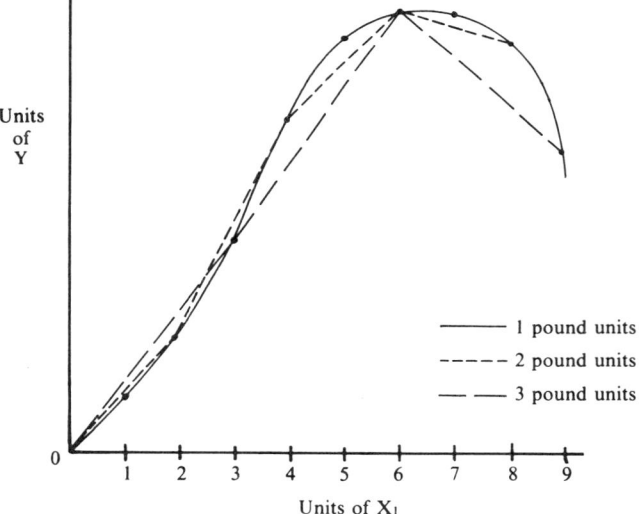

Figure 6-7. The Problem of Indivisibility of Inputs.

MULTIPLE EXPECTATIONS

When considering $Y = f(X_1/X_2 \ldots X_n)$ there can be only one possible value of Y. Using that model—called a *single expectation model*—we held all factors and conditions constant, $/X_2 \ldots X_n$; only X_1 was permitted to change. On farms, however, production has many conditions, always changing and uncontrollable, that affect the productiveness of X_1—for example, diseases, temperature, wind, sunlight, insects. Under such conditions the farmer has a *multiple-expectation model*. He does not produce under conditions of no uncertainty; he is, in fact, uncertain as to production.

FACTOR-PRODUCT RELATIONSHIP—HOW MUCH TO PRODUCE   73

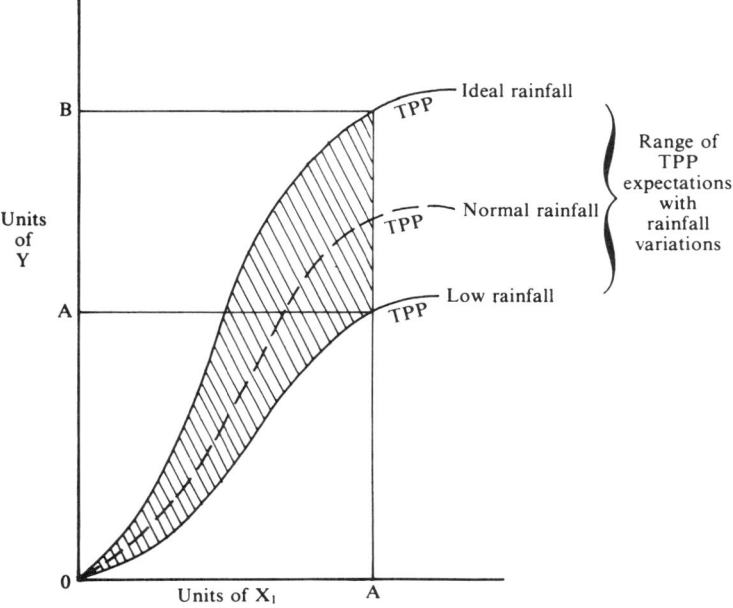

Figure 6-8. Multiple Expectation Model.

In Figure 6-8, a farmer producing product Y (grain sorghum) using OA units of X_1 (fertilizer) would have a yield expectation ranging from Y = OA to Y = OB depending upon rainfall. Under the least favorable rainfall, an OA yield could be expected. (The shaded area represents all possible reasonable yield expectations.) Under such a situation not only is TPP a wide band, but also the MPP is a wide band with many MVP = PX_1 possibilities. Making the right resource-use decision depends on the producer's ability to estimate the true yield within this range of expectations.

TECHNOLOGY

Technology, including its application and results from its use, is complex. *In economics we consider technology to be knowledge applied to improve the production process.* Improvement in the production process is measured by the increase in output per unit of input $\left(\frac{output}{input}\right)$

For a given level of input, it is possible to get a higher output; that is, an improved variety gives a higher per acre yield, as illustrated in Figure 6-9. With the existing technology, we would have the input-output relationship represented by TPP_1. Using OAX_1 would give an output of OAY. Applying technology results in an improved input-output relationship as represented by TPP_2, where we get an output of OBY using OAX_1. Technology increased output by AB.

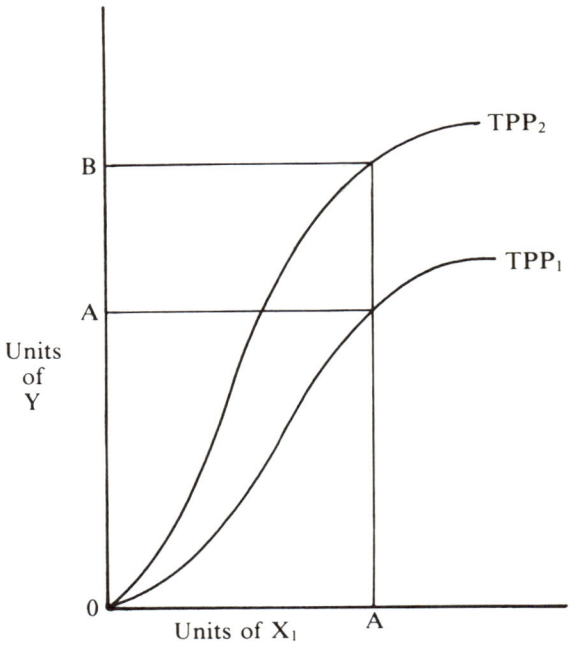

Figure 6-9. Effect of Technology on the Production Function.

YIELD MAXIMIZATION

Agriculturalists are constantly being advised to maximize output. In any farm paper or magazine, we can find articles and advertisements urging increased output. On the surface, the statements seem so reasonable and logical, we may not analyze what is said. Why, if profits are being made, can they not be increased by using more and more inputs? Let us return to the concept of diminishing marginal returns. Remember, each additional unit has its unique effectiveness as an input. As more and more units are used, each additional unit eventually adds less to the total product. If we convert the TPP and MPP information to TVP and MVP by multiplying by the PY, we observe (Figure 6-10) that for maximum production (total value product is highest), TVP = OA, when OB units of X_1 are used. When TVP is highest, MVP = 0. Profits are maximized when MVP = PX_1. If OB units of X_1 are used, then MVP = 0; and for MVP = PX_1, the PX_1 must be equal to zero. We can thus conclude the only time production maximization is consistent with profit maximization is when PX_1 = 0, or when the input is free.

PROFIT MAXIMIZATION IN CONFLICT WITH NONECONOMIC LIFE GOALS

Although we began our discussion of the factor-product relationship

FACTOR-PRODUCT RELATIONSHIP—HOW MUCH TO PRODUCE

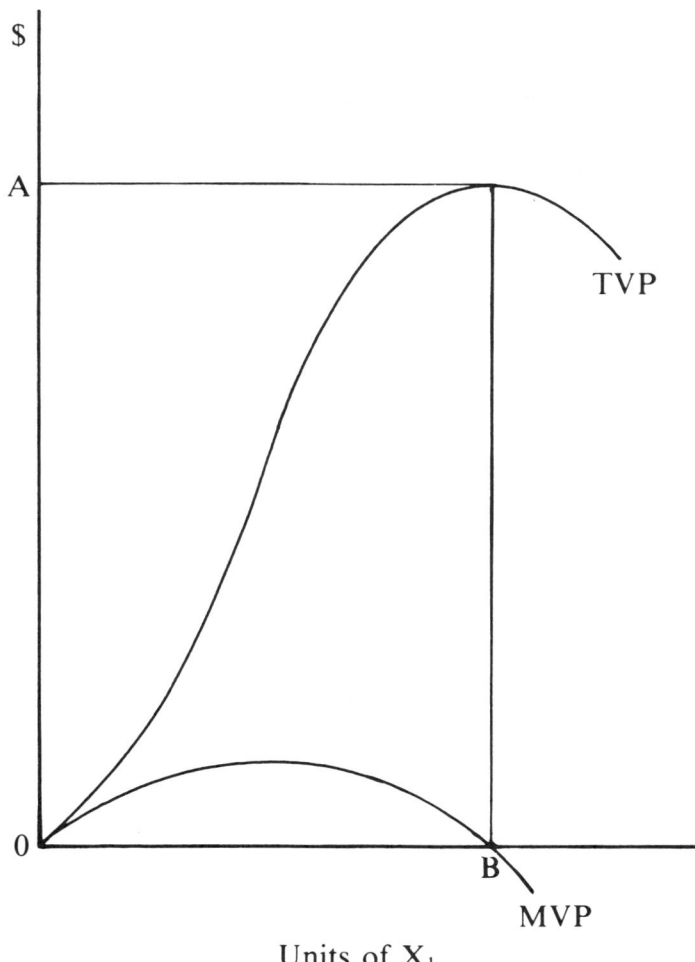

Figure 6-10. Yield Maximization.

on the assumption the producer wants to maximize profits, we must remember producers have other objectives that may be in conflict with profit maximization. To achieve the other objectives, some profits may have to be given up. For each of us leisure, friendships, community activities, and other "noneconomic quality of life" factors deeply affect our economic actions. How much profit is given up willingly depends on how important the other factors are to the individual.

IN SUMMARY

If the business objective is to maximize profits, then continue using additional inputs, thus increasing total cost, as long as the value of the increased output is greater than the increased cost of the input used in getting the additional output.

SUGGESTED READINGS

Doll, John P., Rhodes, V. James, and West, Jerry G. *Economics of Agricultural Production, Markets, and Policy*. Richard D. Irwin, Inc., 1968, Chapter 4.

Heady, Earl O. *Economics of Agricultural Production and Resource Use*. Prentice-Hall, 1952, Chapter 3.

Leftwich, Richard H. *The Price System and Resource Allocation*, 3rd Edition. Holt, Rinehart, and Winston, 1965, Chapter 7.

Samuelson, Paul A. *Economics an Introductory Analysis*, 9th Edition. McGraw-Hill Book Company, 1973, Chapter 27.

Vincent, Warren H., Editor. *Economics and Management in Agriculture*. Prentice-Hall, 1962, Chapter 4.

THE COST OF PRODUCTION 7

In the production process we use scarce resources. Because they are scarce, expenses are incurred in acquiring them. The expense of acquiring resources for producing a good or service is a cost. Costs are related to production and are expressed in terms of expenditures for given levels of output. In this chapter we shall show how costs are classified, how costs are computed, how costs are used to compute profits, the effect of time and technology on costs, and the effect of output on costs.

CLASSIFICATION OF COSTS

CASH, NONCASH, OPPORTUNITY COSTS

Cash costs require an out-of-pocket expenditure: the exchange of money for resources. Cash costs are easily identified. A farmer or agribusiness manager knows when he purchases and pays for fertilizer, grain, oil, or electricity. Noncash costs, a bit more difficult to identify, often go unnoticed. For example, a farmer with a hired employee is aware that this labor is a cost of production. But he is not so aware that his own labor (not a cash cost) is just as real a cost as the hired labor. Among noncash costs are the cost of using his own land (rent) and of using his own capital (interest). When another's land or capital is used, the cost is more obvious because a cash outlay is involved. A third type, opportunity cost, is even easier than noncash costs to overlook. *Opportunity cost is potential income foregone from a resource as a result of using that resource for another line of production.*

An example of cash costs familiar to students is the cash paid for tuition, room, books, and clothing—all associated with enrolling in college. Some noncash costs (at least for the student directly) include the depreciation on his car and the laundry his mother does for him. But the greatest cost of attending college is the opportunity cost, which may not even be recognized. Each student, in forgoing wages that could be earned if he were not in college, must consider those lost wages a part of the cost of the education. In Chapter 9 we will apply opportunity costs to a farm management problem.

FIXED AND VARIABLE COSTS

Fixed costs are those arising from using resources whose quantity cannot be changed during the production period and are used even if no pro-

duction is undertaken. An example of a fixed resource is a 100-animal cattle shed on a farm currently feeding a lot of cattle. That shed is a fixed resource because for that lot of cattle no change can be made in the cost of using the shed. Seed already planted is a fixed cost. The cost is incurred, cannot be recovered or changed, regardless of yield. The interest on a mortgage also must be paid regardless of level of production. Fixed costs need not be considered in many management decisions. For example, the cost of using the cattle shed will not affect the choice of ration to feed cattle.

Variable costs are those that can be changed during the production period. For example, at the time of planting a farmer may choose the amount of fertilizer to apply, and at any time during the growing period he may apply more. It is possible to vary the amount and thus to affect production. Variable costs must be considered in making management decisions.

MARGINAL COSTS

Marginal cost is the change in total cost associated with producing one more unit of output. A feedlot operator trying to decide whether to continue feeding a lot of steers must know his additional cost for getting each additional pound of gain. What is the cost of producing one more unit? Whatever the amount, that amount is the marginal cost.

COMPUTATION OF COSTS

In economic analysis we are concerned with seven types of costs directly related to and derived from the production function. To make production decisions, it is necessary to understand the relationship between the production function and costs and how each type of cost is computed.

In Table 7-1 and Figure 7-1 the computation and relationships are shown. Each cost is expressed in terms of output. Total fixed costs (TFC), total variable costs (TVC), and total costs (TC) are expressed for specific levels of output. Average fixed costs (AFC), average variable costs (AVC), average total costs (ATC), and marginal costs (MC) are expressed in terms of costs per unit of output. Each is computed as follows:

Total fixed cost = Sum of all fixed costs.
Total variable costs = Sum of all variable costs.
Total cost = Sum of all fixed and variable costs,
or
TC = TFC + TVC.
Average fixed costs = $\dfrac{\text{Total fixed costs}}{\text{Units of output}}$,
or
$AFC = \dfrac{TFC}{Y}$.

Average variable costs = $\dfrac{\text{Total variable costs}}{\text{Units of output}}$,

or

$$AVC = \dfrac{TVC}{Y}$$

Average total cost = $\dfrac{\text{Total costs}}{\text{Units of output}}$,

or

$$ATC = \dfrac{TC}{Y}$$

Marginal cost = $\dfrac{\text{Change in total costs}}{\text{Change in output}}$,

or

$$MC = \dfrac{\Delta TC}{\Delta Y}$$

Table 7-1. Costs Computed for An Input-Output Relationship $Y = f(X_1/X_2....X_n)$ when the $PX_1 = \$3.00$.

Input (units of X_1)	Output (units of Y)	Total Fixed Costs (TFC)	Total Variable Costs (TVC)	Total Costs (TC)	Average Fixed Costs (AFC)	Average Variable Costs (AVC)	Average Total Costs (ATC)	Marginal Cost (MC)
0	0	$10.00	$ .00	$10.00	$ ---	$ ---	$ ---	$ ---
1	3	10.00	3.00	13.00	3.33	1.00	4.33	$ 1.00
2	8	10.00	6.00	16.00	1.25	.75	2.00	.60
3	15	10.00	9.00	19.00	.67	.60	1.26	.43
4	18	10.00	12.00	22.00	.55	.67	1.22	1.00
5	20	10.00	15.00	25.00	.50	.75	1.25	1.50
6	21	10.00	18.00	28.00	.48	.86	1.33	3.00

RELATION OF COSTS TO THE PRODUCTION FUNCTION

In studying cost relationships, economists have observed certain relationships always exist between the TPP, MPP, and APP curves and the cost curves. (We can see the relationships in both Table 7-1 and Figure 7-1). Total fixed cost, ten dollars, is unchanged, regardless of output. Diagrammed, it results in a horizontal line. Total variable cost and total costs increase as output increases; they are upward sloping curves. Average fixed costs, as they are spread over more units of output, become smaller as output increases. The AFC curve is downward sloping as long as TPP increases. Average variable costs decline as long as the average physical product is increasing, but they increase after APP begins to decline. Thus, the AVC curve will have a ∪ shape, first declining then increasing. Average total costs first decline because average fixed cost is spread over more units while the efficiency of the variable input is increasing. After the efficiency begins to diminish ATC reaches a minimum and then will turn upward. Marginal costs are influenced by the efficiency of the variable input used. At first MC declines, and as the efficiency of the variable input declines MC begins to increase. The marginal cost curve, like the average variable cost curve, will be ∪ shaped.

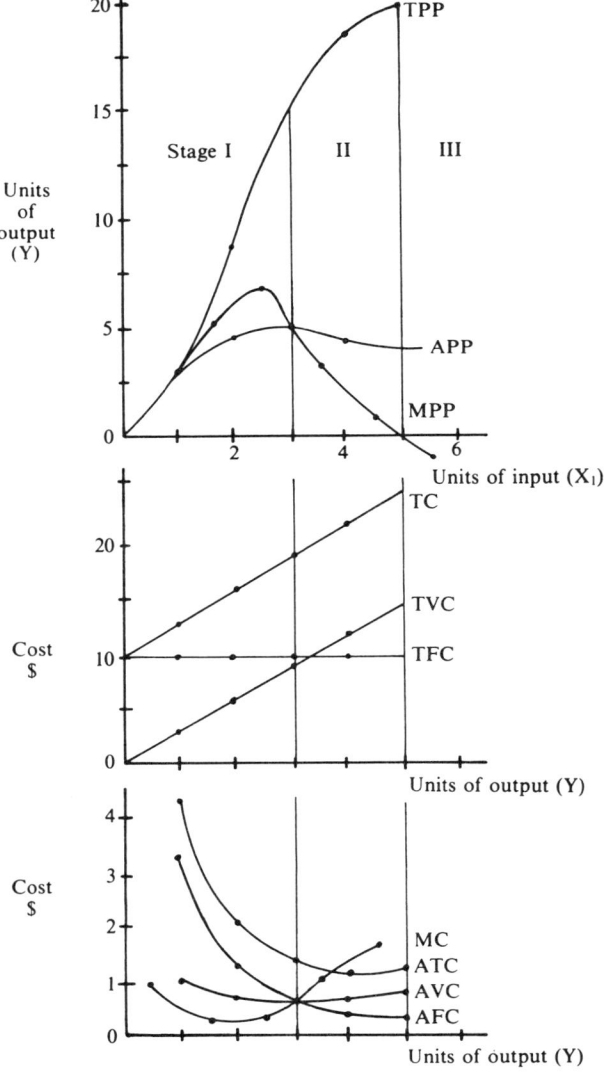

Figure 7-1. Relationship between the Production Function and Cost Curves.

In Figure 7-1 we can further observe that when MPP is greater than APP, APP is increasing, AVC is decreasing, and MC is less than AVC. When MPP = APP, APP is at a maximum, MC = AVC, and AVC is at a minimum. All these characteristics occur in Stage I of production. All per unit costs, except MC, decline throughout Stage I.

When MPP is less than APP, APP is decreasing, MC is greater than AVC, and both MC and AVC are increasing. These relationships are characteristic of Stage II of production. In Stage II, AVC and MC are increasing.

In Chapter 6 we showed that profits can be maximized only in Stage II of production. *This means that profits are maximized when AVC and MC are increasing.* That is contrary to our "everyone-is-an-economist" belief that lower unit costs mean higher profits. In almost every discussion of farm income problems, some will advise that to improve net income, costs must be reduced. But look carefully at the cost curves in Figure 7-1. In Stage II, the profit maximization stage, TC, TVC, AVC, and MC all continue to increase. We must be very careful in our study of costs to understand that usually if unit costs are decreasing, use of the variable input should be increased, thus increasing costs and increasing profits. Profits are increased because the additional output resulting from the use of more resources is worth more than the cost of producing it.

PROFIT MAXIMIZATION

In Chapter 6 we showed a criterion for profit maximization for the factor-product situation: $MVP_y = PX_1$. An alternative criterion for determining the most profitable level of output is to equate the value of one more unit of output with the cost of producing it. As long as the value of the last unit exceeds the cost (MC) of producing it, more input should be used. The value of the last unit is called marginal revenue (MR). Written in a formula we have:

Value of 1 unit of output = Cost of producing that 1 unit of output, or
MR = MC when $MC = \frac{\Delta TC}{\Delta Y}$.

Table 7-2. Profit Maximization for $Y = f(X_1/X_2....X_n)$ When $PX_1 = \$3.00$ and MR = $1.50.

Units of X	Units of Y	ATC	AVC	MC	MR	Profit (TVP-TC)
0	0	—	—	—	—	—
1	3	$4.33	$1.00	$1.00	$1.50	$ −8.00
2	8	2.00	.75	.60	1.50	−4.00
3	15	1.26	.60	.43	1.50	3.50
4	18	1.22	.67	1.00	1.50	5.00
5	20	1.25	.75	1.50	1.50	5.00
6	21	1.33	.86	3.00	1.50	3.50

☐ MC = MR

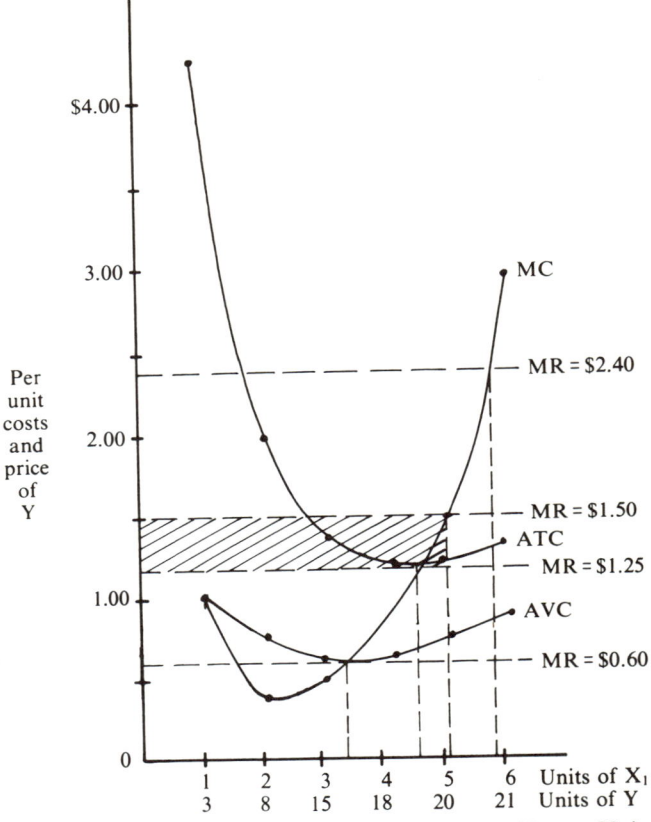

Figure 7-2. Profit Maximization for $Y = f(X_1/X_2....X_n)$
When $PX_1 = \$3.00$ and $MR = \$1.50$.

Table 7-2 illustrates how to determine the most profitable production level. We computed the marginal cost for the output at each level of input. The added cost of producing each of the two units produced with the fourth unit of X was $1.50, which equalled the value of each unit. The most profitable level of output, MC = MR is at that level, X = 5.

Graphically (Figure 7-2), it is easier to visualize why the point, MC = MR, is the most profitable level of output. When MR = $1.50 the shaded area, which extends from the low ATC of $1.25, represents profits. Because a MR equal to any portion of the MC curve above ATC will more than cover all unit costs, that portion may be used for long-term planning. No one would enter into business who did not expect to cover all costs. Sometimes however, we misjudge future prices or yields and find we have fixed costs that cannot be recovered and may exceed possible returns. For example, fertilizer once applied cannot be recovered except by harvesting the crop. Only noncommitted resources remain as costs that can be changed; for example, when wheat is ripe only harvesting and marketing costs are yet variable. Whether one decides to incur those additional costs depends upon the MR. As long as it is greater than the lowest point on the AVC, the additional costs should be incurred, even though total cost might be greater than total revenue. If profits cannot be maximized, the next best alternative would be to minimize losses. Applying the amount of MR that is above AVC against those fixed costs will reduce losses. In the short run a producer will stay in production as long as MR is greater than AVC. Using Figure 7-2 we can illustrate that. If you are already in production, any MR above $.60 will induce you to stay in production and to use at least between 3 and 4 units of X_1. As MR increases, the amount of X_1 used will increase. At MR = $1.22, by using slightly more than 4 units of X_1, a producer would just cover ATC. Profits then would increase and it would pay to use more X_1 as MR increases to $1.50 and $2.40.

CHANGE IN TECHNOLOGY

Adopting new technology results in an improved input-output ratio. The TPP is increased for any level of input use, which means the cost of the variable input is spread over more units of output. We could therefore expect technology to reduce per unit costs, and using more units would increase profits, as illustrated in Figure 7-3.

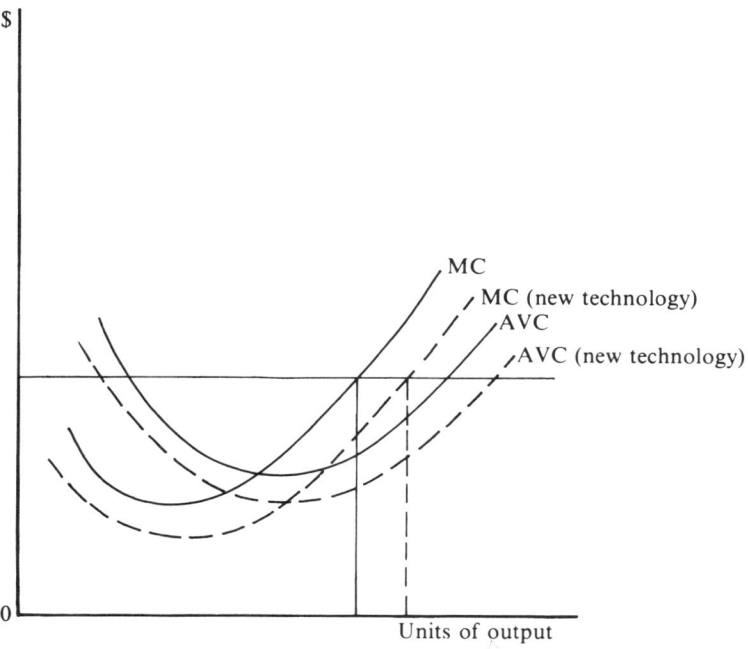

Figure 7-3. Effect of Technology on Unit Costs.

TIME AND COSTS

Costs are classified into variable or fixed costs, categories depending on the time period. The shorter the time, the greater will be the portion of costs that is fixed; the longer the time, the greater the portion that is variable. The economic short run is a time within a production period so short that nearly all costs are fixed and cannot be changed to affect output. The economic long run is a time period long enough so nearly all costs can be changed. This concept of time is not measured in terms of weeks or days, but in terms of whether costs can be changed.

A broiler enterprise in which the entire production period is about ten weeks can be considered a long-run situation. An apple orchard with a production period of twenty years can also be so considered. In the one case it would take ten weeks, in the other twenty years, for a producer to vary most costs.

ECONOMIES OF SCALE

We have limited our study to one production period in which only one resource is varied and all others are fixed. A real-world firm, of course, has successive production periods often running over many years, and so its operator has sufficient time to change several or all resources. Over time he will experiment with businesses of different sizes. So far, in studying $Y = f(X_1/X_2....X_n,)$ the fixed resources, $X_2....X_n$, have limited the firm to just that one size; output can be changed only by changing the amount of X_1 used.

What happens when it is possible to add more land to the business as well as more fertilizer? It is immediately apparent that the remaining fixed costs—tractor, combine, operator's labor—can be spread over more units of output, thus reducing per unit fixed costs. Lower unit fixed costs will influence (lower) the average total costs. For each size or scale of operation, the firm will have a new set of cost curves. Knowing each set of cost curves (short run) provides information for determining the most profitable size of business as well as the best level of variable resource use for each size of business.

The "mass production" of United States industry has made possible the low cost production of appliances, clothing, and automobiles. All such products have large fixed costs. Spreading the fixed costs over more units of output gives us the benefits of *economies of scale*.

Economies of scale refers to reduction in output unit costs as output is increased. (Output unit costs are the average total costs, $\frac{TC}{Y}$). Economies occur when the unit costs decline as output increases. As illustrated in Figure 7-4, a small farm producing 200 acres of wheat would find the most profitable level of resource use associated with ATC_1; 400 acres, with ATC_2; 600 acres, with ATC_3; 800 acres, with ATC_4; and 1,000 acres, with ATC_5. Moving from 200 acres to 400 acres to 600 acres reduced average total cost—each bushel of wheat produced cost less as the size of farm was increased. That is what we call economies of scale. At each production level there are short-run cost curves such as ATC_1, ATC_2, ATC_3, ATC_4, and ATC_5. If we connect them, we have a long-run average total cost (LRATC) curve. Figure 7-4 shows that after ATC_3 the LRATC began to increase. Such increasing cost per unit is called *diseconomies of scale*. Diseconomies arise primarily from losses in efficiency of management. Usually as a business grows, its organization becomes more complex to manage, resulting in diminishing returns to management. A business aware of diseconomies will cut back its size to increase profits. Thus, most businesses will not have diseconomies.

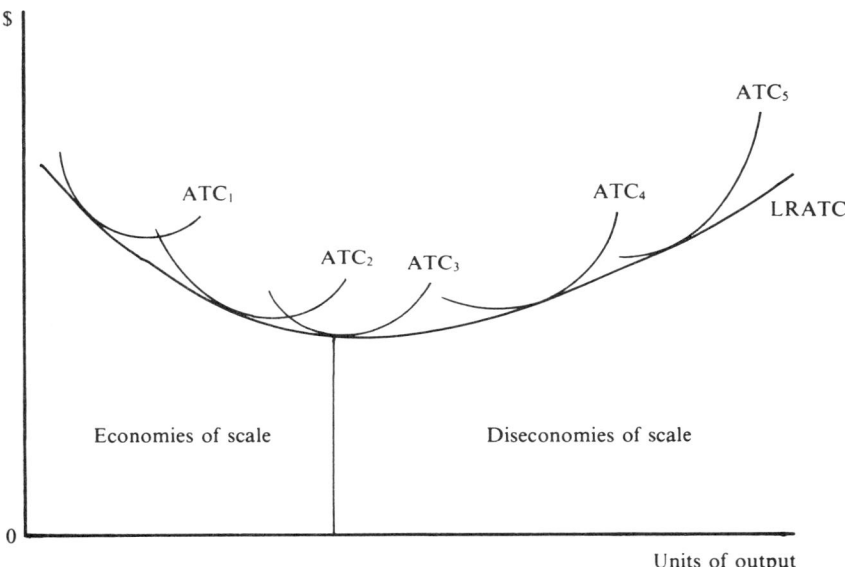

Figure 7-4. Economies and Diseconomies of Scale.

Because diseconomies of scale arise primarily from losses in management efficiency, the optimum size of a business varies according to the managerial skill in that business. A Kansas State University farm management adviser, Clarence Bartlett, once stated that his first task with a new client was to determine whether he was a "20 or 200 cow man." There is a lot of wisdom in that statement. A cow man with the managerial skill to handle 200 cows will have economies of scale up to that point. The cow man who can handle just 20 cows profitably will experience diseconomies of scale if he attempts to handle more. Thus, he will make more on 20 cows than on 200; in fact, 200 might be more than he could handle at all.

PUBLIC SERVICES

Most agriculturalists must deal daily with public services—schools, safety, water districts, waste disposal. Because private industry has benefited so much from economies of scale, there is great interest in applying the concept to the production of public services. Thus, we find pressure to consolidate services and government units. Often, however, consolidation does not noticeably reduce costs, resulting in bewilderment and disappointment. The apparent lack of economies of scale in producing public services can be attributed partly to differences between private and public goods and services. Most public production, unlike private, produces services difficult to measure and to assign value to—education, police protection, and public welfare. Thus, we cannot compute per unit costs to compare organizations of different sizes. Total costs for a consolidated school district are often greater than the sum of costs for the previous several districts, thus disappointing citizens. But because quality and quantity (both difficult to measure) of education may have been improved significantly, there may in fact have been economies of scale. To implement, directly, economies of scale concepts, so useful in private businesses, may be difficult for public organizations.

IN SUMMARY

Costs result from using scarce (expensive) resources in the production process. The various cost functions are derived from the production function. The level of production possible depends on the cost of production. In Chapter 10 we will show how the supply schedule is determined from cost information.

SUGGESTED READINGS

Doll, John P., Rhodes, V. James, and West, Jerry G. *Economics of Agricultural Production, Markets, and Policy*. Richard D. Irwin, Inc., 1968, Chapter 7.

Heady, Earl O. *Economics of Agricultural Production and Resource Use*. Prentice-Hall, 1952, Chapters 11 and 12.

Leftwich, Richard H. *The Price System and Resource Allocation*, 3rd Edition. Holt, Rinehart, and Winston, 1966.

Peterson, Willis L. *Principles of Economics: Micro*. Richard D. Irwin, Inc., 1974, Chapter 7.

Samuelson, Paul A. *Economics an Introductory Analysis*, 9th Edition. McGraw-Hill Book Company, 1973, Chapters 23 and 24.

THE FACTOR-FACTOR RELATIONSHIP — HOW TO COMBINE INPUTS   8

In Chapters 6 and 7 we considered the simplest production situation of producing a single product when one input was varied and all others were fixed. In agricultural production we usually face more complex production situations. Several inputs may vary, even to the case of all resources except one. To understand how variable inputs should be combined to maximize profits, we will consider a simple case when two inputs vary and all others are fixed. If one understands that basic situation, he has the basis for understanding even more complex input combinations.

In economic literature one will find the factor–factor relationship may also be referred to as the least cost principle. Also the term input or resource is often used to mean the same as factor.

FACTOR-SUBSTITUTION

Generally one or more factors can be substituted for any one factor used in production:

Prairie hay for alfalfa hay, silage for alfalfa hay, grain sorghum for corn, silo unloader for labor, cultivator for a hand hoe.

Factor substitution is one of the biggest problems confronting a farm manager. There are literally countless input combinations that will maintain his level of production. For example, take a sheet of paper and try to list all the possible combinations of land, labor, feed, buildings, and equipment that will produce one 200 pound market barrow. Every combination will have its unique technical efficiency (rate of gain) and costs. A manager must sort through the many possibilities to find the one giving the greatest profit on that barrow.

In this chapter we try to simplify the input combination problem and provide criteria for making better resource allocation decisions. In all cases we need to know something about the productivity of the inputs considered. We can modify our basic production function $Y = f(X_1/X_2....X_n)$, to reflect the addition of a second variable resource, $Y = f(X_1 X_2/X_3....X_n)$, where X_1 and X_2 are the variable resources and $X_3....X_n$ are the fixed resources. Our task is to determine the best (most profitable) amounts of X_1 and X_2 to combine with $X_3....X_n$ to produce a given level of output, for example the best combination of grain sorghum and soybean meal to produce 200 pounds of pork.

All the assumptions of the factor–product relationship except the single variable resource assumption will hold. In the factor–factor relationship there will be two variable inputs used to produce a given level of output.

DEFINITIONS

An iso-product curve shows all the possible combinations of two variable resources that will produce the same amount of a product.

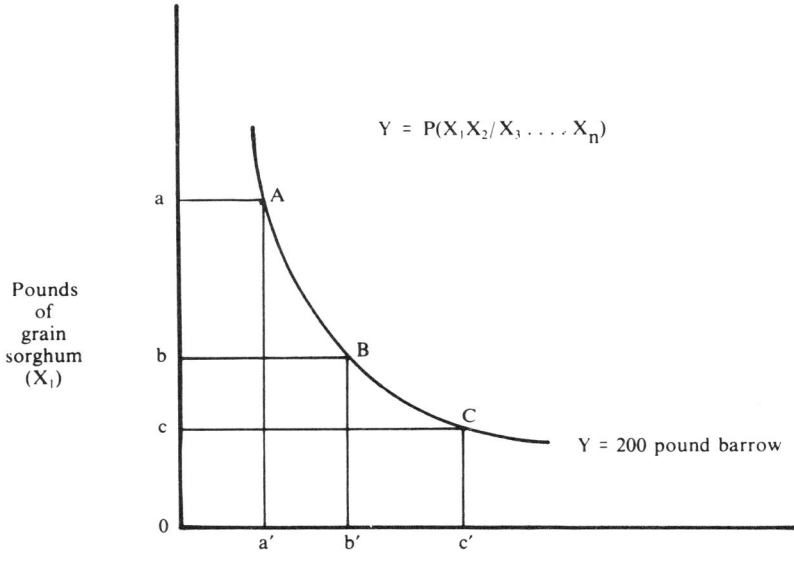

Figure 8-1. The Iso-product Curve.

Figure 8-1 illustrates the iso-product curve when Y = 200 pounds of pork. Every point on Y (A, B, C or any other point) represents 200 pounds of output that can be produced with varying combinations of grain sorghum (X_1) and soybean meal (X_2). To produce 200 pounds at A requires OaX_1 and $Oa'X_2$; at B, ObX_1 and $Ob'X_2$; at C, OcX_1 and $Oc'X_2$.

For every level of production there is an iso-product curve. We illustrated only one, but there is one for 10, 50, 150. . . . .300, 500, etc. units of output.

Note the similarity of the iso-product curve to the indifference curve (Chapter 3).

The marginal rate of substitution (MRS) refers to the amount a resource can be decreased as use of another resource is increased by one unit without affecting the output. Algebraically stated:

$$\text{MRS } X_2 \text{ for } X_1 = \frac{\Delta X_1}{\Delta X_2}$$

The marginal rate of substitution is illustrated in Table 8-1 and Figure 8-2. Each shows how much X_1 must be decreased in order for successive one unit additions of X_2 to maintain 100 units of production.

FACTOR-FACTOR RELATIONSHIP: HOW TO COMBINE PRODUCTS

Table 8-1. The Marginal Rate of Substitution.

To Produce 100 Units of Y		Change in Inputs		MRS of X_2 for X_1
Units of X_2	Units of X_1	ΔX_2	ΔX_1	$\dfrac{\Delta X_1}{\Delta X_2}$
2	10	—	—	—
3	6.5	1	−3.5	$\dfrac{-3.5}{1} = -3.5$
4	5	1	−1.5	$\dfrac{-1.5}{1} = -1.5$
5	4	1	−1.0	$\dfrac{-1.0}{1} = -1.0$
6	3.5	1	−.5	$\dfrac{-.5}{1} = -.5$

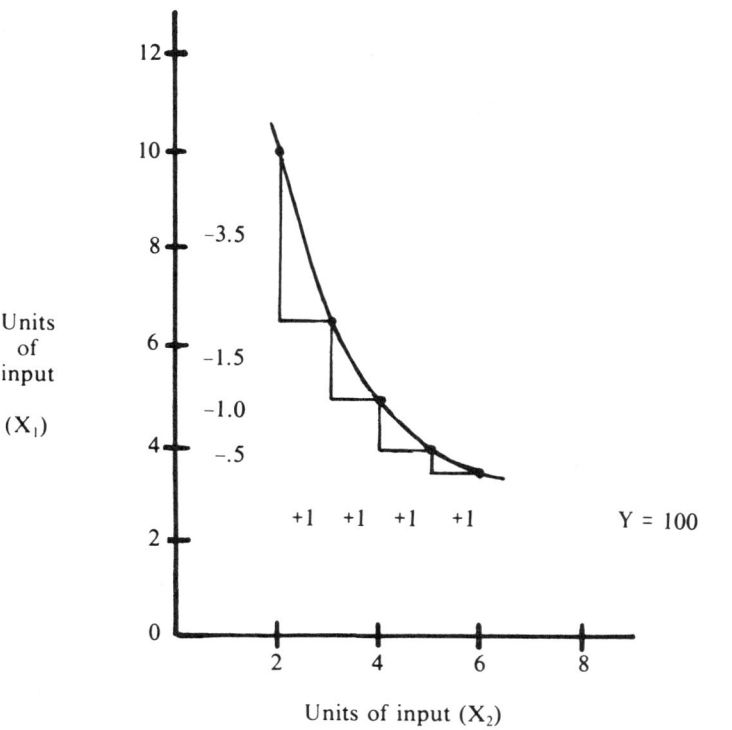

Figure 8-2. The Marginal Rate of Substitution.

The marginal rate of substitution is always stated as a negative; the iso-product curve always slopes downward and to the right.

A diminishing marginal rate of substitution is apparent when successive equal units of a variable input (X_2) are substituted for another variable input (X_1) and the successive equal units of the substitute (X_2) gradually replace less and less of the original variable input (X_1).

We can use Table 8-1 and Figure 8-2 to explain further diminishing marginal rate of substitution. With the first substitution of X_2 for X_1, going from 2 to 3 units of X_2, the one unit of X_2 replaced 3.5 units of X_1; with the second substitution, 3 to 4 units of X_2, one unit replaced 1.5 units; with the third substitution, 4 to 5 units of X_2, one unit replaced 1.0 unit; and with the last substitution, 5 to 6 units of X_2, one unit replaced .5 unit. As more and more X_2 was used in producing 100 units of Y, X_2 gradually became less productive relative to X_1. We could, of course, reverse this process by substituting one unit increments of X_1 for X_2 and observe the same characteristic.

The iso-cost line represents all possible combinations of two variable inputs that can be bought with a given amount of money.

The amount of each that can be bought depends upon the price of each and the money available. Figure 8-3 illustrates an iso-cost line. Let us assume $6 is available to purchase X_1 and X_2 and the PX_1 = $1 and PX_2 =$2; then if the full $6 were spent on X_1, six units of X_1 could be bought. If it were all spent on X_2, then three units of X_2 could be bought. If the $6 were used to buy both X_1 and X_2, then any amount of each whose combined cost was $6 could be bought. When we have such information we can draw the iso-cost line by connecting the two points, X_1 = 6 and X_2 = 3. Any point on that line represents the amount of each that can be bought for $6; for example, with $6 one can buy:

6 units of X_1 and 0 units of X_2

5 units of X_1 and ½ unit of X_2

4 units of X_1 and 1 unit of X_2

3 units of X_1 and 1½ units of X_2

2 units of X_1 and 2 units of X_2

1 unit of X_1 and 2½ units of X_2

0 unit of X_1 and 3 units of X_2

The slope of the iso-cost line is determined by the price ratios. Any change in the prices results in a different slope. For example, (Figure 8-3) if the price of X_2 were reduced to $1, then 6 units of it could be bought with $6. Any change in the funds available results in a new iso-cost line. In Figure 8-3 an iso-cost line for $8 is illustrated: 8 units of X_1 could be bought with $8; or 4 units of X_2 could be bought. For every level of funds there is a separate iso-cost line.

FACTOR-FACTOR RELATIONSHIP: HOW TO COMBINE PRODUCTS

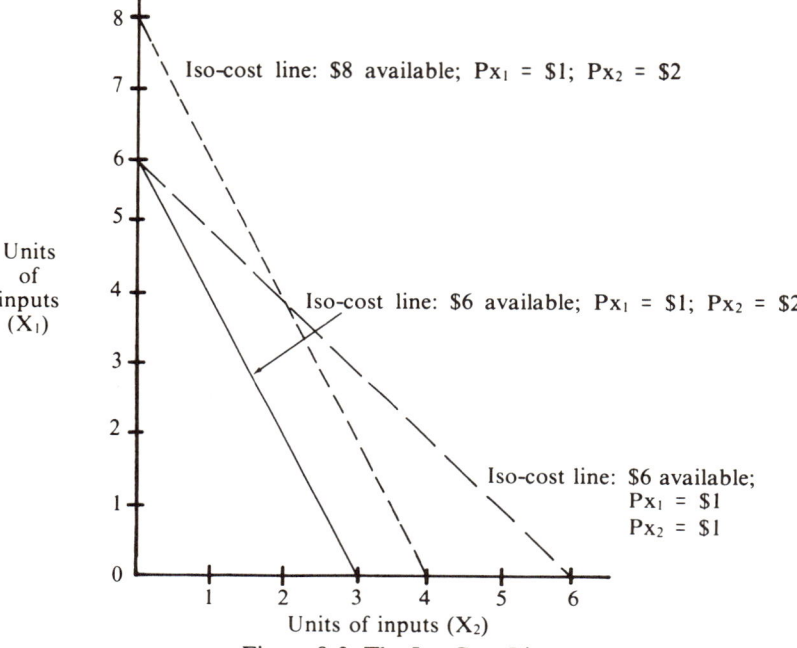

Figure 8-3. The Iso-Cost Line.

CONSTANT SUBSTITUTIBILITY

There are two cases of constant substitutibility between two variable resources. When one unit of a resource can be substituted for one unit of another resource without changing output, the two are perfect substitutes. An example of perfect substitutes is one bag of 10-20-0 fertilizer (brand A) for one bag of 10-20-0 fertilizer (brand B), if a unit of either is equally effective in producing Y. The iso-product line for producing 100 units of Y then will be a straight line.

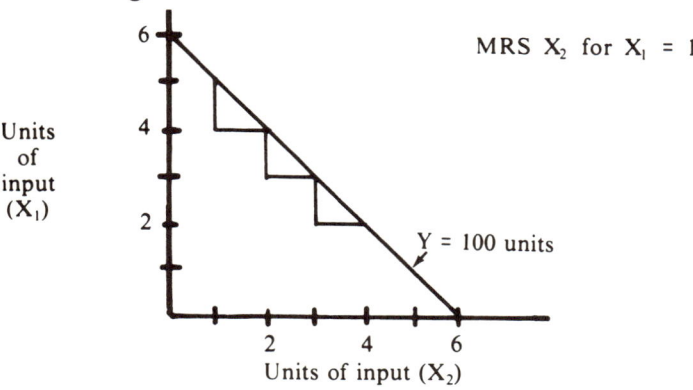

Figure 8-4. Perfect Substitutes.

The other case of constant substitutibility is the situation when the two inputs substitute at a constant rate 1:2 or 1:3 or 1:4 but not at a 1:1. In neither case is there a diminishing marginal rate of substitution.

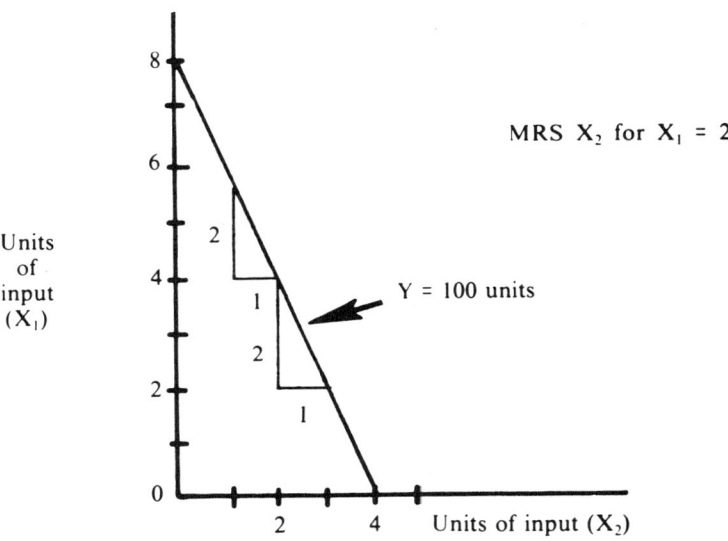

Figure 8-5. Constant Substitutes.

PERFECT COMPLEMENTARITY

At times an agricultural producer is in a production situation that requires that resources be used in some fixed portion. There is no substitutibility. When using a tractor, we must treat the tractor and the driver as a single unit. There is only one way at a given time to combine labor and tractors: 1 man, 1 tractor. Such a resource relationship is called perfect complementarity, and the marginal rate of substitution is zero. The Fixed ratio is not restricted to a 1:1 ratio and could be 1:2, 1:5, 1:20, or even 1:1000.

In Figure 8-6 we show a resource combination of 3 units of X_1 and 3 units of X_2 to produce 100 units of Y. No other combination is possible, therefore the iso-product curve is a single point.

IMPERFECT SUBSTITUTIBILITY

Because of diminishing marginal productivity of resources, we find the most usual resource combination situation is one where the resources are imperfect substitutes. There is a diminishing marginal rate of substitution. The imperfect substitutibility of resources was illustrated in Figure 8-2, Table 8-1 and in the discussion accompanying that figure and table.

FACTOR-FACTOR RELATIONSHIP: HOW TO COMBINE PRODUCTS

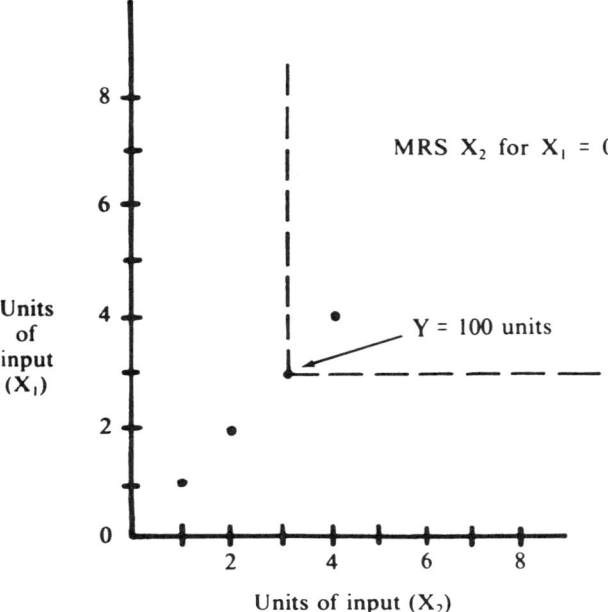

Figure 8-6. Perfect Complements.

In summary, imperfect substitutibility may be explained as follows: As equal successive units of an input (X_2) are substituted for another input (X_1), when almost none of the substitute (X_2) is used, the substitute input (X_2) will replace a relatively large amount of the original input (X_1), but as more units of the substitute (X_2) replace the original input (X_1) the equal unit of the substitute (X_2) replaces less and less of the original input (X_1).

PROFIT MAXIMIZATION CRITERION

If our objective is to maximize profits at a given level of output, say 100 units, we must find the cheapest way to produce the 100 units. It is one case (when output is at a given level) that cost minimization is identical to profit maximization. We will seek the least cost combination of resources to produce the 100 units. A feed mixing plant is confronted daily with acquiring grains and supplements that will meet the minimum nutrient standards specified on the tag. Its profits will be greatest when it finds the least cost combination of ingredients that meet the standards. Similarly a feedlot manager wants to find the least cost resource combination to produce a pound of beef.

To determine the least cost combination, we need to know the price of each factor and the marginal rate of substitution between factors. When that is known, we can determine the profit maximizing combination by finding the point where the marginal rate of substitution is equal to the inverse of the price ratios:

$$\text{MRS } X_2 \text{ for } X_1 = \frac{PX_2}{PX_1}$$

or

$$\frac{\Delta X_1}{\Delta X_2} = \frac{PX_2}{PX_1}$$

We will consider profit maximization for each of the types of resource substitutibility.

PROFIT MAXIMIZATION FOR IMPERFECT SUBSTITUTES

Because it is the most usual case, we will first show the application of the profit maximization criterion to imperfect substitutes. With imperfect substitutes careful consideration must be given to both the price relationship and the marginal rate of substitution. Profits can be increased (costs decreased) whenever the substitute input's price relative to the other input price is less than the rate at which it substitutes for the other. If X_2, the substitute, is twice as costly as X_1, but it is 3 times as productive, costs will be reduced by substituting X_2 for X_1. In Table 8-2 we show a simple hypothetical resource combination where X_2 is an imperfect substitute for X_1 to illustrate profit maximization.

When using 3 units of X_2 and 7 units of X_1, the total variable cost is $11.50 and profits are $38.50. At 4 units X_2 and 5 units X_1, total variable cost is $11 (the least cost situation) and profits are highest, $39. Thus we would select $X_2 = 4$ and $X_1 = 5$ as the optimum input combination. We do not have a MRS that is equal to the inverse of the price ratio $\frac{\Delta X_1}{\Delta X_2} = \frac{PX_2}{PX_1}$. We find the closest to be

X_2	X_1	MRS	$\frac{PX_2}{PX_1}$
3	7	−3	1.50
		1	1.00
4	5	−2	1.50
		1	1.00

therefore we can conclude that somewhere between $X_2 = 3$ and $X_2 = 4$

FACTOR-FACTOR RELATIONSHIP: HOW TO COMBINE PRODUCTS

$$\frac{\Delta X_1}{\Delta X_2} = \frac{1.50}{1.00}$$

and

$$\frac{PX_2}{PX_1} = \frac{1.50}{1.00}$$

and the profit maximization criterion $\frac{\Delta X_1}{\Delta X_2} = \frac{PX_2}{PX_1}$ is fulfilled. From the data we would select $X_2 = 4$ and $X_1 = 5$ as being the best combination. The possibility exists that more data would reveal a least cost combination of slightly less than $11.

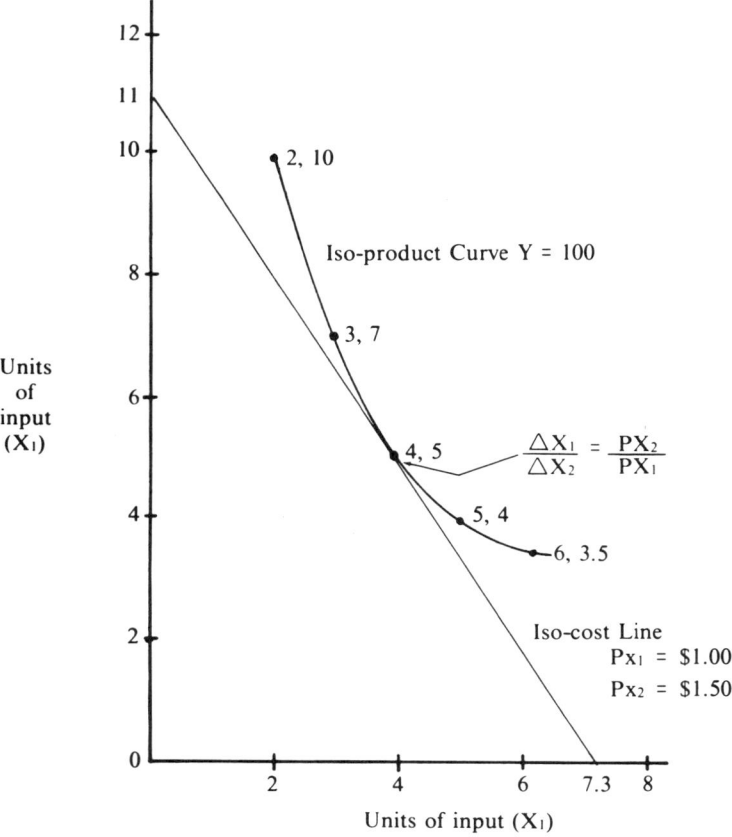

Figure 8.7. Profit Maximization When $Y = f(X_1 X_2 / X_3 \ldots X_n)$ and X_2 is an Imperfect Substitute for X_1.

Table 8-2. Profit Maximization When $Y = f(X_1, X_2/X_3 \ldots X_n)$ and X_2 is an Imperfect Substitute for X_1, $PY = \$1.00$, $PX_1 = \$1.00$, $PX_2 = \$1.50$.

Inputs to Produce 100 Units of Y		MRS X_2 for X_1 $\left(\dfrac{\Delta X_1}{\Delta X_2}\right)$	$\dfrac{PX_2}{PX_1}$	Cost of X_2 $(PX_2 \cdot X_2)$	Cost of X_1 $(PX_1 \cdot X_1)$	Total Variable Cost (Col. 4 & 5)	Fixed Cost	Total Cost (Col. 7 & 8)	Value 100 Units Y	Profit (Col. 10-9)
X_2	X_1									
2	10	--	1.50/1.00	$3.00	$10.00	$13.00	$50.00	$63.00	$100.00	$37.00
3	7	−3/1	1.50/1.00	4.50	7.00	11.50	50.00	61.50	100.00	38.50
4	5	−2/1	1.50/1.00	6.00	5.00	11.00	50.00	61.00	100.00	39.00
5	4	−1/1	1.50/1.00	7.50	4.00	11.50	50.00	61.50	100.00	38.50
6	3.5	−5/1	1.50/1.00	9.00	3.50	12.50	50.00	62.50	100.00	37.50

FACTOR-FACTOR RELATIONSHIP: HOW TO COMBINE PRODUCTS

The data in Table 8-2 can be plotted on a diagram as in Figure 8-7. By connecting the input combination points we can construct an iso-product curve. Using the least cost, $11, we can construct the iso-cost line. The point of tangency shows us the optimum resource combination. In our example any time the production value of X_2 is greater than 1½ times that of X_1, we continue to substitute X_2 for X_1 because we can lower the cost of producing 100 units of Y.

PROFIT MAXIMIZATION FOR CONSTANT SUBSTITUTES

Determining the least cost combination is simpler for constant substitutes than for imperfect substitutes. From a cost standpoint only, a producer will find using one input, the cheapest one, will maximize profits so there is no incentive to combine the two inputs. We will illustrate both the perfect substitute and the constant substitute situation. If the prices are $1 for each when the MRS = $\frac{1}{1}$ at any combination the $\frac{\Delta X_1}{\Delta X_2} = \frac{PX_2}{PX_1}$, the producer would be indifferent to the combination because profits would be the same regardless of the amount of each used. However, any time prices differ, then only the cheapest would be used; for example, when the price of X_2 = $2 and X_1 = $1, no X_2 will be used.

Table 8-3. Profit Maximization When $Y = f(X_1 X_2 / X_3 \ldots X_n)$ and X_2 is a Perfect Substitute for X_1.

To Produce 100 Units of Y		MRS $\frac{\Delta X_1}{\Delta X_2}$	Price Ratio	
X_2	X_1		$PX_1 = \$1.00$ $PX_2 = \$1.00$	$PX_1 = \$1.00$ $PX_2 = \$2.00$
2	4	--	1.00/1.00	2.00/1.00
3	3	1/1	1.00/1.00	2.00/1.00
4	2	1/1	1.00/1.00	2.00/1.00

Table 8-4. Profit Maximization When $Y = f(X_1 X_2 / X_3 \ldots X_n)$ and X_2 Substitutes for X_1 at a Constant Rate — (2/1).

To Produce 100 Units of Y		MRS $\frac{\Delta X_1}{\Delta X_2}$	Price Ratio	
X_2	X_1		$PX_1 = \$1.00$ $PX_2 = \$2.00$	$PX_1 = \$1.00$ $PX_2 = \$3.00$
2	12	--	2.00/1.00	3.00/1.00
3	10	2/1	2.00/1.00	3.00/1.00
4	8	2/1	2.00/1.00	3.00/1.00

The constant substitute situation is very similar to the perfect substitute case. In Table 8-4 we show that one unit of X_2 substitutes for two units of X_1—that is X_2 is twice as valuable in the production process as X_1. As long as its price is less than two times that of X_1 use all X_2 and no X_1, and when the price is more than twice that of X_1 use no X_2 and all X_1. When PX_2 is just two times the price of X_1 either one or any combination of the two will give equal profits.

PROFIT MAXIMIZATION FOR PERFECT COMPLEMENTS

Perfect complements is a special case when the inputs must be used in fixed proportions to produce the product. For example, to produce water, two parts of hydrogen must be combined with one part of oxygen. There is no other way to produce water so the price of each will not affect how those two inputs are combined. If you choose to produce the product, the inputs must be used in fixed proportions.

THE EFFECT OF A CHANGE IN INPUT PRICES

Whenever there is a change in the price relationship between two inputs, there will be a new least cost combination of the two. The cheaper one will be substituted for the more expensive one until once again the MRS equals the inverse of the price ratio.

Using the example in Table 8-2 we can show what would happen if the PX_2 were reduced by 50 cents to $1. First we would note that $\frac{\Delta X_1}{\Delta X_2} = PX_2$ at $X_2 = 5$ and $X_1 = 4$: $\frac{-1}{1} = \frac{\$1.00}{\$1.00}$. Profits can be increased by substituting X_2 for X_1. If PX_2 were raised to $3.00 then we would use less X_2, 3 units, and more X_1, 7 units. We will illustrate the adjustments necessary in Table 8-5 and Figures 8-8 and 8-9.

Table 8-5. Affect of a Change in Price Relationships.

To Produce 100 Units of Y		MRS X_2 for X_1	Affect of Price Changes					
			$PX_1 = \$1.00$ $PX_2 = \$1.50$		$PX_1 = \$1.00$ $PX_2 = \$1.00$		$PX_1 = \$1.00$ $PX_2 = \$3.00$	
X_2	X_1		PX_2/PX_1	TVC	PX_2/PX_1	TVC	PX_2/PX_1	TVC
2	10	--	1.50/1.00	$13.00	1.00/1.00	$12.00	3.00/1.00	$16.00
3	7	-3/1	1.50/1.00	11.50	1.00/1.00	10.00	3.00/1.00	16.00
4	5	-2/1	1.50/1.00	11.00	1.00/1.00	9.00	3.00/1.00	17.00
5	4	-1/1	1.50/1.00	11.50	1.00/1.00	9.00	3.00/1.00	19.00
6	3.5	-.5/1	1.50/1.00	12.50	1.00/1.00	9.50	3.00/1.00	21.50

When X_2 is substituted for X_1 when PX_2 is lower, note that the least cost combination of producing 100 units is $9. The $2 savings may be used to expand production of Y or elsewhere. If used to expand production,

FACTOR-FACTOR RELATIONSHIP: HOW TO COMBINE PRODUCTS   99

more than 100 units can be produced with the original $11. That is called the expansion effect. Using more X_2, when its price falls, and less X_1 is the substitution effect. With an increase in PX_2 less X_2 would be used, and it would require at least $16 to produce 100 units, thus the producer must either cut back output or raise more cash.

In Figures 8-8 and 8-9 that concept is presented geometrically. Figure 8-8 shows the decrease in PX_2 and the necessary adjustments to have the least cost combination. The original situation is given in solid lines. With $PX_2 = \$1.00$, $11 will now buy 11 units of X_2 giving a new iso-cost line, the highest broken line. At no point is this new iso-cost line tangent to the original iso-product curve. The producer, if he chooses to spend the full $11, can move to a higher iso-product line or if he chooses to remain at 100 units, he can save $2.

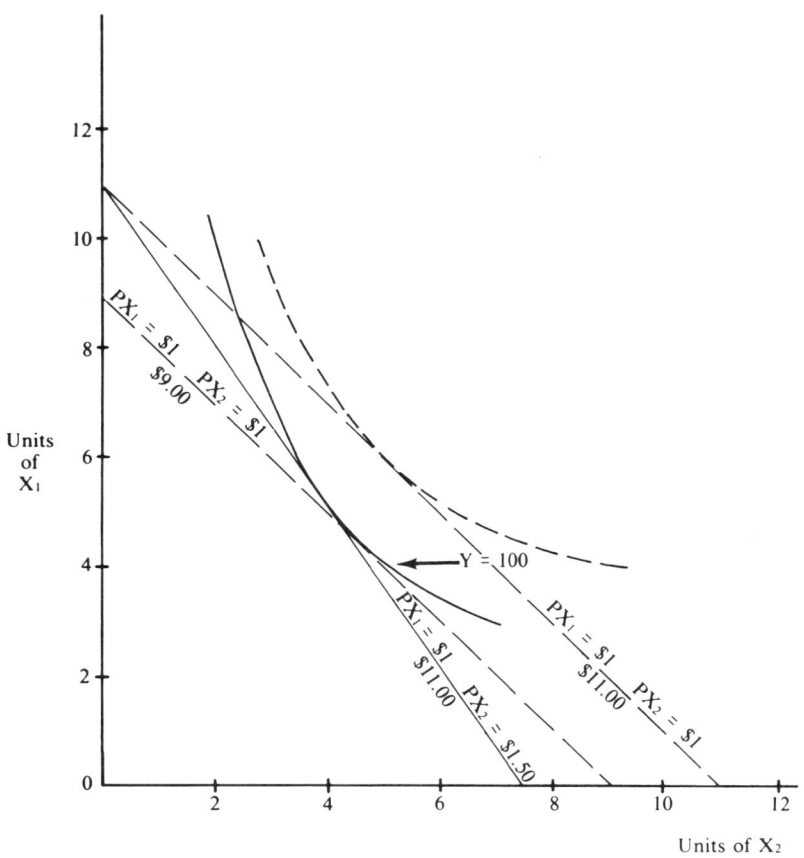

Figure 8-8. Effect of a Decrease in PX_2.

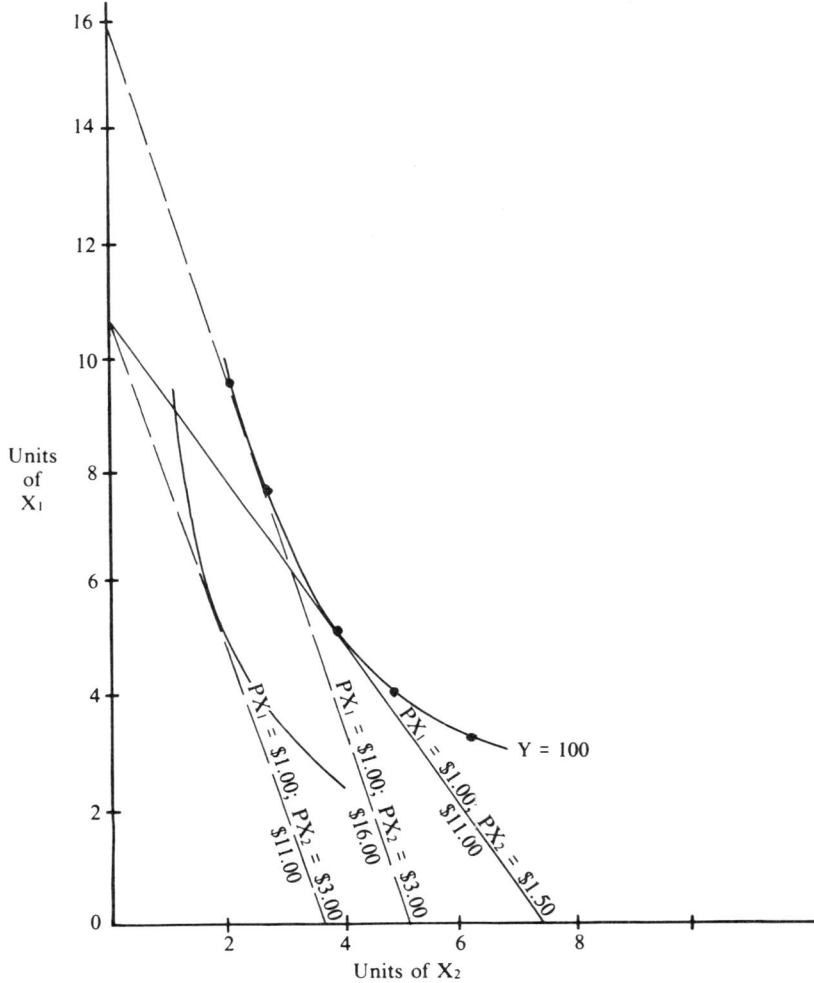

Figure 8-9. Effect of an Increase in PX_2.

In Figure 8-9 the same type of illustration is used to show a rise in the PX_2 and the resource use adjustment accompanying that change. Originally 100 units of Y were produced when the PX_1 = $1.00 and the PX_2 = $1.50. The solid iso-cost line gives the least cost combination, $11, at those prices. An increase of PX_2 to $3 ($PX_1$ unchanged) results in a new iso-cost line (the dotted one). The $11 no longer buys enough X_1 and X_2 to remain on the Y = 100 iso-product curve. Output must be reduced to the new iso-product curve if no more funds (over the $11) are available to

FACTOR-FACTOR RELATIONSHIP: HOW TO COMBINE PRODUCTS

arrive at a new least cost combination $\frac{\Delta X_1}{\Delta X_2} = \frac{PX_2}{PX_1}$. To remain at Y = 100, more funds ($5) will be necessary to buy the new combination of X_1 and X_2; X_1, now cheaper relative to X_2, will be substituted for X_2.

EXPANSION OF BUSINESS SIZE

At no time in our consideration of the factor-factor relationship have we made any claim that 100 units was the most profitable level of production. We have only explored the most profitable way to produce 100 units. Now we would like to raise a question about determining the most profitable level of production. How can a business using two variable resources expand?

For any factor-factor relationship there can be any number of iso-product curves, depending upon the amounts of X_1 and X_2 used. We chose just one possibility, Y = 100. In Figure 8-10 we have shown several iso-product curves. For every level of expenditure there is also a new iso-cost line. For every iso-product curve, there will be an iso-cost line just tangent to it. Thus we can show the optimum input combination for several levels of production. Each point that $\frac{\Delta X_1}{\Delta X_2} = \frac{PX_2}{PX_1}$ gives the least cost combination for producing that level of Y. By connecting the points, we determine the expansion path. Any point on the expansion path gives a least cost combination, which guides us in expanding output.

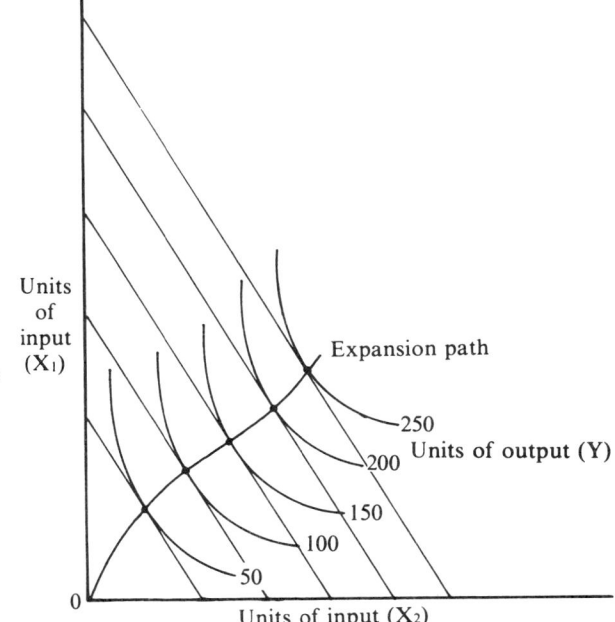

Figure 8-10. Expansion of a Business.

We can carry the expansion path a step further. If we find the best combinations of X_1 and X_2, we can then think of X_1X_2 combined as a single input. Farmers buying a mixed ration do just that. There is also a price for the mixed ration. If X_1X_2 combined are treated as a single variable input, the expansion path becomes a production function where $Y = f(X_1X_2)/X_3 \ldots X_n$. It is possible to compute the MPP and if we know the PY, we can determine the MVPY. We now have all that is needed to determine the level of production that fulfills the profit criterion $MVP = P(X_1X_2)$.

APPLICATIONS

The least cost concept has a wide range of applications. Understanding it well enough to make effective use of it in agricultural production is well worth your time and effort. Any time a manager is confronted with resource allocation decisions, he will find the factor-factor principle basic to his decision-making. Examples of producers who almost daily are purchasing resources used in producing a product that combines those resources are persons who manage: feed mixing plants, dairies, feedlots, broiler plants and hoglots. Other producers also make such decisions about resource combinations.

SUGGESTED READINGS

Doll, John P., Rhodes, V. James, and West, Jerry G. *Economics of Agricultural Production, Markets, and Policy*. Richard D. Irwin, Inc., 1968, Chapter 5.

Heady, Earl O. *Economics of Agricultural Production and Resource Use*. Prentice-Hall, 1952, Chapters 4, 5, and 6.

Leftwich, Richard H. *The Price System and Resource Allocation*, 3rd Edition. Holt, Rinehart, and Winston, 1966, Chapter 7.

Vincent, Warren H., Editor. *Economics and Management in Agriculture*. Prentice-Hall, 1962, Chapter 4.

THE PRODUCT-PRODUCT RELATIONSHIP—HOW TO COMBINE ENTERPRISES

9

We have provided a basis for answering the first two of the three basic production questions: how much to produce? how to produce the product? what to produce? The third, "what to produce," is the topic of this chapter. When producers desire to maximize profits, they try to find those lines of production that add most to profits. Their resources will be allocated to the enterprises that give the highest returns. Our objective here is to provide an understanding of how to determine the combination of enterprises that maximizes profits.

In Chapter 6 we considered the case of a single firm having enough resources to attain $MVP = PX_1$ for a single product. In real situations agricultural producers usually have the opportunity to produce several products but it would be rare, indeed, if any producer had enough resources to push each production possibility to the point where $MVP = PX$. If that were possible the factor-product analysis would be adequate to answer combination questions. We would combine enterprises so that:

$$MVPY_1 = PX,$$

$$MVPY_2 = PX, \text{ and}$$

$$\vdots$$

$$MVPY_n = PX$$

The producer not having enough resources to do that has a much more complex enterprise-combination problem. He must find the enterprise that adds most to profits for each unit of his limited resources. For example, if a farmer has 400 acres of crop land, he may find that he gets higher returns on the first 200 acres in corn than for any other crop. Because of time limitations, he may find another crop, such as wheat, with a different and less intense cultural practice schedule, would return less per acre than the first 200 acres of corn, but more than another 200 acres of corn would. Thus a combination of corn and wheat may be more profitable than corn alone. The farmer's problem is to determine the best use of each of the 400 acres—to use each acre to produce the crop that adds the most profits. In an agricultural business our objective is to maximize profits for the whole business not for any one enterprise alone.

Keep in mind that land used for corn cannot be used for wheat production. If the land resource is used for corn, the opportunity for profits on wheat are given up. Thus a cost of using the land for corn production is the loss of the income from wheat. So long as the profits given up by not raising wheat are less than those gained by raising corn, that land should be used to produce corn. The profits will be greatest when each unit of resource is used in the enterprise that adds most to profits.

DEFINITIONS

As has been the case with each new concept, we will introduce new terms that need to be carefully defined so each of us uses them in the same way.

A production possibility curve represents all possible combinations of two products (Y_1 and Y_2) that can be produced with a given amount of resources.

Table 9-1. Combinations of Output from Two Enterprises (Y_1 and Y_2) When 100 Units of Input Are Available.

Units of Output	
Y_2	Y_1
25	0
23	5
20	10
16.5	15
10	20
0	25

In Table 9-1 we have illustrated the production possibility curve using 100 units of input. The 100 units will produce any of the combinations of Y_2 and Y_1 listed, for example, 25 units of Y_2 and 0 units of Y_1 or 16.5 units of Y_2 and 15 units of Y_1 or any of the other combinations listed. Note Y_1 output can be increased only by giving up Y_2 output.

Such enterprise combination data can be plotted on a diagram, Figure 9-1. Here we will plot Y_1, the output being substituted in equal increments for Y_2, on the horizontal axis and Y_2, the output being substituted out of the business, on the vertical axis. We can then plot each of the output combinations. A line connecting the points gives us a production possibility curve. For every level of resource use, there would be a new production possibility curve. We have selected just one for our example.

PRODUCT-PRODUCT RELATIONSHIP—HOW TO COMBINE ENTERPRISES 105

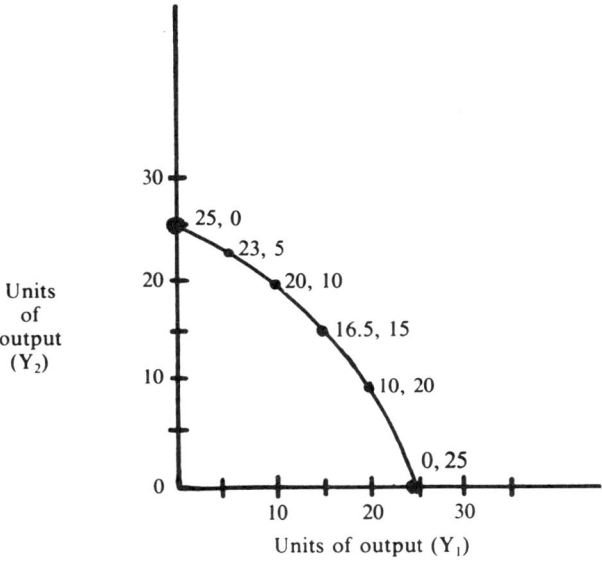

Figure 9-1. The Production Possibility Curve.

An iso-revenue line represents all possible combinations of two products that, if sold, will give a fixed amount of revenue. For example, if the PY_1 = $2 and PY_2 = $1, then a $60 income can be obtained by selling:

Units of Y_1	Units of Y_2
0	60
10	40
20	20
30	0

When those data were plotted in Figure 9-2, the straight line connecting Y_2 = 60 and Y_1 = 30 is the iso-revenue line. The slope of this line is determined by the price ratios, in this case $2 : $1. The iso-revenue line is very similar to the iso-cost line; both indicate a constant value.

Opportunity cost is potential income foregone from a resource as a result of using that resource for another line of production. In Chapter 7, we previously defined and explained opportunity cost.

Equi-marginal returns refer to allocating resources so that the last unit of resources gives the same returns from each product produced. We can express the idea algebraically: $MVPY_1 = MVPY_2 \ldots = MVPY_n$. That formula tells us that we have allocated X_1 among all our enterprises so that the value of the output resulting from using one more unit of X_1 would be the same for any one of the enterprises; if there were unlimited

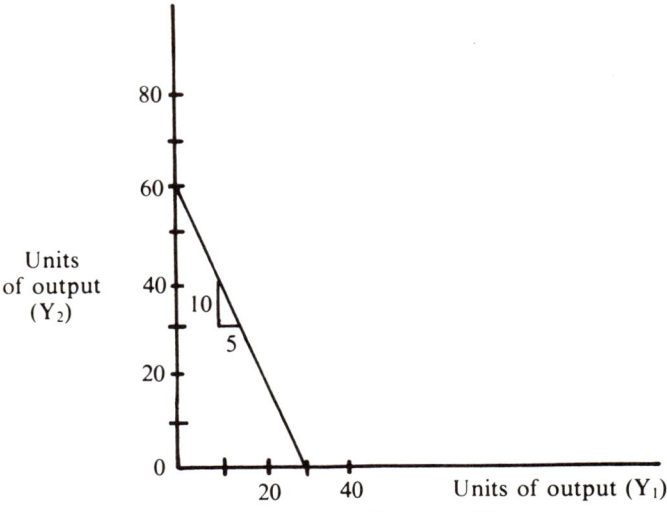

Figure 9-2. The Iso-Revenue Line.

resources, that would be true when the $MVPY_1 = MVPY_2 = \ldots = MVPY_n = PX_1$. When resources are limited the equi-marginal returns will occur before $MVPY = PX$.

The marginal rate of product substitution (MRPS) is the amount one product (Y_2) changes in quantity when the other product (Y_1) is increased by successive equal units, when total resources used remains constant. The MRPS is computed by using this formula:

$$\text{MRPS } Y_1 \text{ for } Y_2 = \frac{\Delta Y_2}{\Delta Y_1}.$$

It shows how a producer can substitute one enterprise for another in working out his business organization. To familiarize us with determining MRPS, it is illustrated in Table 9-2.

Table 9-2. Computation of the Marginal Rate Product Substitution, X = 100.

Units of Output		Computation			MRPS Y_1 for Y_2
Y_2	Y_1	ΔY_2	ΔY_1	$\Delta Y_2 / \Delta Y_1$	
25	0	--	--	--	--
23	5	– 2	5	–2/5	– .4
20	10	– 3	5	–3/5	– .6
16.5	15	– 3.5	5	–3.5/5	– .7
10	20	– 6.5	5	–6.5/5	–1.3
0	25	–10	5	–10/5	–2.0

The data from Table 9-2 are presented graphically in Figure 9-3. The MRPS gives us the slope of the production possibility curve.

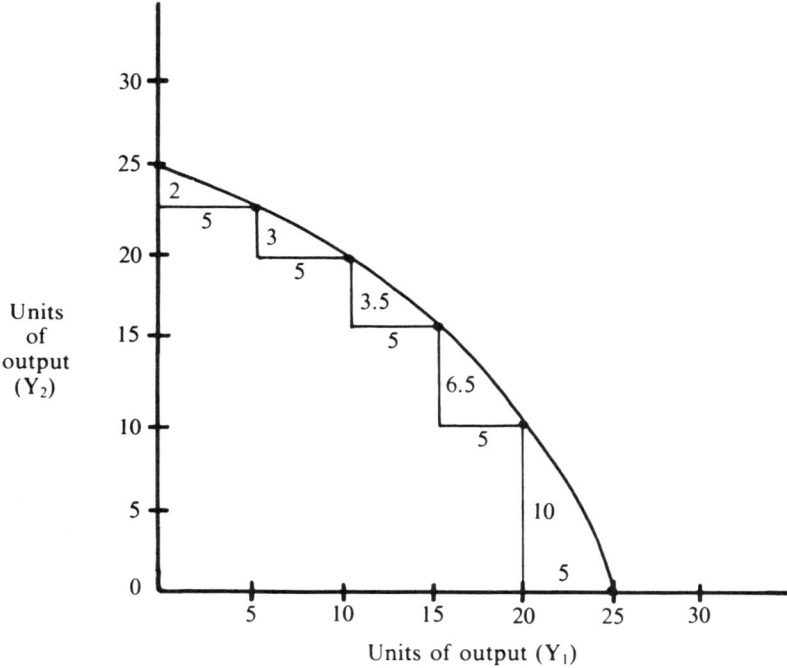

Figure 9-3. Marginal Rate of Product Substitution.

When using a given amount of resources an increasing marginal rate of product substitution is apparent when equal units of a product (Y_1) are substituted for another product Y_2 and gradually the successive equal units of (Y_1) replace more and more of the other product (Y_2). That can be seen in both Table 9-2 and Figure 9-3. Note that the equal units of Y_1 (5) replace successively larger amounts (2, 3, 3.5, 6.5, 10) of Y_2. The increasing MRPS tells us the production possibility curve will be concave to the point of origin.

TYPES OF PRODUCT-PRODUCT RELATIONSHIPS

When substituting enterprises within a business, the enterprises may help, compete, or have no effect on each other. When an enterprise helps another; that is, when resources are taken from one enterprise and placed in another and output of both increases, there is a *complementary* relationship. Because of their nitrogen fixing ability legumes are beneficial to other crops. Taking land from corn production and putting it into legumes not only produces leguminous hay but also increases output of corn. When enterprises have no effect on one another, there is a *supplementary* relationship. The most illustrative example of such a relationship comes from the time of your grandfathers when it was a common practice "to run hogs after cattle." Feedlot cattle then were fed whole corn much of which passed through the animal only partially digested. Hogs could be run in the same lot, to salvage the partially digested corn. Pork could thus be produced without affecting beef production. Today, use of a combine for wheat and sorghum harvesting may result in a supplementary relationship between the two crops for the use of the combine. The most usual relationship however, is a competing one. Enterprises *compete* when the addition of one reduces the output of the other.

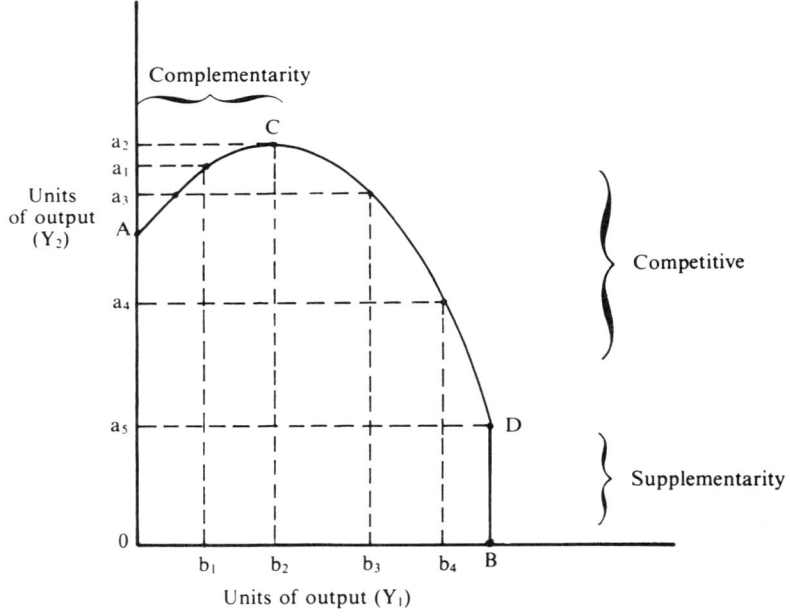

Figure 9-4. Complementarity, Supplementarity, and Competitiveness among Products.

In Figure 9-4 we are producing two products Y_1 and Y_2 with a given set of resources. We can use the resources to produce only Y_2, OA units, or all Y_1, OB units. If we use some resources for producing each instead of only Y_2, then we can produce Ob_1 of Y_1, and Oa_1 of Y_2 or Ob_2 of Y_1 and Oa_2 of Y_2. We have increased the output of both Y_1 and Y_2 by shifting resources from producing Y_2 to Y_1. That happens between A and C on the production possibility curve because Y_1 is complementary to Y_2.

Instead of producing only Y_1, OB units, we can shift some resources to producing Y_2. Without giving up any Y_1 we can gain Oa_5 units of Y_2. That supplementary relationship exists between B and D on the production possibility curve.

PRODUCT-PRODUCT RELATIONSHIP—HOW TO COMBINE ENTERPRISES 109

Between C and D a shift of resources from Y_2 to Y_1 results in a loss of output from Y_2 in order to gain output from Y_1. This portion of the curve represents a competitive relationship in which Y_1 competes with Y_2 for the resources.

PROFIT MAXIMIZATION

Profits can be maximized only in the competitive portion of the production possibility curve. Think for a moment about the complementary and supplementary portions. Because we are considering output for a given level of resources, cost of production is equal at any point on the curve. By shifting resource use (there is no change in cost) from one enterprise to another when you can gain output from the new enterprise without giving up output (or even gaining some output from the original enterprise), profits are bound to increase (or losses to decrease) regardless of prices. Therefore we will concentrate on explaining profit maximization for the competitive portion of the curve.

Before presenting the profit maximization criterion, we shall show that profit maximization of individual enterprises does not give the highest profit for the whole agricultural business. Because it is easy to understand that interest rates are a return on investment we have chosen a savings bank example. Ordinarily we would not expect banks to have similar interest rate policies, but for illustrative purposes let us assume they do. Let us consider a case of having $10,000 to put in savings accounts. It can be placed in any of three banks, and each bank has a different interest rate depending on the size of deposit. Each bank could be looked upon as a separate farm enterprise. We want to maximize our income on the $10,000 invested. The banks have these interest rates:

Interest rates for the:	Interest rates paid by					
	Bank A		Bank B		Bank C	
First $1,000 deposit	(1st)	6.00%	(9th)	5.25%	(2nd)	5.80%
Second $1,000 deposit	(3rd)	5.75	(10th)	5.20	(4th)	5.60
Third $1,000 deposit	(5th)	5.50		5.00	(6th)	5.40
Fourth $1,000 deposit	(7th)	5.35		5.00	(8th)	5.30
Fifth-tenth $1,000 deposit		5.00		5.00		5.00

The circled numbers refer to the sequence of the $1,000 deposits.

If for each $1,000 unit we use the bank giving the highest interest rate for that unit, we would make our savings as follows:

Deposit units by banks

Bank A
First $1,000 at 6%	= $60.00
Third $1,000 at 5.75%	= 57.50
Fifth $1,000 at 5.50%	= 55.00
Seventh $1,000 at 5.35%	= 53.50

Bank B
Ninth $1,000 at 5.25%	= $52.50
Tenth $1,000 at 5.20%	= 52.00

Bank C
Second $1,000 at 5.80%	= $58.00
Fourth $1,000 at 5.60%	= 56.00
Sixth $1,000 at 5.40%	= 54.00
Eighth $1,000 at 5.30%	= 53.00

After the tenth unit there would be equi-marginal returns, and one would be indifferent to which bank to use. Total profits, if all $10,000 were placed in Bank A would have been $525.50; in Bank B $504.50; in Bank C $521.00. Total profits with each unit of resource, $1,000, placed where it brought the highest returns were $551.

Different rates of return to resources are similar among agricultural enterprises. Also because of the diminishing marginal productivity of variable resources the rate of return will decrease as more of a resource is used in agricultural enterprises. Eventually the rate of return will probably go below the returns possible from some other enterprise. It will pay then to use some of the remaining resources on the new enterprise rather than to push the original one to the point MVPY = PX.

PROFIT MAXIMIZATION CRITERION

To determine profit maximization, we must know the marginal rates of product substitution and the price of the products. The profit formula gives us a guide to determine whether the returns from an enterprise are greater than the opportunity costs of giving up other enterprises. It is written $\frac{\Delta Y_2}{\Delta Y_1} = \frac{PY_1}{PY_2}$ when considering just two enterprises. If considering more enterprises it can be stated $\frac{MVPX(Y_1)}{PX} = \frac{MVPX(Y_2)}{PX} = \ldots = \frac{MVPX(Y_n)}{PX}$.

When we allocate each resource among the enterprises in such a way that the marginal return to each resource is the same in each enterprise, profits are maximized. If the return for a resource is higher in one enterprise than in other enterprises, expanding that enterprise will increase profits and cause the marginal return to the resource to fall. When the fall

PRODUCT-PRODUCT RELATIONSHIP—HOW TO COMBINE ENTERPRISES 111

brings the marginal return below that in other enterprises, shifting the resource to those higher returning enterprises will increase profits.

Table 9-3. Profit Maximization for Two Enterprises When the $PY_1 = \$3$ and $PY_2 = \$5$.

Units of Output				MRPS	Revenue		
Y_2	Y_1	ΔY_2	ΔY_1	$\Delta Y_2 / \Delta Y_1$	$PY_2 \cdot Y_2$	$PY_1 \cdot Y_1$	Total
18	0				$90.00	$ 0.00	$90.00
20	5	+2	5	2/5	100.00	15.00	115.00
18	10	−2	5	−2/5	90.00	30.00	120.00
15.5	15	−2.5	5	−2.5/5	77.50	45.00	122.50
12.0	20	−3.5	5	−3.5/5	60.00	60.00	120.00
0	20	−12	0	−12/0	0.00	60.00	60.00

In Table 9-3 we illustrate profit maximization for the product–product situation. We have $\dfrac{PY_1}{PY_2} = \dfrac{\$3}{\$5}$. By looking down the MRPS column, we find no $\Delta Y_2 / \Delta Y_1$ exactly equal to the price ratio. However, we can find $\Delta Y_2 / \Delta Y_1 = -2.5/5$ and $\dfrac{\Delta Y_2}{\Delta Y_1} = -3.5/5$. Between those two, ($Y_2 = 15.5$ and $Y_2 = 12$) there must be a point where $\$3/\$5 = -3/5$. By computing total revenue we found that the highest income, $122.50, was with $Y_2 = 15.5$ and $Y_1 = 15$. Remember we used a given set of resources so that total costs were equal for all enterprise combinations; thus profits will be greatest where total revenue was highest.

We can also determine the type of relationship that exists between Y_2 and Y_1 from those data. With the first substitution of Y_1 for Y_2 the output of both increase a complementary relationship. If we read up the Y_2 and Y_1 columns, we note a supplementary relationship. Resources can be taken from Y_1 to produce Y_2 without affecting the output of Y_2. Between those two points Y_2 can be increased only by giving up Y_1, so the relationship is competitive.

Using the data in Table 9-3, we have prepared a diagram, Figure 9-5, illustrating profit maximization. The production possibility curve gives us the MRPS, and the iso-revenue line gives us the price ratio. The point where the two are just tangent fulfills the profit maximization criterion and tells us the most profitable combination of the two enterprises.

The iso-revenue line was determined by taking the highest revenue possible, $122.50, dividing it by the PY_2, $\dfrac{\$122.50}{\$5} = 24.5$, and by PY_1, $\dfrac{\$122.50}{\$3} = 40.8$. That gives us the number of units required to generate $122.50 income if only one were produced. By locating each of the quantities on the Y_2 and the Y_1 axis and connecting the two points we have the iso-revenue line. No combination of Y_2 and Y_1 production will give $122.50 income except where $\dfrac{\Delta Y_2}{\Delta Y_1} = \dfrac{PY_1}{PY_2}$.

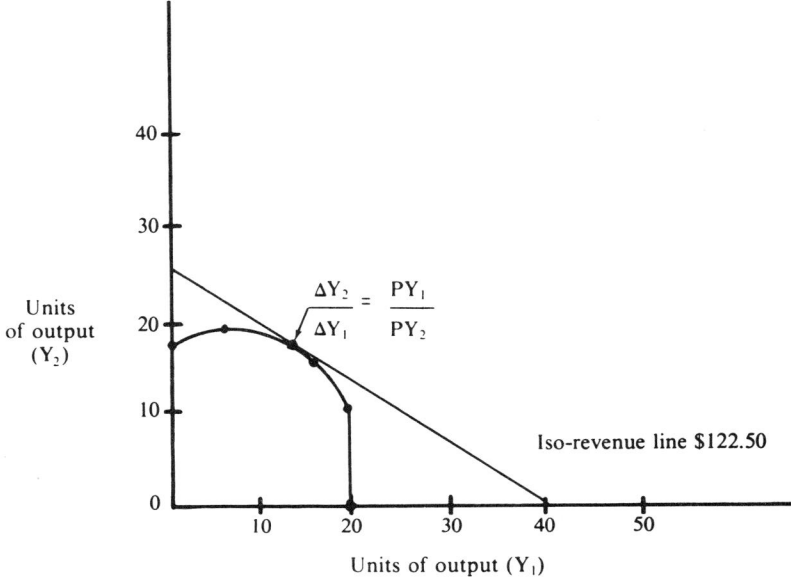

Figure 9-5. Profit Maximization for Two Enterprises When the $PY_1 = \$3$ and $PY_2 = \$5$.

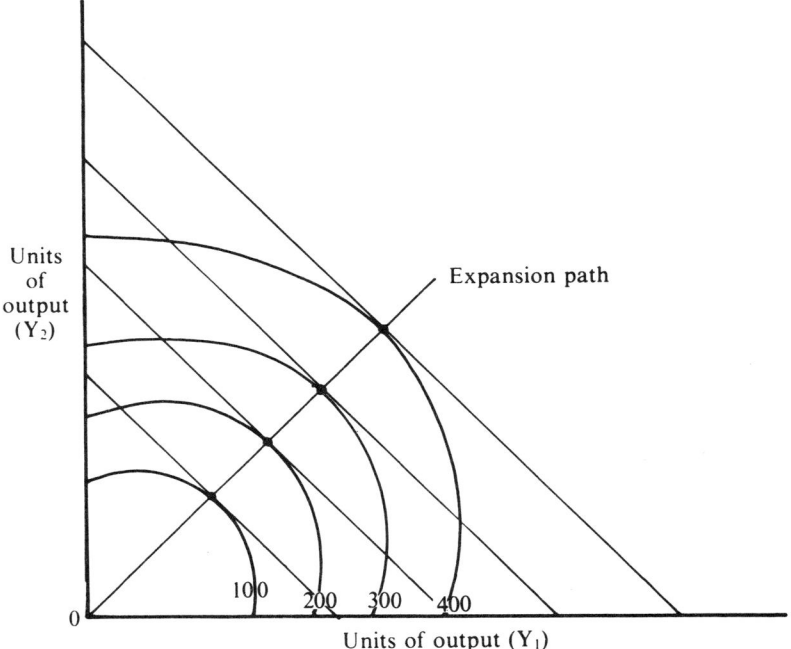

Figure 9-6. Business Expansion.

BUSINESS EXPANSION

In our example we considered a single level of resource use. For every resource level there would be a new production possibility curve, and every level of production would give a new iso-revenue line. For example, in Figure 9-6 let us assume each production possibility curve represents the output of two crops, Y_2 and Y_1, that can be raised on 100, 200, 300, or 400 acres. For each acreage level there will be a new iso-revenue line, and the most profitable enterprise combination can be determined for that level by discovering the point $\frac{\Delta Y_2}{\Delta Y_1} = \frac{PY_1}{PY_2}$. A line connecting each of those points gives the "expansion path" or how to increase the size of business when there are only two production possibilities.

IN SUMMARY

As is so often the case in introductory courses, we have only scratched the surface of the problems of enterprise combination. Seldom will an agricultural producer be limited to only two alternative enterprises. The complexity of decision making increases greatly as the alternatives increase. We have not dealt with the problems of using the product of one enterprise to produce another product. For example, a dairyman must determine the best combination of pasture, forage, and grain to feed cows to produce the product, milk, which he sells.

Gaining an understanding of such basic and admittedly over-simplified cases is necessary to understand the more complex production situation in a real world of price and yield uncertainty, a large number of alternatives, changes in technology, and changes in institutions.

SUGGESTED READINGS

Doll, John P., Rhodes, V. James, and West, Jerry G. *Economics of Agricultural Production, Markets, and Policy*. Richard D. Irwin, Inc., 1968, Chapter 6.

Heady, Earl O. *Economics of Agricultural Production and Resource Use*. Prentice-Hall, 1952, Chapters 7, 8, and 9.

Leftwich, Richard H. *The Price System and Resource Allocation*, 3rd Edition. Holt, Rinehart, and Winston, 1966.

Vincent, Warren H., Editor *Economics and Management in Agriculture*. Prentice-Hall, 1962, Chapter 5.

CONCEPT OF SUPPLY   10

Supply, like demand, is a price-quantity relationship. We must be able to distinguish between supply and the quantity supplied. So often in our everyday lives we call both supply.

SUPPLY DEFINED

Supply is a schedule of the quantities of a good or a service producers are willing and able to sell at a given time at different price levels in a given market. There is a separate supply schedule for each product, and, in fact, for each quality of each product. Supply tells us how the producers behave in a market. It tells us how willing and how able they are to commit their limited resources to meet demands of consumers. They try to allocate the resources in a way to maximize profits. The satisfaction derived from the profits arising from production is the end goal of most producers. The hope for that satisfaction is what motivates producers to offer products to the consumer. Supply and demand together provide the mechanism in a market economy for price determination. The quantity supplied is the amount the producers offer for sale.

THE LAW OF SUPPLY

The law of supply states the quantity of goods and services offered by producers on a market varies directly with price. The producers are responsive to prices. An increase in price of a product motivates producers to produce and sell more of that product. A decrease in price causes a reduction in output.

THE SUPPLY SCHEDULE

We can illustrate both supply and the law of supply by using a supply schedule. A supply schedule is a table or a diagram showing the relationship between the quantity of a good or a service and its prices. The supply schedule, Table 10-1, represents the responsiveness of a milk producer to various prices. In Table 10-1 we have shown a possible schedule of the quantities of milk a producer would be able and willing to offer for sale on a given day. Figure 10-1 shows the same information in a graph. Note that quantity moves in the same direction as price—the law of supply. The diagram shows an upward sloping supply curve as contrasted to the downward sloping demand curve (Chapter 4). If we consider both the demand curve and the supply curve together, we know how consumers and producers respond to prices. When we know that, we then have the basic information to determine price (Chapter 11).

Table 10-1. A Supply Schedule.

Price (Per Quart of Milk)	Quantity (Quarts of Milk)
$.50	1000
.40	875
.30	725
.20	550
.10	310

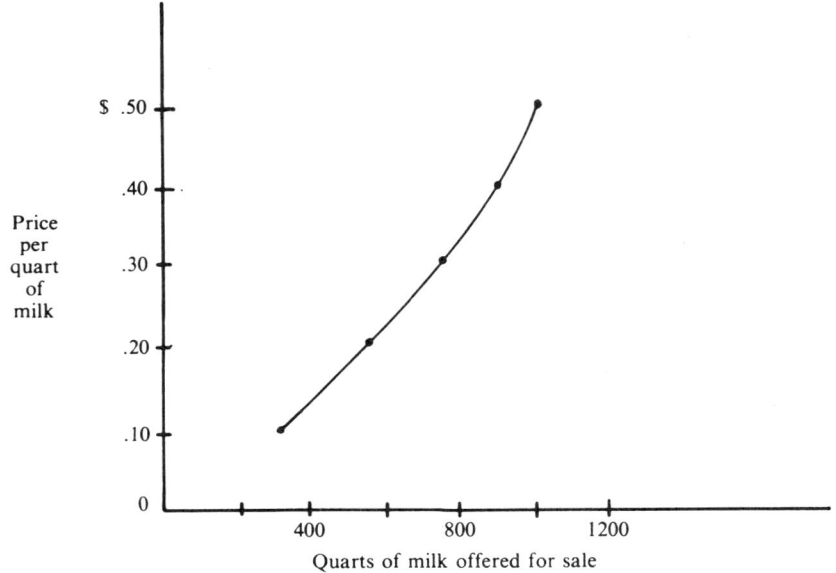

Figure 10-1. A Supply Schedule.

DETERMINING A SUPPLY SCHEDULE

Our supply schedule for milk is a hypothetical one. You may ask where in a real situation would one get the information to determine any individual producer's supply schedule. Think back to the cost concepts. There we had shown that producers trying to maximize profits will produce at the point that MC = MR. In Figure 10-2 we have presented that relationship again with the milk example. Let us assume the producers have the cost structure given in the diagram. We would find at different prices of milk the producers could maximize profits by producing different

CONCEPT OF SUPPLY 117

levels of milk. The higher the price, the more milk can be produced to equate its price (marginal revenue) to the marginal cost. Below 20 cents there would be net losses so the producer would not plan to enter production below that price. At 20, 30, 40, or 50 cents a quart he can make and maximize profits producing 550, 725, 875, and 1000 quarts, respectively. That tells us what the producers are willing to produce at different prices. Assuming they are also able to produce, we now know his supply schedule. The portion of the MC curve above AVC becomes his supply schedule as it gives the same price quantity relationship as required to know supply.

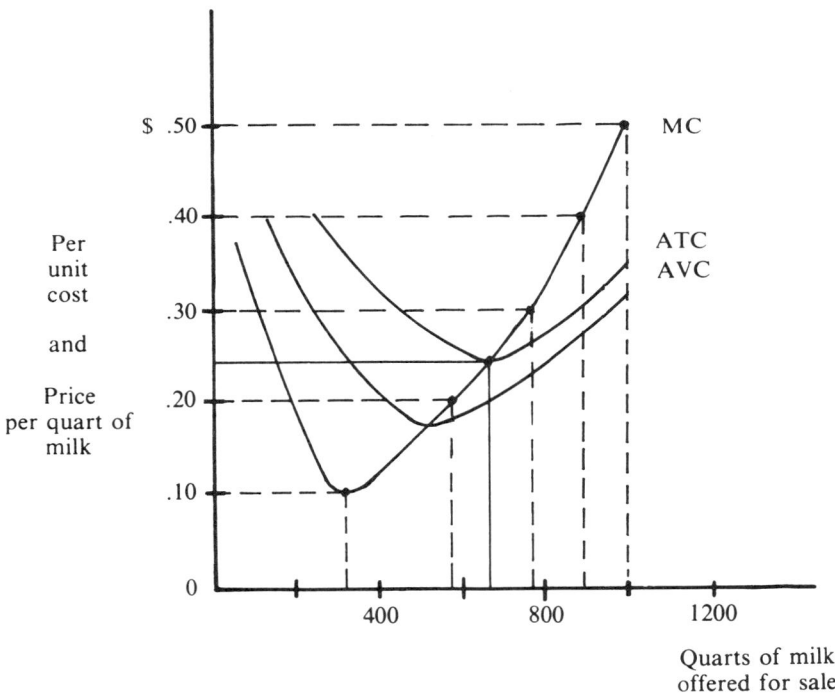

Figure 10-2. Determination of a Supply Schedule

MARKET SUPPLY

To determine market prices, we must know the aggregate of all producers' supply schedules. Each producer has his own unique supply schedule as illustrated in Figure 10-3. At 30 cents a quart producer A will, and is able to, sell 725 quarts, B 900 quarts, and C 500 quarts. By adding the quarts each will deliver at 30 cents, we have that point on the market supply curve. We can repeat that for each price and determine the aggregate supply schedule for all producers—market supply.

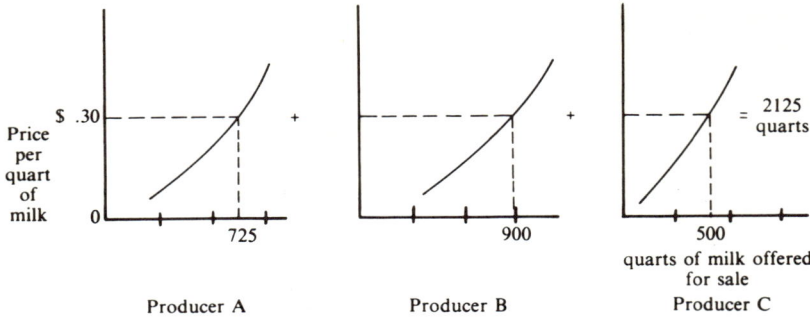

Figure 10-3. Market Supply for Three Producers.

CHANGE IN SUPPLY

In Chapter 4 we considered what is meant by a change in demand. We shall find a change in supply is similar to a change in demand. Movement along a supply schedule does not represent a change in supply. Only a shift from one schedule to another schedule represents a change in supply. That is illustrated in Table 10-2 and Figure 10-4.

Table 10-2. A Change in Supply

Price of Milk (quart)	Quarts Marketed	Change in Supply Quarts Marketed	
		Increase	Decrease
$.50	1000	1200	800
.40	875	1100	700
.30	725	1000	580
.20	550	825	350
.10	310	600	150

FACTORS CAUSING A CHANGE IN SUPPLY

A change in supply may be caused by a change in the price of inputs, a change in prices of other products, a change in producer price expectations, a change in the number of producers, and a change in technology.

Any change in the price of inputs will affect the MC. A rise in PX will increase MC, then MC = MR will occur at a lower level of production —a decrease in supply. A fall in PX will lower MC, thus increasing supply.

A change in the price relationship between the product produced and other products affects their relative profitability. If other products enjoy a price increase, the incentive is to shift resources to produce those products. A fall in the price of other products will cause a shift of resources from their production.

Actual price changes are not even necessary since most production decisions must be made before prices are known. Producers usually decide how much to produce based on input and product price expectations. A change in producer price expectations affects supply.

If more producers start producing a product, the market supply curve will shift to the right. An expanding economy usually has a supply curve that is moving to the right (an increase in supply).

A change in technology, as observed in Chapters 6 and 7, causes an increase in productivity of resources and a reduction in unit costs. Expectations of high profits cause a shift of resources to that line of production and increasing supply.

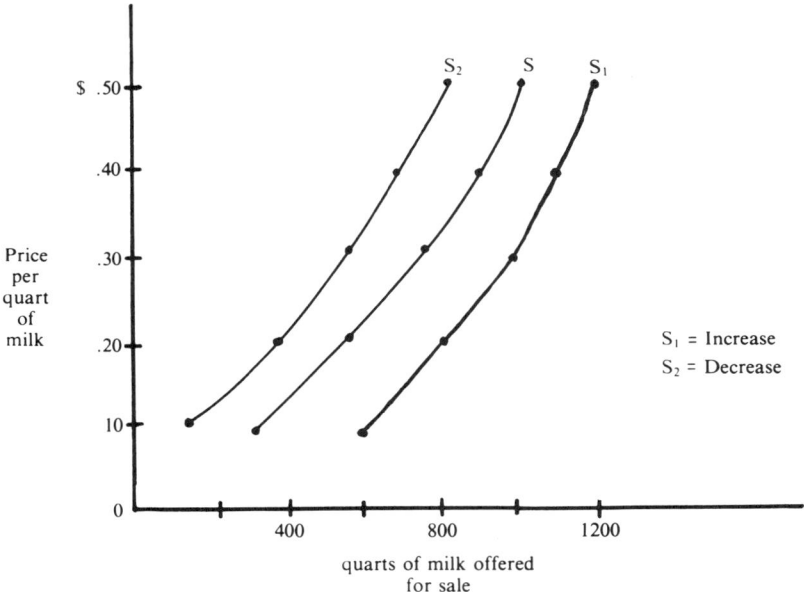

Figure 10-4. A Change in Supply.

ELASTICITY OF SUPPLY

Our discussion of supply attempted to explain producer behavior in the market. We have tried to determine how the producer responds to prices. Thus far we have shown producers will produce more if prices rise and less if prices fall, but we have not given any way to measure producer responsiveness to price changes. The supply curves in Figures 10-1, 10-2, 10-3, and 10-4 each have a specific slope. The steeper the curve, the less responsive are producers to a price change; the flatter the curve, the more responsive are producers to a price change. The slope of the curve is a measure of price responsiveness of producers, but we need a more precise measure than just "eye-balling" a supply curve.

Elasticity of supply (Es) is a measure of a percentage change in the quantity supplied resulting from a percentage change in price. It is usually expressed as the percentage change in quantity resulting from a one percent change in price. As price elastacity of supply is so similar to the price elasticity of demand, rather than make a repeat presentation, we suggest that section of Chapter 4 should be reviewed.

We use the same formula as for price elasticity of demand:

$$Es = \frac{\frac{Q_1 - Q_2}{Q_1 + Q_2}}{\frac{P_1 - P_2}{P_1 + P_2}}$$

Elasticity of supply greater than 1 is elastic; unit elastic if equal to 1; and inelastic if less than 1.

However, there are differences in the two concepts. First since, for supply, price and quantity move in the same direction, the elasticity coefficient will be positive rather than negative. Second, the degree of elasticity will not determine whether total revenue increases, stays the same or decreases. Because price and quantity move in the same direction, any change in price will result in the same direction change in income.

Understanding elasticity of supply is particularly useful when trying to estimate output of a farm product when prices change. It helps determine the amount farmers will increase output of that product when its price rises. For example, if we want a 10 percent increase in the production of oranges, how big a price increase is needed to do that?

SUGGESTED READINGS

Peterson, Willis L. *Principles of Economics: Micro*, Revised Edition. Richard D. Irwin, Inc., 1974, Chapters 5 and 6.

Leftwich, Richard H. *The Price System and Resource Allocation*, 3rd Edition. Holt, Rinehart, and Winston, 1966.

Samuelson, Paul A. *Economics an Introductory Analysis*, 9th Edition. McGraw-Hill Book Company, 1973, Chapter 20.

Vincent, Warren H., Editor *Economics and Management in Agriculture*. Prentice-Hall, 1962, Chapter 7.

PART IV

MARKETS AND PRICE DETERMINATION

ORGANIZATION AND STRUCTURE OF AGRICULTURAL MARKETS   11

Our emphasis in previous chapters has been to explain consumer and producer behavior. The behavior of the consumer was summarized in a demand schedule, of the producer in a supply schedule. The schedules showed the reaction of each to price changes. In our explanation of the demand and supply schedules, we assumed certain prices without showing how a market price is determined. In this and the next chapter we explain what a market is and how supply and demand determine prices.

ROLE OF PRICES

Price is the per unit value of a good or service. Price is expressed in dollars (or cents) per unit (bushels, pounds, gallons, or each). Prices in a market system are important, as they measure consumer and producer preferences. A consumer choosing a product "votes" for that product by the price paid, a higher price represents a "bigger vote." The price paid is a message to producers; a higher price encourages them to produce more; a lower price, less. Prices affect profitability of production, and determine who uses resources for what lines of production.

Prices perform three functions in our economy. First, they guide and regulate consumption. Second, they guide and regulate production. Third, they guide and regulate distribution of income among the owners of production resources.

CONSUMERS AND PRODUCERS MEET IN THE MARKET

In a simple economy consumers and producers meet at a known time and place to trade. It may be just two people—one with a bag of wheat, the other with a box of apples—who wish to exchange their goods. Before they can trade they must determine to their mutual satisfaction how many apples are equal in value to the bag of wheat. In a more advanced economy the value of a unit of each would be expressed in monetary units—called price. Usually all the sellers want to sell everything they carried to the trading place. If they cannot sell their commodity at their original price, they reduce the price until a buyer takes it. Likewise, the prospective buyer will adjust what he will pay depending upon how difficult he believes it will be to buy what he wants.

We have described a market. True, a very simple one, but one that functions as do our complex markets of today.

MARKET DEFINED

A market is a place where buyers and sellers come together to exchange goods and services. In a modern market money is used as a medium of exchange. In addition to the buyers and sellers there may be individuals and groups in the market who negotiate and facilitate the exchange of the goods, for example, salesmen, commission men, brokers. A market is limited to an area in which there is one price for a given commodity. For example, Omaha, Chicago, and Kansas City are each separate markets for choice steers because each has its own price. For each type, class, and grade of livestock there will be separate markets for each location having a different price. There are many markets; every commodity has as many markets as there are places with different prices. A market may cover a small or a large area. Size depends on how far a commodity can be shipped without shipping costs and product deterioration affecting price.

A marketing system provides the organization to bring together buyers and sellers so that they may exchange goods and services directly or for money.

THE FLOW OF AGRICULTURAL PRODUCTS AND INPUTS

From the time production begins, either for products or inputs, many individuals and groups contribute to readying a final product for consumption or use in farm production. A farmer's 200 pound market barrow is a vastly different product from the pork chops the consuming family wants. Further production activities—processing, storing, and transporting—plus market activities are required to meet the consumers' wants.

Agriculturalists deal with the production and marketing of both the product produced by farmers and inputs used by farmers in their farm operations. We shall show the total production and marketing organization through which products and inputs flow.

PRODUCT FLOW

In Figure 11-1 we have developed a flow chart to show what happens to a farm product from the time it leaves the farm until it is purchased by the consumer. Let us continue with our market barrow example and follow it through the diagram.

One or more farmers may have had a part in producing the barrow; for example, one farmer may specialize in producing feeder pigs, another in feeding, or one may produce his own feeder pigs and feed them out. The feeder pigs may have come from sows raised on the farm or from sows purchased from someone specializing in raising breeding gilts. The feeder may produce his own feed, or he may buy it from other farmers directly or through a feed mill.

When the barrow is ready for market, the farmer will transport it to a local sales barn where a commission buyer will buy it for a meat packer.

ORGANIZATION AND STRUCTURE OF AGRICULTURAL MARKETS

At that point, if the farmer raised the barrow, came the first transfer of ownership and a determination of price. The packer must transport the barrow to his plant where it is slaughtered, dressed out into pork sides, cooled, and stored waiting for an order. The packer risks changes in prices while holding the pork. The slaughtering took place under government regulation and was graded on standards set by the government. The packer, besides continuing the process begun by the farmer, of producing a package of pork chops, was a part of the market process.

The sides of pork are purchased by wholesalers; thus there is another transfer of ownership and a price determination. The wholesaler may transport and store the sides of pork under his ownership.

The sides of pork move from the wholesalers to retail stores. Once again there may be a change in ownership and price determination. The

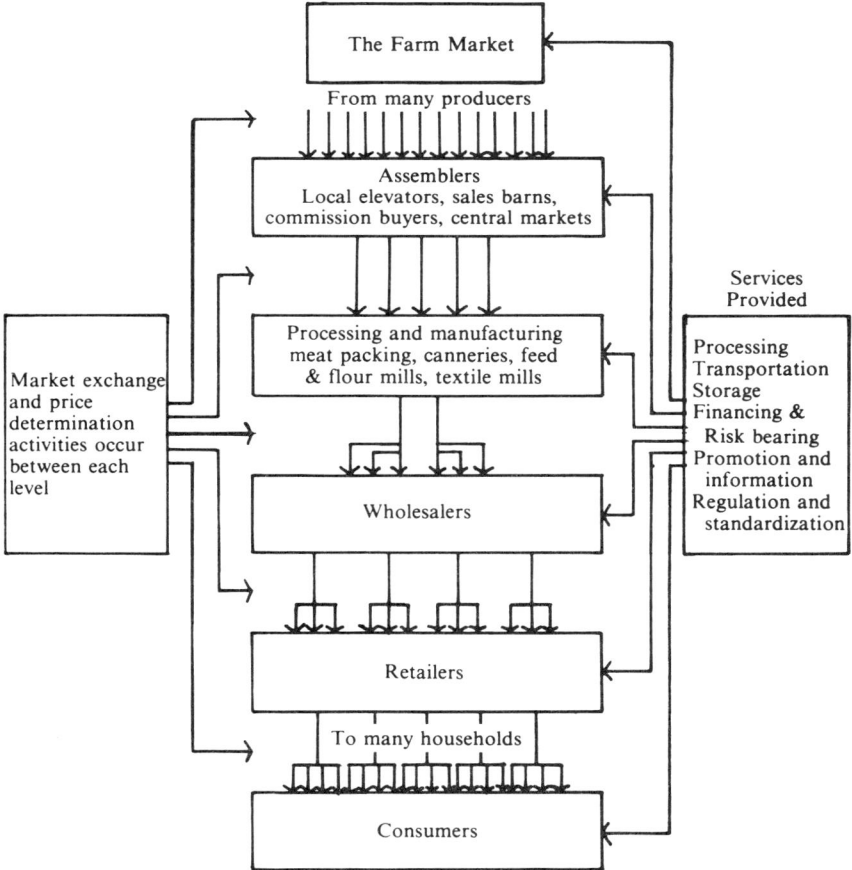

Figure 11-1. The Flow of Farm Products from the Original Producer to the Final Consumer.

retailer will cut down the sides into retail cuts, package the cuts, store the packages, and advertise the pork. One of the packages will contain four pork chops and will meet the needs of a final consumer. The retailer has continued the production and marketing process begun by the farmer.

Finally the four pork chops, in their cellophane wrapping, are chosen by a shopper, who must transport them home, store them in a refrigerator, and prepare them for eating. Once again there was a transfer of ownership and price determination, both a part of the market process. But the consumer, in storing and cooking the pork chops, concluded the production process begun by the farmer from whose litter that barrow came.

INPUT FLOW

To produce the barrow that provided those pork chops required the use of many resources, some coming from the same farm as the barrow, some from other farms, and some from nonfarm sources. Let us take one input, say the gasoline used to haul the pig to the sales barn, and trace it through the production and marketing process. Figure 11-2 summarizes the flow of inputs from the original producer to the final users. As with the product flow, there can be many variations to the more or less direct flow illustrated.

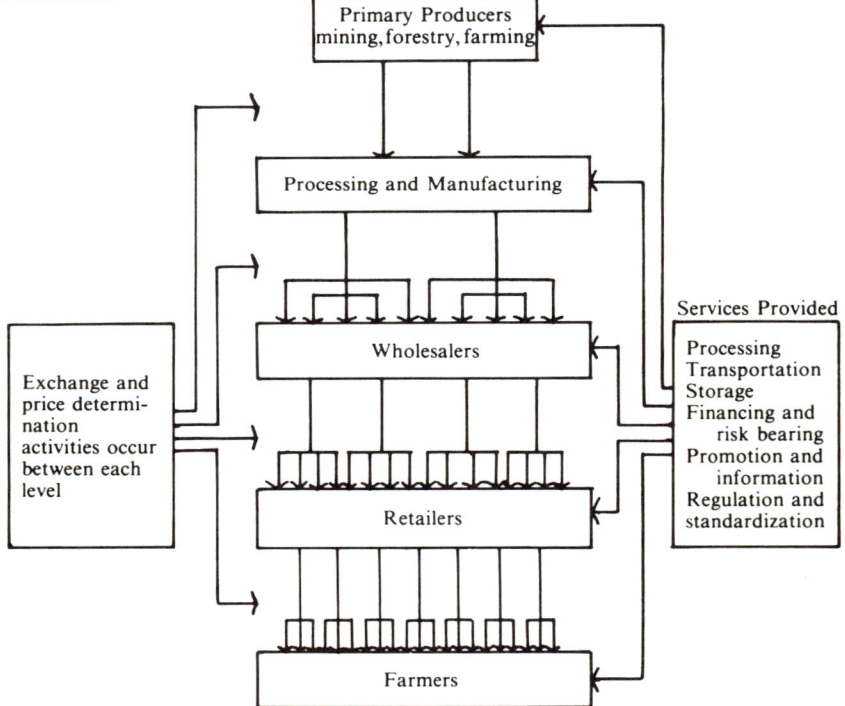

Figure 11-2. The Flow of Farm Inputs from the Original Producer to the Farm User.

Some oil driller produces crude oil that may move through a pipe line to a refinery. The refinery may store the crude oil before producing the gasoline and may then store the gasoline. If the refinery is a separate firm from the driller, there has been a transfer of ownership and a price determination.

The gasoline then moves to wholesalers. It is stored and transported again before going to the retailer who delivers the gasoline to the farmer. The farmer stores the gasoline until he pumps it from his storage tank into his truck before loading his hogs for the trip to the sales barn.

Like the product flow, there were possibilities for several transfers of ownership and price determination. The production process was a continuing one from the oil well to the farmer's truck tank. A similar pattern would exist for feeds, fertilizers, seeds, veterinary supplies, or other inputs.

AGRICULTURAL MARKETING

Historically, agricultural marketing has been broader than our definition of a market as being a place where a transfer of ownership occurs. In the past, agricultural marketing has included all that happened to a farm product from the time it left the farm until it reached the consumer. That means that besides the exchange and price function agricultural marketing has been thought of as providing place utility, as in transportation; time utility, as in storage; and form utility, as in processing.

In a strict sense transportation, storage, and processing are a continuation of the production process begun on the farm, in the forest, or in the mine and should be treated as economics-of-production problems. It is easy to understand how nonfarm production came to be viewed as a part of marketing. Agricultural economics, early in its history, was divided into two parts, farm management and farm marketing. Farm management stopped at the farm gate; farm marketing began at the farm gate and followed the product to the consumer. Traditionally, Figures 11-1 and 11-2 would have been considered as agricultural market flow diagrams. In this text we are showing that the production and marketing processes move together continuously from the very beginning of production until the product is consumed.

At one time little production, such as processing, storing, and transporting, occurred after the product left the farm. The little that did was included as a part of the ownership transfer and price determination functions of the market. As more and more off-farm processing, storing, and transporting became necessary, agricultural marketing became more and more production oriented. The number of individuals and groups contributing to readying farm products for consumers increased as consumers demanded nonfarm processing. Those who provide the production and market activities between the farmer and the consumer are commonly called middlemen.

In this text we consider marketing as being primarily an exchange and pricing activity occurring repeatedly during the full production process. The nonfarm processing, storing, and transporting are treated as agribusiness production and will be covered more fully in Chapter 16.

MARKET EFFICIENCY

In previous chapters we measured production efficiency by the input-output ratio. Increased efficiency results from reducing inputs (costs) relative to output (value). The same analytical process can be used to measure efficiency of storage, transportation, and processing which we consider a continuation of the production begun on the farm.

The exchange and pricing functions of the market are somewhat different. We find that the output of a market is the satisfaction of consumers. Satisfaction, as discussed in Chapter 3, is difficult to measure. Market output can be measured only subjectively and not in precise quantitative units. That does not mean we must abandon all attempts to measure and improve market exchange and pricing efficiency. Any change that reduces marketing costs without reducing satisfaction is, of course, an improvement in efficiency. If the reduced costs result in lower consumer satisfaction, there may be lower efficiency. Increased marketing costs, if more than offset by increased consumer satisfaction, could result in improved efficiency.

One of our best estimates of consumer satisfaction is his return to buy a product again. Thus, if consumers continue to buy as much or more product at the stated price, that clearly demonstrates consumer satisfaction.

MARKET STRUCTURE

All of us are familiar with the term competition. We may think of the competition that exists at a track meet. It is the desire and will of the competitor to be first that makes a track meet a thrilling experience. In such a race each competitor must have a free and an equal chance to compete. If someone sets up and is able to enforce a rule limiting the race to 16-year-old boys, then all girls and any boys other than 16-year-olds would not be free to enter the competition. Competition would be restricted. Only a few could compete.

COMPETITION AMONG PRODUCERS DETERMINES MARKET STRUCTURE

We use the term competition similarly in economics but with some special meanings. Competition among sellers and buyers determines the structure of the market. Competition varies inversely with imperfections and restraints existing in a market. A competitive market is one with few imperfections and restraints on the activities of buyers and sellers. A market with little competition is one that has many imperfections and restraints on sellers and buyers.

Based on the degree of competition, market economists have observed four types of market structure in selling and buying markets:

Types of Market Structure

	Selling Market	Buying Market
Increasing imperfection in the market ↓	Perfect competition Monopolistic competition Oligopoly Monopoly	Perfect competition Monopolistic competition Oligopsony Monopsony

Characteristics associated with each type of market structure follow. We should keep in mind that there is no clear cut criteria to classify a market. Instead there is a steady progression from perfect competition to monopoly. Any one industry may have characteristics of more than one of the types of market structure, but this classification will be particularly helpful in understanding price determination.

PERFECT COMPETITION—COMPETITION AMONG MANY

In a market system perfect competition is often viewed as the "ideal market condition." However, in practice it is impossible for perfect competition to exist in all markets. Those who argue for letting a "free market" determine prices envision the "free market" as being one that is perfectly competitive, in which many unrestrained and informed producers and sellers come together to exchange goods. No buyer or seller has an advantage over any other buyer or seller.

An industry market to be classified in the perfect competition group must have:

1. Such a large number of individual sellers that no one seller can influence price or, from the buying viewpoint, such a large number of buyers no one buyer can influence the price
2. Sellers and buyers who all have both equal and perfect knowledge of all market conditions
3. All sellers offering a nearly identical product so that any seller's product is a perfect substitute for any other seller's product.
4. No restrictions on entry or exit of producers and resources to or from the industry
5. Sellers and buyers who behave in an economically rational manner, that is, they try to maximize their own self interest.
6. No effective collusion among either buyers or sellers

Most of us would immediately recognize that few, if any, industries meet all of the above characteristics. There are some that come close and nearly all of them are in agriculture. One of the best examples is the hard red winter wheat producers. There are so many that individually or in groups the producers have not been able to influence prices. On the buyer's side, the terminal markets, there are few enough so that buyers have not operated in a perfectly competitive market. Individual farmers can sell all their wheat at the market price but none at any higher prices. Thus we often say wheat farmers are "price takers." Each sells such a minute portion of the total hard red winter wheat sold that his sale alone does not affect the market. A wheat grower has no reason to advertise or promote his wheat as all other growers' products are nearly a perfect substitute for his.

Under perfect competition the sellers have little market power so we find such industries usually seek ways to make their market less competitive by forming cooperatives, seeking market orders, requesting legislation, and finding other market restraints.

MONOPOLY-MONOPSONY—NO COMPETITION

The least "free" of the four market structures is a monopolistic market. A monopoly, a selling market, or a monopsony, a buying market, has these characteristics:

1. There is only one firm and by determining the amount produced (or bought for monopsony), it can affect prices.
2. There are no close substitutes for the product.
3. There is not freedom for new firms to begin producing the product; through control of the market or raw materials the existing firm can prevent new entries.

Monopolies in the United States are illegal; in industries that tend to be monopolies the firm may operate, but only under government franchise and regulation. Examples of monopolies are the public utilities which are provided either by government or by private firms franchised and regulated by government. Other monopolies are the postoffice and public road system, both government owned and operated. In agriculture there are no clear cut cases of monopoly, but farmers may purchase from monopsonies—for example, electricity, telephone. Monopolies, although usually big, need not be big. A monopoly may be small and may occur because of a particular situation. The 24-hour grocery store, because it is the only one open in town from 10 p.m. to 7 a.m. may be a monopoly during that time. The rest of the day it is not a monopoly. Similarly a doctor in an isolated community may have a monopoly because it is too far to drive to another doctor. Such small monopolies are not illegal.

OLIGOPOLY-OLIGOPSONY—COMPETITION AMONG THE FEW

Just above the monopoly in degree of competition are the oligopoly/oligopsony firms. An oligopoly/oligopsony has these characteristics:

1. A small number of large firms each producing (or buying) a large enough portion of the total to affect prices and the pricing policies of other firms.
2. The product produced has no close substitute; if there are close substitutes, such as among automobiles, through advertising and promotion the firm will attempt to convince consumers there are differences among the cars.
3. There is limited entry into the industry by new firms; entry is limited by capital investment requirements, market organization needs,

control of patents and raw materials by existing firms, and economies-of-scale advantages of established large firms.
4. There may be little actual collusion among firms, but each must consider what effect its policies will have on other firms and what effect policies of other firms will have on itself; price competition is futile for the oligopoly or oligopsony firm because if one cuts prices, all others must follow and all are worse off.

Oligopolistic competition has dominated United States industry. Because of the economies-of-scale advantages for large firms, most industries are dominated by a few large firms. Examples of oligopolistic competition include firms producing automobiles, electrical appliances, petroleum products, fertilizers, and farm machinery. A number of agricultural processing firms such as cereal grain processors and textile mills operate in an oligopoly market. Even a few farm producers through joint marketing efforts have characteristics of an oligopoly. They include producers of milk, cranberries, English walnuts, and other specialty crops.

MONOPOLISTIC COMPETITION—COMPETITION AMONG MANY

True to its name, monopolistic competition has characteristics of both perfect competition and monopoly. We rank it next to perfect competition in terms of degree of competition existing in the industry. A monopolistic competition industry has the following characteristics:

1. Many small firms, each producing a small enough portion of the total industry output to have little influence on price.
2. Output among firms not highly standardized, but the output of each is a fairly good substitute for the output of others; the firms, through promotion and advertising, attempt to convince consumers there is a real difference between their product and all others.
3. Little or no collusion among firms; each generally ignores the existence of other firms.
4. Little restriction for new firms entering the industry.

Examples of monopolistic competition are the clothing industry, furniture industry, and some food processing industries.

IN SUMMARY

Criteria for distinguishing among the four market structures overlap. There is no clear-cut final way to classify markets. Market structure is a continuum—moving from one classification to another without a clear distinction between the most similar markets. Where to separate one structure from another is difficult, but Robert W. Taylor, Purdue University, uses this simple test.

"To be perfect competition, no producer can influence price; to be monopolistic competition, a producer can influence his price, but is ignored by all competitors; to be oligopoly, a producer can influence his price and affects the actions of his competitors; and to be monopoly, there can be no good substitute for the producer's product."

The structure of a market, depending upon the degree of competition, affects determination of market prices. In Chapter 12 we show how prices are determined under different market structures.

SUGGESTED READINGS

Doll, John P., Rhodes, V. James, and West, Jerry G. *Economics of Agricultural Production, Markets, and Policy.* Richard D. Irwin, Inc., 1968, Chapters 10, 11, 12, 13, 14, 15, 16, and 17.

Kohls, Richard L., and Downey, W. David. *Marketing of Agricultural Products*, 4th Edition. The Macmillan Company, 1972, Chapters 1 and 2.

Leftwich, Richard H. *The Price System and Resource Allocation*, 3rd Edition. Holt, Rinehart, and Winston, 1966.

Vincent, Warren H., Editor. *Economics and Management in Agriculture.* Prentice-Hall, 1962, Chapter 9.

Wilcox, Walter W., Cochrane, Willard W., and Herdt, Robert W. *Economics of American Agriculture*, 3rd Edition. Prentice-Hall, Inc., 1974, Chapters 7, 8, 9, and 10.

PRICE DETERMINATION   12

In previous chapters we have shown that prices in a market economy are fundamental to guiding consumption and production, which, in turn, influence the nature of our economic growth. We have developed demand schedules, Chapter 4, supply schedules, Chapter 10, and considered market structures, Chapter 11. Understanding demand, supply, and market structure are necessary to explore how prices are determined. As we have so often done in explaining economic concepts, we will select the simplest and most ideal situation as a beginning and work to the more complex price determination situations. The perfectly competitive market, where all buyers and sellers have equal market power and information, would permit prices to be determined by the forces of demand and supply only. That would be the simplest pricing situation.

PRICING UNDER PERFECT COMPETITION

The perfectly competitive market with so many buyers and sellers, all having equal knowledge of the market conditions so that no one individual or group can influence the market, is a simple market in which demand and supply determine prices. We must remember, however, that the perfectly competitive market is a special case that can seldom be found. Generally a market has many imperfections and restraints that affect pricing. The imperfections arise from some industries having only a few buyers and sellers, unequal market power among the buyers and sellers, government regulations, trade union influences, labor union influences, and consumer organizations. Before we can hope to understand pricing under such imperfect situations we need first to study our simple, perfect competition situation.

Under perfect competition every buyer will be trying to buy at the cheapest price, and every seller will be trying to sell at the highest possible price. The market provides the place for the buyers and sellers to come together to negotiate the price that will satisfy both enough to cause them to make a trade. Each buyer has a demand schedule that determines his willingness to buy at different prices. Each seller has a supply schedule that determines his willingness to sell at different prices. If we know that information, we can determine the market price.

PRICE DETERMINATION

Using the demand and supply information given in Table 12-1 and Figure 12-1, we can demonstrate price determination under perfect competition. By combining the supply and demand information into a single diagram, Figure 12-2, we can show that at some point the demand schedule will intersect the supply schedule. That happens because consumers demand less and producers supply more as prices are higher (the law of demand and the law of supply). With the resulting upward sloping supply curve and downward sloping demand curve, it is inevitable that they will intersect. At the point of intersection, point P in Figure 12-2, the quantity the producer is willing and able to sell, 15 eggs, is just equal to the number of eggs the consumer is willing to buy, 15 eggs, at 4 cents each. At that point supply equals demand. The price satisfactory to both buyers and sellers for 15 eggs is 4 cents each. Price for those two, one buyer and one seller, has been determined.

Table 12-1. A Hypothetical Demand and Supply Schedule for Eggs.

Number of Eggs Wanted (demand)		Number of Eggs Offered for Sale (supply)	
Price Per Egg	Number of Eggs	Price Per Egg	Number of Eggs
$.02	25	$.02	10
.04	15	.04	15
.06	10	.06	20
.08	5	.08	22
.10	3	.10	24
.12	1	.12	25

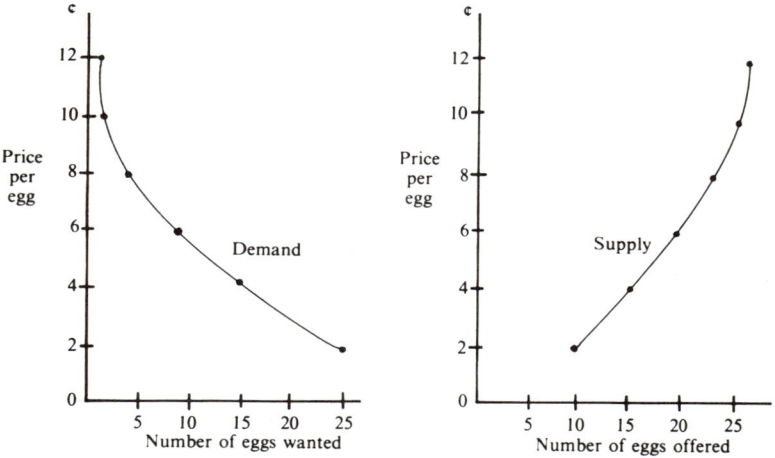

Figure 12-1. A Hypothetical Demand and Supply Schedule for Eggs.

EFFECT OF CHANGES IN DEMAND AND SUPPLY ON PRICE

As demand and supply under perfect competition determine prices, we can expect that any change in consumer and producer behavior that changes demand or supply will affect prices. Prices will rise if:

PRICE DETERMINATION   135

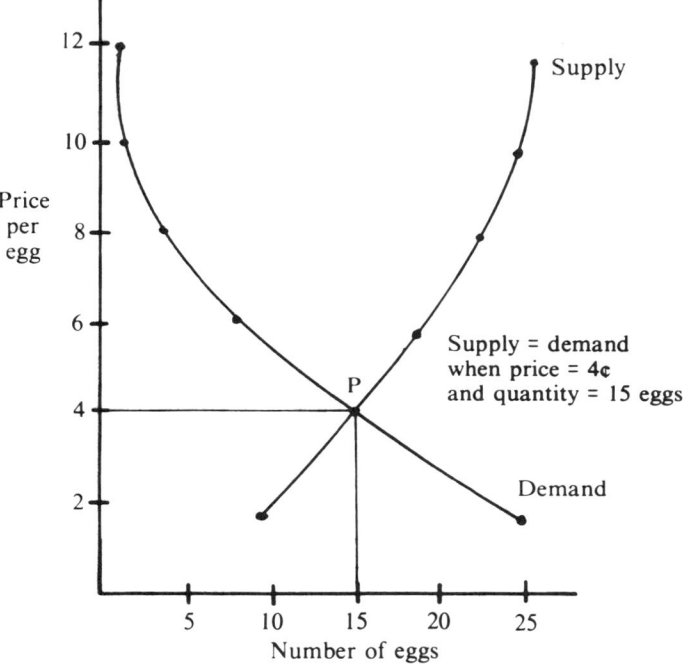

Figure 12-2. Price Determination of Eggs.

1. Demand increases and there is no change in supply, Figure 12-3 a
2. Supply decreases and there is no change in demand, Figure 12-3 b
3. Supply decreases and demand increases, Figure 12-3 c.

Prices will fall if:

1. Demand decreases and there is no change in supply, Figure 12-3 d
2. Supply increases and there is no change in demand, Figure 12-3 e
3. Supply increases and demand decreases, Figure 12-3 f.

Prices may either rise, fall, or remain the same depending on the size of change when demand and supply move in the same direction. If:

1. Both demand and supply decrease,
   a. Price will rise if supply decreases relatively more than demand decreases, Figure 12-3 g
   b. Price will fall if supply decreases relatively less than demand decreases, Figure 12-3 h
   c. Price will remain the same if supply decreases the same as demand decreases, Figure 12-3 i.

2. Both demand and supply increase,
   a. Price will rise if demand increases relatively more than supply increases, Figure 12-3 j.
   b. Price will fall if demand increases relatively less than supply increases, Figure 12-3 k.
   c. Price will remain the same if demand increases the same as supply increases, Figure 12-3 l.

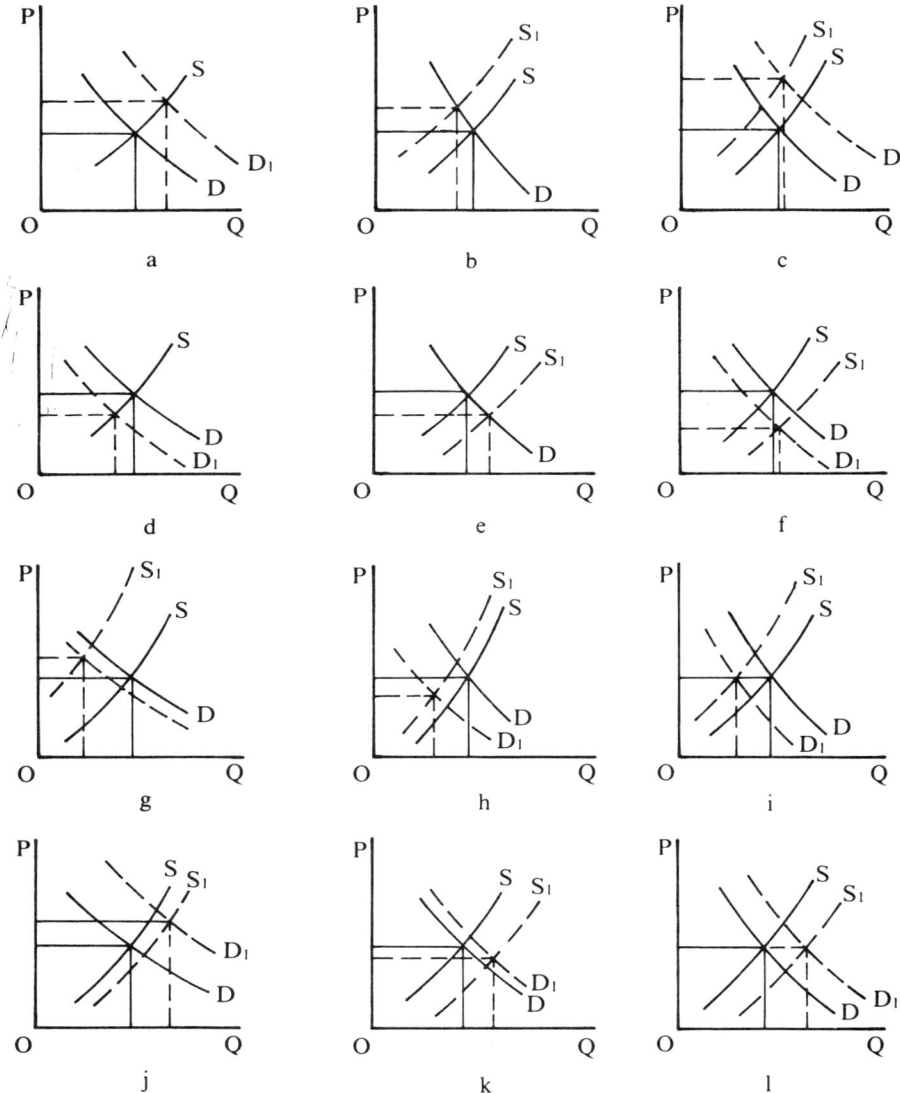

Figure 12-3. Effects on Price of Changes in Demand and Supply.

PRICING UNDER IMPERFECT COMPETITION

Monopoly. We have identified three types of markets with imperfect competition—monopoly, oligopoly, and monopolistic competition. If we had any monopolies that were free to set their own prices, we would find such firms seeking the price that would maximize their profits. In Chapter 7 we showed a firm would maximize profits when MC = MR. In Chapter 10 we showed the MC curve was the same as the individual producing firm's supply curve. In Figure 12-4 we have illustrated profit maximization. MC = MR when the firm is producing Oy_1 units of Y. To find the price it can charge when producing Oy_1 units, the firm must know the demand schedule for the product. In Figure 12-5 we have added the demand schedule, which represents all the quantities of Y the consumer will buy at different prices.

The monopoly can determine the price consumers are willing and able to pay for Oy_1 units by extending a vertical line from the point y_1 until it intersects the demand curve. A line drawn from that point to the vertical axis will give the price, Op_1. Such a monopoly firm will set Op_1 price if left free to do so. However, monopoly prices are regulated and usually set somewhat lower than the one equating MC to MR. For example, a regulated price of Op_2 will require an output of Oy_2 by the firm. The justification for regulating prices of monopoly firms is that they are in a position to take advantage of the consumer. Even monopolists have limits

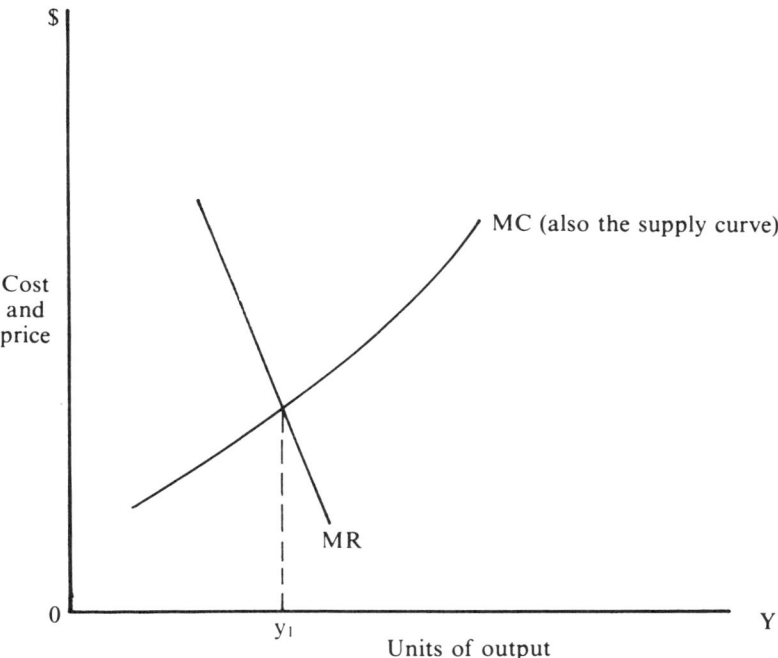

Figure 12-4. Profit Maximization for a Monopoly.

to prices they can set as determined by its consumers' demand schedule. A monopolist setting the price Op_1 while producing Oy_2 of Y would find it could not sell Oy_2 of the product. Rather it would be limited to selling the amount the consumer demanded at the higher price, Oy_1.

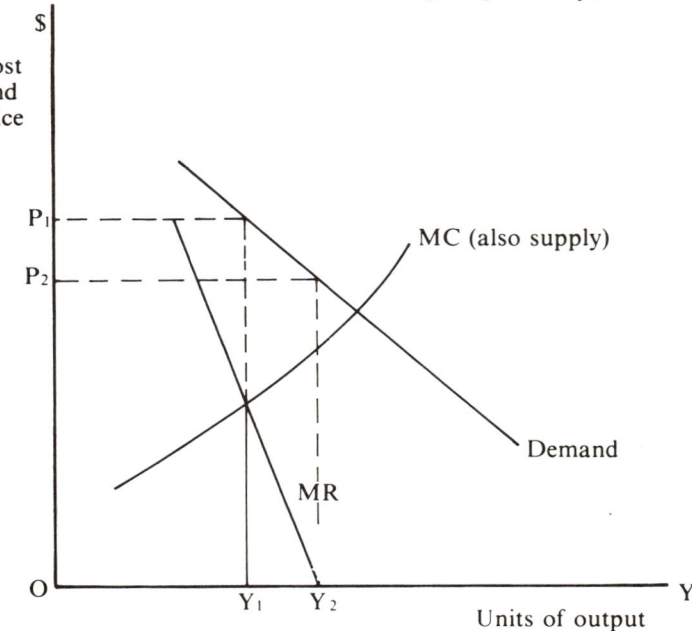

Figure 12-5. Monopoly Price Determination.

Oligopoly. Under oligopoly conditions an individual firm can influence prices in the market; therefore no one firm can have prices much above or below those of its competitors—if above, it will lose customers, if below it will take all the customers. Each firm soon realizes that to get along, that is, stay in business, it must follow pricing policies similar to those of its competitors.

Often in an oligopoly market one firm emerges as the price leader. It will probably settle for a price somewhat close to the one that will maximize its profits, MC = MR. Unlike the monopolist, the oligopolist price leader must consider the effect of his price on his competitors' prices. If its price forces its competitors to have quite different pricing policies, in order to retain their part of the market or to assure them some profits, its role as price leader is jeopardized. Thus the price leader will seek a price assuring its competitors a share of the market. Usually competition among the few concentrates upon product competition rather than on price competition.

Price determination by the price leader may begin from the same basis, Figure 12-5, as the monopolist, but, for the oligopolist, price determination will be modified by the impact that price would have on other producers.

Monopolistic Competition. Like perfect competition, a market under monopolistic competition has so many sellers that no one firm has much affect upon price. The forces of demand and supply in the market place largely determine prices. We must bear in mind that although the perfectly competitive pricing model, Figure 12-3, is basic to monopolistic competition pricing, imperfections do exist. Some firms alone can have some small effect on the market, thus they can, by their actions, influence prices. Advertising, promotion, and product development are techniques used to try to change (increase) demand for their output. To the extent their efforts succeed they can affect prices. Their "market power" to affect prices is usually limited.

IN SUMMARY

A characteristic of the United States market seems to be the positive actions taken to move away from either extreme—pricing under perfect competition or under monopoly. Monopoly, unregulated, is illegal in the United States. As citizens we have insisted there must be competition among producers. In industries, such as the public utilities where many or even a few companies would not be possible, we franchise one firm and regulate its prices. Under oligopoly, where there are only a few firms, we have made it illegal for the firms to collude in setting prices. But even if there is no overt collusion, each firm's reactions to its competitors cause each to end up with almost identical pricing policies.

In those sectors of the economy operating under nearly perfect competition, like farming, the industries have, through organization and government, attempted to introduce some imperfections into their markets. Price supports, market orders, minimum wages, and cooperative marketing all are examples of policies to reduce competition. A current issue in agriculture has been the apparent lack of bargaining power among farm producers.

Generally in the United States we have sought public policies that reduce the effects of the two extremes, monopoly and perfect competition, on price determination.

SUGGESTED READINGS

Doll, John P., Rhodes, V. James, and West, Jerry G. *Economics of Agricultural Production, Markets, and Policy.* Richard D. Irwin, Inc., 1968, Chapters 10, 11, 12, 13, 14, 15, 16, and 17.

Kohls, Richard L., and Downey, W. David. *Marketing of Agricultural Products*, 4th Edition. The Macmillan Company, 1972, Chapters 1 and 2.

Leftwich, Richard H. *The Price System and Resource Allocation*, 3rd Edition. Holt, Rinehart, and Winston, 1966.

Vincent, Warren H., Editor. *Economics and Management in Agriculture.* Prentice-Hall, 1962, Chapter 9.

Wilcox, Walter W., Cochrane, Willard W., and Herdt, Robert W. *Economics of American Agriculture*, 3rd Edition. Prentice-Hall, Inc., 1974, Chapters 7, 8, 9, and 10.

Part V

AGRICULTURAL BUSINESS MANAGEMENT AND ORGANIZATION

THE ROLE OF MANAGEMENT IN ECONOMIC ACTIVITY 13

As our society has increased in complexity, more and more human effort has been required to organize resource use and to guide the operation of our activities. Those providing the human effort have become known as managers. Each of us has his own management activities, but there has arisen a group of professional managers who organize and guide much of our private and public activities. This chapter is devoted to explaining management and its role in our private and public economic activities.

MANAGEMENT DEFINED

Management is the organization and operation of affairs to achieve some predetermined objective. Management is an abstract concept that applies to many types of human endeavor. It is an intangible human behavioral activity. As with all human behavioral activities, management is difficult to identify and to measure. There is no unit measure of managerial effort. We do not understand much about managerial effectiveness or what characteristics are associated with good management. Good management seems, like beauty, to be easier to recognize than to describe or to measure. Management is largely a learned skill. Some seem to be much more effective managers than others—they seem to be more efficient in achieving their predetermined objectives. Good managers are those who pay special attention to the management process rather than only letting things happen. Managerial skill can be improved. We are capable of learning management techniques; thus we offer management courses, for example, farm management, financial management, business management.

Each of us has been engaged in management since we first learned to cry to get attention. As students we must organize and use our time to get our studies completed. Planning and setting up a 4-H club booth is a management activity. Seeking, finding, and marrying a lifetime mate, setting up a home, rearing children, and planning for retirement require managerial skills. Organizing and operating a farm, a commercial orchard, a machinery dealership, or a bank are management tasks. We see that management pervades throughout our lifetime and all our activities.

MANAGEMENT—A PART OF ECONOMIC ACTIVITY

In neither our discussion of the economics of consumption or production have we considered management. Yet management is essential to achieving either our consumption objective of utility maximization or our production objective of profit maximization. Many individuals may have additional, competing, and noneconomic goals that must be considered in applying management even to our economic activities. But for the sake of simplicity let us assume there are some consumers and some producers who have those single objectives.

Remember we earlier assumed all producers had perfect knowledge in the factor-product, factor-factor, and product-product cases. We made the same assumption for the consumer. Thus in considering, for example, the production function $Y = f(X_1 \ldots X_n)$, we did not designate any X as a managerial resource. There was no need to identify the management input because every producer had perfect knowledge. Every producer knew for now and always exactly what the results for every resource combination would be. Under such conditions there is no need for management; without it every producer knew his results, so why bother with management. Every producer would always get the same results as every other producer when using the same set of resources.

IMPERFECTIONS IN KNOWLEDGE

Experience tells us that no producer or consumer has perfect knowledge about what will happen in his production or consumption activities. Each of us is confronted with knowledge imperfections, which we speak of as uncertainty. We are uncertain at planting time what our yields will be. We are uncertain about future prices and costs. Every way we turn, we are confronted with uncertainties.

The need for management arises because there is uncertainty. The function of the manager is to organize and to operate a business when the exact results are unknown. It is the manager who must take all the resources, $X_1 \ldots X_n$, and use them in a way that will come closest to producing the quantity of Y that will maximize profits.

THE EFFECT OF MANAGEMENT ON
THE PRODUCTIVITY RESOURCES

Management does affect output. All producers do not achieve the same level of output with a similar set of resources. Observe managers you know—farmers, bankers, agribusinessmen—and you will find great differences in the input-output ratios each achieves. Quality of management does affect the productivity of the resources used.

MANAGEMENT AND LABOR

In many small businesses, particularly farms, one individual provides both the management and the labor. In such instances labor and management tend to merge and it is difficult to separate the two. Often both are done simultaneously. For example, a farmer may be planning his next year's organization (management) while driving a tractor (labor).

Large businesses are able to have two separate groups of employees, one specializing in labor and the other in management. But even then we find the managers may spend time laboring or laborers managing. Planning a bookkeeping method is clearly management; recording information in the books is labor. Either a bookkeeper or a manager may be involved in both activities. A machine operator in a feed mixing firm may be a laborer, but in planning his day's grinding schedule for filling orders he is a manager. At all levels of activities some management is required. Only those jobs that are strictly repetitive are limited to using only labor.

FUNCTIONS OF MANAGEMENT

In trying to organize resources and then to carry out day-to-day operations to achieve some objective when the results are uncertain, a manager is confronted with many problems. Students of management have noted that managers are essentially problem solvers. They also noted a similarity between managers' problem solving and the problem solving of research scientists. The objectives, of course, were different. The researcher sought new knowledge; the private business manager sought profits. Scientists had developed a problem solving process called the scientific method to guide them in their search for knowledge. Those studying the managerial process found that the scientific method could be useful in describing management. The scientific method for scientists and the functions of management derived from that method are useful guides for solving perplexing problems.

FARM AND AGRIBUSINESS MANAGEMENT

In agricultural economics we deal with management of two types of businesses—the farm, usually a one-man operation dealing with biological and weather uncertainties, and agribusiness firms usually employing several managers dealing with human relationships and physical uncertainties. The nature of the management problems of each is similar, yet in practical application the problems are quite different. As a result of the difference, the early agriculturalists, who specialized in farm management, did not base their work on the writings in business administration. The early agricultural economists, who had scientific training, soon saw a strong similarity between the problem-solving activities of a scientist working alone and a farmer also working alone. Therefore, we find they developed a set of functions describing the management process that are very similar to the scientific method.

In agribusiness firms there may be many people who share in the management process. There are also perhaps hundreds of people providing the labor input. The emphasis of management under such conditions was quite different from that applicable to the one-man farm. People in agribusiness found business administration writings that emphasized the interpersonal relationships well suited to agricultural processing firms. In the one-man business the manager has only one individual, himself, to direct and supervise, so the problem of control is much less critical.

As students in agricultural economics you should not be perplexed by what seems to be a different approach to management on your farm and the approach given in agribusiness management courses. You will be dealing with the problem-solving techniques best adapted to each.

COMPARISON OF THE FUNCTIONS OF MANAGEMENT

In Table 13-1 we have listed the steps of the scientific method and the functions of management in farm and agribusiness firms. Farm management and business management texts give different functions of management. Table 13-1 gives both. Both describe the same process. Managers, whether of farms or agribusinesses, are involved in all the activities in either list of functions. We will stress the similarities between farm management and agribusiness management rather than their differences. As farm businesses increase in size and complexity, management problems become indistinguishable from agribusiness management problems.

Table 13-1. The Functions of Management and the Scientific Method Compared.

The Scientific Method	Functions of Management	
	Farm Management Text List	Agribusiness Management Text List
Identify and Formulate a Problem	Observation Goal Specification Problem Identification	Organizing
Develop a Hypothesis	Gather Relevant Data	Planning
		Leading
Collect Data and Information	Analysis—Identify Alternative Solutions	Controlling
Test Hypothesis	Decision—Choose Among Alternatives	
Accept or Reject Hypothesis	Action	
Report Results	Bear Responsibility	

FARM MANAGEMENT

The farm management process has been broken into five separate functions. A danger of any such list is that the reader may think each function is separate and that one can progress from function to function down the list. Actually each function is related to each other function, and a manager may do two or more simultaneously. For example, the data needed depend upon the analysis so that a manager in the analysis function may find he needs more data and may have to return to the observation function. A tentative decision may be made, but more analysis and more data are needed before making a firm decision for action. A farm manager soon will find management necessitates the continuous use of

THE ROLE OF MANAGEMENT IN ECONOMIC ACTIVITY 147

all five functions simultaneously. He alone is responsible for the five functions, whereas a larger business may have managers specializing in a single function.

Using the five functions, we see a manager is a learner, a decision maker, a strategist, and a bearer of risk, as illustrated below:

Observation ⎱ Analysis ⎰	Learning
Decision	Deciding
Action	Strategy
Bear Responsibility	Risk

As a learner he sets goals and objectives for his farm. He identifies problems, that is, things occurring that are inconsistent with the objectives set. He seeks information relevant to the solution of the problem.

As a decision maker he must select the solution that he believes will come closest to fulfilling the business objectives. We often think in terms of decision making as the heart of management. In a large business, decision making is usually reserved for "top" management. The learning activities may be delegated to technical staff, for example, a research department. Carrying out a decision may also be shared, for example, by supervisors and foremen. On most farms one individual has all those functions.

Strategy comes into play when action is taken. By strategy we refer to the control of the conditions under which decisions are implemented. The finest decisions not put into effect never bear results. A manager can ill afford inaction, because a decision not carried out has exactly the same affect as no decision.

It is management that must bear the risk. It reaps the rewards (profits) for good management, and the failures (losses) for poor management.

AGRIBUSINESS MANAGEMENT

The management process takes on a new dimension when a second person joins a business. Then the manager must emphasize the coordination of other people's efforts in the organization and operation of the business. The new emphasis results in a different classification of functions from those used for the one-man farm.

In Table 13-1 we identified four functions of agribusiness management: organizing, planning, leading, and controlling.

A multiman business, besides organizing its resource use, must develop an organization that assigns work responsibilities to, and coordinates the work of different people. Thus we find the large business is made up of divisions and departments each with its assigned activities.

Planning entails establishing goals for the business, developing policies and programs to achieve the goals, and finding strategies to implement the policies and programs. It is in this function that we find the similarity to the five functions of farm management. The learning, the deciding and the acting are also fundamental to "large business" management.

Leading refers to the methods management uses in its relationship to the people in the organization. Management seeks the cooperation of the staff, motivates the staff to fulfill the firm's goals, and fosters mutual trust between management and staff. In short it sets an example for all employees.

Controlling a business is seeing that the firm is moving toward its objectives. A manager continuously determines how closely the operation is to meeting its goals, or how far it is missing them. After identifying weakness, he implements corrections that bring the business back on course.

All four functions are interrelated and must be carried out continuously. No one of them, or all of them together, are ever completed.

THE RETURN TO MANAGEMENT

Each of the factors of production claims its returns from the production process: land, rent; capital, interest; and labor, wages. Management, as the bearer of risk for organizing and operating a business under uncertainty, is rewarded through profits (or losses).

SUGGESTED READINGS

Bradford, Laurence A., and Johnson, Glenn L. *Farm Management Analysis*. John Wiley and Sons, 1953, Chapters 1, 2, and 3.

Cohen, Morris P., and Nagel, Ernest. *An Introduction to Logic and Scientific Method*. Harcourt, Brace and Company, 1934, Chapter 20.

Johnson, Glenn L., and Haver, Cecil B. *Decision-Making Principles in Farm Management*. Kentucky Agricultural Experiment Station Bulletin 593, 1953.

Johnson, Glenn L. *Managerial Concepts for Agriculturalists*. Kentucky Agricultural Experiment Station Bulletin 619, 1954.

Newman, William H., Summer, Charles E., and Warren, E. Kirby. *The Process of Management: Concepts, Behavior, and Practice*, 2nd Edition, Prentice-Hall, 1967, Chapter 1.

Vincent, Warren H., Editor. *Economics and Management in Agriculture*. Prentice-Hall, 1962, Chapters 1 and 2.

TYPES OF BUSINESS ORGANIZATION   14

The conduct of economic activity is through some type of organization. The organization can be either private or government. In this chapter we describe the types of business organizations used by private businesses. In some instances government establishes semiautonomous, or even completely autonomous, organizations, such as the Tennessee Valley Authority, the Commodity Credit Corporation, or the Federal Land Bank System, to conduct specific economic activities. State and local governments also organize some economic activities into business organizations similar to the private ones. Generally the government's economic activity is carried out directly by governmental agencies.

TYPES OF BUSINESS ORGANIZATION

Businesses are organized on both legal and economic bases. The organization establishes the relationship between the business and the person or persons who own and control the business, among the owners (when there is more than one), and between the business and government. A business organization is for the benefit of its owners who provide ownership capital, organize and direct it, and accept the risk.

No one type of business organization is best for all businesses. The type selected should depend on the needs of a specific business. On a legal basis all businesses are either unincorporated or incorporated. An unincorporated business under law exists only as a part of its owners and has no separate legal identity. An incorporated business by law has a legal identity separate from its owners. The incorporated business is endowed by law with most of the rights and obligations of a person. An unincorporated business has no legal rights or obligations apart and separate from its owners. An unincorporated business may define relationships among the owners through oral or written contractual relationships. An incorporated business, through its articles of incorporation, specifies the relationships, unique to each business, subject to the laws of the particular state in which it is incorporated.

The types of business organizations for agricultural business activities are:
    Unincorporated
        Sole proprietorship
        Partnership
            Regular partnership

Table 14-1. Characteristics of Types of Private Business Organizations Compared.

Characteristic	Unincorporated Business			Incorporated Business		
	Sole Proprietorship	Partnership[1]		Ordinary Corporation	Tax Option Corporation	Cooperative Corporation
		Regular	Limited			
Nature of entity	Single person	Two or more persons	Two or more persons	Legal person separate from owners	Legal person separate from owners	Legal person separate from owners
Life of business	Terminates at death of owner	Agreed term; terminates at death of a partner	Agreed term; terminates at death of a partner	Fixed term or perpetual	Fixed term or perpetual	Fixed term—specified in state laws
Liability	Personally liable to extent of all assets	Each partner liable for all partnership obligations to extent of all assets	Limited partners liable only for their investment, regular partners liable for all partnership obligations	Shareholder liable only to extent of ownership; not liable for corporation's obligations	Shareholder liable only to extent of ownership; not liable for corporation's obligations	Shareholder liable only to extent of ownership; not liable for corporation's obligations
Sources of capital	Owners' investment and loans	Partner's investment and loans	Partners' investment and loans	Contribution of shareholders for stock; sale of stock and bonds; loans	Contribution of shareholders for stock; sale of stock and bonds; loans	Contribution of members for stock and/or other equity capital; loans from members and/or financing agencies—especially banks for cooperatives
Management decisions	Proprietor	Agreement among partners	Agreement among partners	Shareholders elect directors who manage the business	Shareholders elect directors who manage the business	Shareholders elect directors who manage the business
Limits to business activities	Discretion of proprietor and laws	Partnership agreement and laws	Partnership agreements and laws	Articles of incorporation and laws	Articles of incorporation and laws	Articles of incorporation and laws
Transfer of interest	Terminates the proprietorship	Dissolves partnership; if all agree, new partnership may be formed	Dissolves partnership; if all agree new partnership may be formed	Transfer of stock does not affect continuity of the business	Transfer of stock does not affect continuity of the business	Transfer of stock back to coop—to be reissued to new members
Effect of death	Terminates the proprietorship	Terminates the partnership or sale by heirs to surviving partners	Terminates the partnership or sale by heirs to surviving partners	No effect on corporation; stock passes to heirs	No effect on corporation; stock passes to heirs	No effect on cooperative; stock redeemed by cooperative to be issued to new members
Distribution of earnings	All to the proprietor	Divided among partners as specified in partnership agreement	Divided among partners as specified in partnership agreement	Retained in the corporation or distributed as dividends to shareholders, based on per share amount set by board of directors	Retained in the corporation or distributed to shareholders, based on per share amount set by board of directors	Some retained as cooperative reserves, some as dividends on stock; major part distributed to members in proportion to amount of business done with the cooperative (patronage dividends)
Income taxes	Income taxed to proprietor	Partnership files information return, pays no tax; each partner pays tax on his share as an individual	Partnership files information return, pays no tax; each partner pays tax on his share as an individual	Corporation pays tax on income; shareholders pay tax on dividends distributed	Corporation pays no tax; each shareholder pays tax on share of income	Cooperative pays corporation income tax on income accruing to the cooperative; members pay personal income tax on stock dividends and on patronage refunds

1—Few cooperatives have used the partnership type of business organization.

Source: North Central Regional Extension Publication No. 11, (Revised 1967) and the author.

Limited partnership
Cooperative (Usually cooperatives are incorporated, but incorporation is not necessary).

Incorporated
  Ordinary corporation
    Public corporation
    Family corporation
  Tax option corporation
  Cooperative corporation

SOLE PROPRIETORSHIPS

As an economy developed, the basic producing unit (a family) gradually began to produce more and more for a market rather than to meet its direct consumption needs. The family became a basic business unit. Usually the head of the household owned and controlled all the family assets and thus became the proprietor of the business unit.

A sole proprietorship is a business owned and controlled by a single individual. There may be many laborers, either hired employees or members of the family, but the management remains with that one individual. The sole proprietorship continues to be an effective type of business organization in agriculture. In agriculture, particularly the farm sector, there are many one-man operations. It is the type of business organization that dominates in perfectly competitive industries. Although usually each is small and their number is large, a sole proprietorship could be extremely large and there could be few in the industry. When a business becomes large, other types of business organization offer significant advantages.

A sole proprietorship can be formed by any one of legal age to enter any type of legal production without chartering or permission from any government agency. The owner is the sole decision maker. He may consult with and share decision making with his family or others, but the owner is finally responsible for decisions. The proprietor is liable for all business activities to the full extent of his business and personal assets. There is no legal distinction between his business and personal wealth and earnings. The business has no legal identity separate from its owner. The business terminates with the death of an individual and a new business must then be formed by the new owners. For income tax purposes all of the business earnings are taxed as individual earnings of the owner.

A sole proprietorship has these advantages:

1. Provides for independent decision making and action
2. Easy to organize and to dissolve
3. Simplicity of operation

It has these disadvantages:

1. Unlimited liability.

2. Termination of business upon death of owner makes continuation of business from generation to generation difficult.
3. Impossible to take others into the business, for example, a son, without changing the type of business organization.
4. Difficult to transfer partial ownership to anyone else.
5. Limited to own wealth or credit for financing operations.

PARTNERSHIPS

As the need for sharing ownership responsibilities in a business increases, an alternative to the sole proprietorship is the partnership form of business organization. *A partnership is a business with two or more owners who contribute their assets to the business, and share the gains and losses of the business.* It is the usual type of business organization used when close family members enter into a joint business venture. It is like a sole proprietorship in all respects except the shared ownership and responsibilities. There can be any number of partners. The basis for a successful partnership is the faith, confidence, and trust each partner has for each other partner as each stands liable for the actions of all other partners.

The partnership is commonly used by agricultural businesses, particularly farm firms. A partnership is formed when those becoming partners agree upon the terms of the partnership. The agreement can be either oral or written. Preferably, it should be written and recorded. No chartering by a government agency is needed in most states. Decisions are by the mutual consent of all partners; if there are several, the partnership may establish a voting procedure. At any time a partner may withdraw, subject to the terms of his partnership contract with the other partners. Each partner has unlimited liability for the obligations of the partnership and may also be liable for some personal obligations of each other partner. The unlimited liability feature can be avoided if a limited partnership is used. *In a limited partnership one or more partners' liability is limited to their investment in the business.* A limited partnership must have at least one partner responsible for management and who is liable for partnership obligations.

The death of a partner terminates a partnership. The remaining partners may form a new partnership, including buying the deceased partner's share from his heirs. If one partner transfers his interest in the partnership, the partnership is terminated.

A partnership does not pay income tax, but must file an information return that shows the distribution of income among the partners. Each partner pays the tax on his share as a part of his personal tax.

The advantages of the partnership are:

1. Provides for pooling of assets, a larger business, and the benefits of economics of scale
2. Provides pooling management and technical skills; each partner can specialize in what he does best

3. Ease of organization
4. Possibilities of expansion

The disadvantages of the partnership are:
1. Unlimited liability
2. The interpersonal strains of shared responsibilities
3. Uncertainty of duration
4. Difficulty in withdrawing investment

CORPORATIONS

A corporation is a business that has a legal entity separate and apart from its owners and managers with its own responsibilities and rights. It is an artificial legal person established under state corporation laws. It pays taxes, makes contracts, holds property, borrows money, and can sue or be sued. There are three common types of private corporations: ordinary, tax option, and cooperative. All must be chartered under some state corporation statutes. There are no federally chartered private corporations.

ORDINARY CORPORATION

The ordinary corporation may be either a public or a family corporation. The distinction between the two is the availability of stock for purchase. A public corporation offers its stock for sale to anyone wishing to buy it. A family corporation does not offer its stock for sale to the highest bidder. The stock is held by a small group, usually the members of a single family and usually the original incorporators. Except for that distinction, public and family corporations have the same characteristics. A corporation may be either a profit or nonprofit corporation. We deal here only with the profit corporation.

The ordinary corporation is owned by the shareholders who have purchased shares of stock in the business. Stock represents the portion equity the investor has in the business; for example, owning 100 shares in a corporation that has issued 10,000 shares means the owner has a $\frac{100}{10,000}$ or 1 percent equity in the business. Shares do not specify the assets owned by the stockholders, but represent a 1 percent equity in all the corporation's assets and liabilities. Shares of stock are a means of raising capital for the firm. The initial purchaser buys them from the corporation, and his payment is available for use by the corporation. The corporation has no obligation to repurchase any stocks issued and sold. The owner of the stock must find another investor willing to buy the stock if he wants to sell. The price of the stock varies depending upon the demand for, and supply of, the stock at any particular time. Stocks, like a good, can be repeatedly sold and bought, so it is relatively easy for an investor to acquire ownership in and to divest ownership in a corporation. Transfer of stock ownership does not affect the continuity of the business. Because it has an entity separate from its owners, a corporation's continuity of operation is not affected by the death of one or more of its owners. The deceased owner's stock goes to the legal heirs and may be retained or sold by them.

Unlike a sole proprietorship or a partnership, a corporation must be chartered by some state government to operate in that state.

A corporation must pay taxes on its income. It is subject to a different set of tax rates from individual tax rates. The dividends distributed are taxed as a part of the personal income of the stockholders.

The advantages of the corporation form of business organizations are:

1. Continuity of operation—the life of the corporation is independent of the life of the owner
2. Transfer of ownership is simplified
3. Liability is limited
4. Greater diversification in raising capital—sale of stock and bonds, loans.

The disadvantages of the corporation are:

1. Additional costs—legal fees, filing fees, stock issuance fees, incorporation fees, annual meetings
2. Additional paper work—annual reports
3. Control of business—particularly in small corporations the operator-manager, if he owns less than 50 percent of the stock, may not be able to control the business.

TAX OPTION CORPORATION

The tax option corporation has all the characteristics of an ordinary corporation except its income tax status. In the federal income tax legislation, subchapter S provides for the formation of corporations that may be exempted from income taxes. A corporation must have the unanimous consent of its shareholders to become a tax option corporation in which they choose that all corporate earnings are taxable to shareholders in proportion to their shareholdings. The corporation is treated as a partnership for tax purposes. It must file an information tax form, but pays no tax. Each shareholder reports his share of the corporation's earnings, both distributed and undistributed, and is taxed on it as a part of his personal income.

Such a tax arrangement may have advantages for some businesses, particularly a smaller family corporation.

COOPERATIVE CORPORATION

A cooperative may be either incorporated or unincorporated. If unincorporated, the cooperative is a partnership. Because of the unlimited liability feature of a partnership, few cooperatives choose to be unincorporated. An incorporated cooperative must secure its certificate of incorporation in the state in which it is located. Cooperatives are not federally chartered.

TYPES OF BUSINESS ORGANIZATION 155

The cooperative type of business in the United States was first authorized by state governments in the last half of the nineteenth century. Even today all cooperatives are authorized under state laws. Federal legislation that clarified and improved the legal status of cooperatives was the Federal Land Bank Legislation of 1916, the Capper-Volstead Act of 1922, the Cooperative Marketing Act of 1926, and the Agricultural Marketing Act of 1929.

The Capper-Volstead Act is often considered the farmers' cooperative "Magna Carta." It made legal the association of farmers to carry out their marketing activities. Under it and other federal and state legislation, three basic characteristics must exist in a cooperative.

1. The ownership and control of the business must be with the members who do business with the association. Generally each member is limited to one vote rather than one vote for each share of stock owned. Most of the business must be with members.
2. The objective must be to minimize costs rather than to make profits. Returns above costs are returned as patronage refunds to the patrons in proportion to their volume of business.
3. The return on investors' capital must be limited to ensure that the primary benefit occurs to the patron-user.

The cooperative must operate its business on cost of operation basis; therefore, no profits can be made. Any return above cost must be returned to the patrons. Therefore, the cooperative is treated much like a partnership for income tax purposes. Patronage refunds, however, are taxable income for the members.

A cooperative has these advantages:

1. Provides the advantages of the corporate organization
2. Is entitled to special tax considerations
3. Permits group marketing efforts that help small farmers to compete more effectively

A cooperative has these disadvantages:

1. Restricted freedom of action of individual members
2. Difficulty of hiring efficient managers
3. Lack of profit incentive.

SPECIAL TYPES OF BUSINESS ORGANIZATIONS

All legal business organizations are subject to the individual state laws relevant to that particular type of organization. Consequently differences among business organizations exist from state to state. Even within a state there may be special legislation applicable to particular situations, so differences may exist among partnerships and among corporations within a state.

Some special types of business organization used much less frequently than those discussed include:

The *joint venture partnership* is organized to fulfill a specific and temporary activity. Upon completion of the venture the partnership is dissolved. This type of partnership is often used in development and sale of real estate. *The underwriting syndicate*, often used for the sale of stocks and bonds, is similar to the joint venture except the partners have limited liability.

The *limited partnership association* has some of the features of a partnership and some of a corporation. The owner partners are issued stock certificates that are not freely transferable. No charter is necessary, but articles of association must be filed with the designated government unit. The principal advantage is limited liability for the partners. Only five states, Michigan, New Jersey, Ohio, Pennsylvania, and Virginia provide for this type of partnership.

The *joint stock company* in some states is treated as a partnership, in others, as a corporation. It is a voluntary association of individuals joined together by articles of agreement. It issues transferable stock. Its stockholders are subject to unlimited liability.

The *business trust* is a special arrangement in which the owners of property deed the property to trustees for management. The owners receive income from the trust, are not liable for the debts of the trust, and have no management responsibility. Trusts are often used as means for corporations to legally acquire real estate holdings when state law prohibits direct ownership.

The *holding company* is a corporation that owns stock in other corporations, usually enough to control them. The other corporations are called subsidiaries. This form of business has permitted corporations to gain control of great masses of resources. It was often used by utility companies in the past.

The *private nonstock corporation* is used by religious, charitable, and educational institutions. It does not seek profits and does not issue stock.

The *government (public) corporation* is used by governmental units to establish corporations to provide public services, for example, city water or power; state, city, or county hospitals or universities.

BUSINESS ORGANIZATION FOR AGRICULTURE

All of the types of business organization discussed are available for agricultural firms. The nonfarm agricultural firms—processors, distributors, and suppliers—follow practices of other businesses and tend to select the legal organization that best fits their economic organization. Because there are so many alternatives, and even variations for any one alternative, selection of a legal business organization is a complex process —so complex most individuals need expert advice on their legal and business organization options.

Farmers are much less likely to consider alternative organizations. The customary and accepted farm organization has been the sole proprietorship. Farmers who decide to take a son into the business or join a brother in a joint operation continue the basic organization, usually without any well defined agreement among the participants. Such "sloppy" organization of partnerships has led to much grief in farm partnerships. Legally the result is a regular partnership. Farmers generally have been distrustful of "legal entanglements" so avoid contracts. The corporation has been viewed as a threat to the family farm. That, along with misunderstanding the corporate organization, has kept many farmers from incorporating their farm businesses. In a few states past legislatures have even restricted the use of the corporate organization for farm businesses. However, as farm businesses have grown more complex, as the need for expansion capital has increased, and as farmers have recognized economies-of-scale associated with larger size, they have turned to the corporation as a business organization alternative.

THE FARMER AND THE CORPORATION

As students of agriculture it is important for you to learn about the place of the corporation in farming. Generally farmers have feared the corporate business organization because they have associated incorporated farms with the idea of huge nonfarm corporations becoming engaged in farming operations. They view such corporations as a threat to the family farm and fear that they will dominate United States farming. Consequently, farmers have often overlooked the possible usefulness of the corporation for even small family farms. It should be viewed along with the sole proprietorship and partnership as alternative forms of business organization. When their economic organization is such that the corporation is a useful means of fulfilling their economic goals, it may be the best alternative.

Let us review the role corporations play in U.S. farming.

In 1975 about 1 percent of all farms were incorporated and operated about 7 percent of all the land. Eight of ten incorporated farms were family corporations. That means about 0.2 percent of our farms were owned and operated by public corporations, that is, offered stock for sale to the public. It was the 0.2 percent of the corporations, thought of as the "big" corporate farms, that were believed to threaten the family farm. They were larger than most farms and accounted for about 2 percent of all farm sales. More than one-third of the "big" corporate farms were located in California, Florida, Texas, and Montana. They have concentrated in beef cattle production, feedlot operations, poultry and egg production, and fruit and vegetable production. Figure 14-1 shows the use of the corporation and other business organizations by farmers.

Use of the corporation by nonfarm investors has made "corporation farming" an economic and political issue. Although the "big" corporate farms are few, their number is increasing, and their control of agricultural production is increasing at a more rapid rate than their numbers. However, an individual family farmer should not let his dislike or fear of "big corporations" keep him from considering the corporate organization if it fits his needs.

We should not confuse "bigness" and corporate organization. Corporations can be small or big, have one owner or thousands, and their stock may be family or publicly held. A corporation is just a type of business organization. However, it is only when a family farm becomes large that its owner or owners begin to develop an interest in incorporation. The tax option corporation often fits the needs of a family farm quite well as it provides for the best business organization features of the corporation and the tax features of a partnership.

A farmer's economic and legal organization of his business is so important to him that he should seek expert advice on both. This chapter only calls attention to each type. Much more thorough study is needed for decisions on the most suitable business organization.

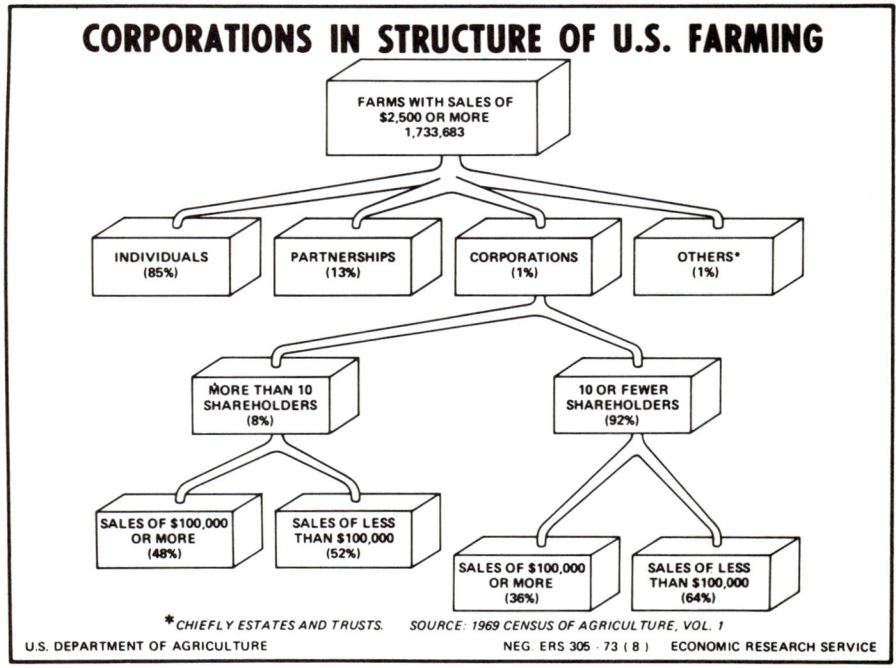

Figure 14-1. Business Organizations in the Structure of United States Farming.

SUGGESTED READINGS

Doane's Agricultural Report. *New Names Enter Corporate Farming, Part 1.* Business Issue, Vol. 32, No. 16, May 1, 1970, page 24.

Doane's Agricultural Report. *More Corporate Farming in the Future, Part 2.* Business Issue, Vol. 33, No. 21, June 5, 1970, page 32.

Kohls, Richard L., and Downey, W. David. *Marketing of Agricultural Products,* 4th Edition. The Macmillan Company, 1972, Chapter 14.

Musselman, Vernon A., and Hughes, Eugene H. *Introduction to Modern Business: Analysis and Interpretation,* 5th Edition. Prentice-Hall, 1969, Chapter 4.

North Central Workshop, Proceedings of. *Corporation Farming: What Are the Issues.* Department of Agricultural Economics Report No. 53, University of Nebraska, April 21-23, 1969, Chicago.

O'Byrne, John C., Krause, N.G.P., Harl, Neil E., Jurgenson, Hein, *The Farm Corporation.* North Central Regional Extension Publication No. 11, Revised 1967, Iowa State University, 1967.

Phillips, Richard. *Managing for Greater Returns in Grain, Feed, and Other Retail Businesses Serving Agriculture,* 3rd Edition. Ag Press, Manhattan, Kansas, 1970, Chapter 11.

Plant Food Review. Corporation Farming U.S.A., Volume 15, Number 1, 1969. National Plant Food Institute, Washington, D.C.

Roy, Ewell Paul. *Cooperatives: Today and Tomorrow.* The Interstate Printers and Publishers, Inc., Danville, Illinois, 1964.

Wheeler, Bayard O. *Business: An Introductory Analysis.* Harper & Brothers, 1962, Chapter 8.

Part VI

WORLD AGRICULTURE

WORLD AGRICULTURE 15

In Chapter 2 we considered the changing structure of United States agriculture. Today's world is too small to limit our inquiry into the agricultural economy of just one nation. To be a knowledgeable agriculturalist requires some understanding of conditions in other nations.

Today we know instantly what is happening around the earth. Within a few hours we can be in the most distant land. What happens in the remotest land concerns and affects us. Famine in Asia, political turmoil in the Middle East, drouth in Africa, or devaluation of the British pound is known at once and quickly affects our lives. Drouth in the Midwest and Great Plains, as in the summer of 1974, affects food prices and diets of people around the world. The 1973 upsurge in U.S. grain prices came when the Soviet Union and other nations made large grain purchases in grain producing nations. The prolonged sub-Sahara drouth in Africa could not go unnoticed or be ignored. The people of this earth depend so much on one another that they must find one world of peace and cooperation. To be just one world each of us must improve our understanding of other people, their problems, and their ways of living. In this chapter we consider the most important features of worldwide economic development in agriculture.

Growing up in the United States, even on a farm, is poor preparation for understanding the world agricultural situation. Your concept that a farm is highly productive land, complex machinery, mechanical power, fertilizer, insecticides, highly developed crops, and livestock is yet a dream of most of the world's farmers. To help other lands to fulfill a dream of agricultural abundance is perhaps the greatest challenge of our times. You, as students in agriculture, have a great opportunity to be a part of mankind's great task of assuring there will be enough food for everyone.

THE TWO WORLDS

Our world is divided into two parts: one with adequate, even abundant food production; and the other short of food, even to the point of starvation. Economists have called one part the developed countries, the other, the less developed countries. The usual measure of economic development is per capita national income. National income is an estimate of the total interest, rent, wages, and profit earnings of a nation. Per capita national income is national income divided by population. The developed countries have a high per capita national income with a farm sector characterized by high crop and livestock yields, high labor productivity, large capital investment relative to labor, and a small portion of the people well educated farmers. The less developed countries have a low per capita national income and a farm sector characterized by low crop and livestock yields, low labor productivity, low capital investment relative to labor, and a high portion of the people poorly educated farmers. In the developed countries the nonfarm sector of agriculture is large relative to the farm sector; many people are employed in processing, storing, and distributing farm products. In the less developed countries few are employed in such agribusiness activities. Differences between the two groups of nations are illustrated in Table 15-1. You should note particularly the inverse relationship between an individual's economic well-being as measured by per capita national income and the percentage of people in farming. Nations with a large portion of their people in farming usually have a lower per capita output. If most of the labor force is tied up in producing food for itself, not much else can be produced. Usually increasing the productivity of farmers is a first step in improving a nation's economic well-being. Then fewer farmers can meet the nation's food needs, thus releasing farm labor to enter other lines of production, that is, industrial goods and services.

Also note that a ten percent increase in per capita national income for the United States adds $500, which is more than the total per capita national income of the least developed nations. India would have to have a 500 percent increase to equal the U.S. dollar increase and would still have only a $600 per capita national income. For the least developed nations to catch up will require a mighty effort over many years. Some pessimistic agriculturalists ask, "Shall the rich grow richer and the poor poorer?" They see strong evidence to support this. As both the less developed countries and the developed countries increase their absolute incomes, the relative increase of the developed countries is greater than of the less developed ones.

THE ROLE OF AGRICULTURE IN ECONOMIC GROWTH

Economic growth improves the output of goods and services relative to population. More goods and services per person are usually considered as economic growth. Adding together all the goods and services is a problem unless a common unit of measure is used. That common unit of measure can be a monetary value; by multiplying the units of output times their price we can arrive at a value. This value can be converted to a common currency value, for example, the U.S. dollar. To avoid the effects of inflation, the value of the production can be adjusted by the amount of inflation. We then have output expressed in a common, constant currency value. By dividing by the population we can compute the per capita output. One of the most common per capita output measures is per capita national income. From this many comparisons can be made.

The average per capita income may not always truly reflect the whole economic situation. We should also look at distribution of income among

Table 15-1. Per Capita National Income and Caloric Intake, Percentage of Population in Farming, and Percentage of People Literate for Selected Nations.

Nation	Per Capita National Income in U.S. Dollars[1]	Per Capita Caloric Intake[2]	People in Farming 1970	People Literate[3]
United States	$4,981	3,300	4%	98%
Canada	4.231	3,200	8	n.a.
Germany	3,739	3,180	12	n.a.
Japan	2,462	2,470	21	78
Soviet Union	n.a.	3,180	32	99
Argentina	1,171	3,160	15	91
Yugoslavia	n.a.	3,130	47	80
Spain	1,239	2,770	34	86
Venezuela	1,085	2,430	26	63
Mexico	681	2,620	47	76
Columbia	426	2,140	45	73
Philippine Islands	254	2,040	70	72
Kenya	151	2,200	80	14
Nigeria	<100	2,290	67	12
India	<100	1,990	68	28

[1] Most data are for 1972.
[2] Most data are for 1970.
[3] Literacy is defined as the ability to read and to write of those over 15 years of age.

Source: Per capita national income—Statistics Yearbook 1973, Statistical Office, United Nations.
Percentage literate—Demographic Yearbook 1970, United Nations and Statistical Papers, 1967, United Nations.
Per capita caloric intake and percentage in farming—*Production Yearbook, 1971,* Vol. 25, F.A.O. of the U.N.

the people. Wide distribution usually is considered better for economic growth than a concentration of income in a small portion of the people. For example, a small nation of ten million people and a national income of fifty billion dollars has a very high average per capita income, $5,000. But if ten percent of the people get ninety percent of the income, the top ten percent would have a per capita income of $45,000, $\left(\frac{\$45,000,000,000}{1,000,000}\right)$ Ninety percent would have an average per capita income of $555 $\left(\frac{\$5,000,000,000}{9,000,000}\right)$. A small portion of the people are rich, but most are in poverty.

In the less developed nations, usually those with the lowest income and often with the lowest productivity are farmers. Yet the farm sector, while having a low capital investment per farmer, controls a high portion of all the capital resources available. The farm sector uses most of the land resource. Thus we see that farming, often low in output per unit of input, controls and uses most of the total labor, capital, and land resources in a less developed country.

A first step in economic development is to increase agricultural productivity. That contributes to economic well-being by:

1. Providing more food to meet the needs of a rapidly increasing population or to improve the nutritional standards.
2. Providing surplus agricultural commodities for export, enabling the nation to earn foreign exchange to buy capital inputs needed in economic development, for example, motor transport equipment, manufacturing equipment, energy, etc.
3. Providing a manpower pool to use in developing other industries, transportation, and services
4. Providing capital that can be used in developing other sectors of the economy
5. Providing increased incomes to the farmers who can then buy the output of the newly established industrial plants, thus stimulating industrialization of the economy

Simultaneously with increased agricultural productivity, industrialization must occur—to provide employment for resources released from farming, particularly the labor resources. Without industrialization, the released farm labor will be unemployed. In many less developed countries the surplus farm labor (often without the skills required by industry) seeking off-farm employment have migrated to cities without sufficient industrialization to provide employment for them. Massive unemployment and poverty among the migrants results.

AGRICULTURAL RESOURCES

The wealth and development potential of a nation is closely tied to the amount and quality of its agricultural resources. For that reason we shall consider the land, capital, and human resource situation of the earth.

THE LAND RESOURCE

Man depends on land (including the seas) for his food. The amounts of land available and suitable for food production are limited. At the present level of technology we cannot bypass land as the basis for food production. As population increases and land remains fixed, the pressure on land use increases. Land suitable for agricultural uses is not necessarily distributed according to population concentration; the disparity in diets among the people of the world is explained by differences in the quantity and quality of land available as well as by population densities and increases. In Tables 15-2, 15-3 and 15-4 we have presented data to illustrate such disparities.

Table 15-2. Land, Population, Yields, Nitrogen Fertilizer, and Tractors by Geographical Regions and Selected Countries.

Geographical Regions	Total Land Area (1,000 acres)	Cropland (1,000 acres)	Population (1,000)	Cereal Crop Yields (1 lbs./acre)	Nitrogen Fertilizer Used (1,000 tons)	Farm Tractors
Developed Countries						
Northern America	4,776,980	582,920	231,300	3,080	8,190	5,110
Western Europe	965,770	242,060	360,070	2,810	7,050	5,520
Oceania	1,966,120	111,150	15,920	900	130	440
Other	397,670	44,460	131,220	2,350	1,100	510
Total	8,106,540	980,590	738,510	2,770	15,870	11,580
Less Developed Countries						
Africa	5,883,540	466,830	287,370	770	360	130
Latin America	5,078,320	293,930	299,750	1,280	1,460	590
Near East	2,976,350	209,950	181,650	1,220	870	200
Far East	2,203,240	664,430	1,056,140	1,190	2,930	120
Other	222,300	2,470	4,330	1,830	10	0
Total	16,363,750	1,637,610	1,829,240	1,130	5,630	1,040
Centrally Planned Countries						
Asia and China	2,825,680	286,520	838,790	1,600	3,540	140
East. Europe and U.S.S.R.	5,784,740	689,130	354,190	1,500	8,130	2.820
Total	8,610,420	975,650	1,192,980	1,550	11,670	2,960
World	33,080,710	3,593,850	3,760,730	1,630	33,170	15,580
Selected Countries						
U.S.A.	2,312,750	475,030	209,170	3,480	7,590	4,470
U.S.S.R.	5,533,340	574,500	247,350	1,280	5,100	2,050
India	807,220	406,590	563,000	1,000	10	70
Nigeria	228,170	53,830	58,020	690	10	1

Source: Food and Agriculture Organization of the United Nations, Production Yearbook, 1972.

The developed countries have 27.2 percent of all cropland from which to support 19.7 percent of the people, while the less developed countries have 48.6 percent of all the people on earth, but only 18.5 percent of the cropland. To make their food problems even more critical compared with those of developed countries, crop yields in the less developed countries are much lower. Cereal grain output per acre is often used to compare productivity. In the developed countries an acre produces an average of 2,770 pounds. In the less developed countries the yield is less than half that figure—1,130 pounds per acre. The higher yields result not only from more productive land, more favorable climatic conditions, better technology, but also the use of more capital. The developed countries use 47.8 percent of all nitrogen fertilizer; the less developed, 17.0 percent.

Seventy-four percent of all farm tractors are in the developed countries, with only 7 percent in less developed countries.

The centrally-planned countries, often spoken of as the Communistic Bloc, have 27 percent of the world cropland; 31.7 percent of the people; use 35.2 percent of the nitrogen fertilizer; and have 19.0 percent of the tractors.

Table 15-3. Percentages of World Population, Cropland, Fertilizer, Tractors and Total Land in Cropland by Geographical Regions and Selected Countries.

Geographical Regions	World Population	World Cropland	World Fertilizer Used	World Farm Tractors	Total Land in Cropland
Developed Countries					
Northern America	6.2%	16.2%	24.7%	32.8%	12.2%
Western Europe	9.6	6.7	21.2	35.4	25.0
Oceania	.4	3.1	.4	2.8	5.6
Other	3.5	1.2	3.3	3.3	2.3
Total	19.7	27.2	47.8	74.3	12.1
Less Developed Countries					
Africa	7.6	13.0	1.1	.8	7.6
Latin America	8.0	8.2	4.4	3.8	5.8
Near East	4.9	5.8	2.6	1.3	7.1
Far East	28.0	18.5	8.8	.8	30.1
Other	.1	.1	.1	.0	.9
Total	48.6	45.6	17.0	6.7	10.0
Centrally Planned Countries					
Asia and China	22.3	7.9	10.7	.9	10.1
East. Europe and U.S.S.R.	9.4	19.1	24.5	18.1	11.9
Total	31.7	27.0	35.2	19.0	11.3
Selected Countries					
U.S.A.	5.6	13.2	22.9	28.7	20.5
U.S.S.R.	6.6	16.0	15.4	13.2	14.6
India	15.0	11.3	<.1	.4	50.4
Nigeria	1.5	1.5	<.1	<.1	23.6

Source: Computed from Table 15-2.

A review of per capita resource use and agricultural production also showed the disparity between the two groups of nations, Table 15-4. Worldwide there was 0.9 crop acre for each person in 1970. The developed countries have 1.3 crop acres per capita; the less developed countries, 0.9 acre; the centrally-planned countries 0.8 acre. The United States has 2.3 crop acres per capita; the Soviet Union, 3.3; Nigeria, 0.9; India, .07.

Per capita crop acres alone do not fully indicate agricultural production. Fertilizer use is another indicator. In the developed countries 42.9

Table 15-4. Crop Acres, Nitrogen Fertilizer Use, and Tractors Per Capita by Geographical Areas and Selected Countries.

Geographical Regions	Crop Acres Per Capita	Nitrogen Fertilizer Use Lbs. Per Capita	Farm Output[1] Lbs. Per Capita
Developed Countries			
Northern America	2.5	65.6	7,762
Western Europe	.7	39.2	1,889
Oceania	7.0	16.3	6,283
Other	.3	16.8	796
Total	1.3	42.9	3,678
Less Developed Countries			
Africa	1.6	2.5	1,250
Latin America	1.0	9.7	1,255
Near East	1.2	9.5	1,410
Far East	.6	5.5	748
Other	.6	4.6	1,043
Total	.9	6.2	1,012
Centrally Planned Countries			
Asia and China	.3	8.4	546
East. Europe and U.S.S.R.	1.9	45.9	2,918
Total	.8	19.6	1,267
World	>.9	17.6	1,557
Selected Countries			
U.S.A.	2.3	78.3	7,903
U.S.S.R.	3.3	41.2	4,166
India	.7	.1	722
Nigeria	.9	.3	640

[1]These figures represent per capita output of cereals if all cropland were planted to cereal crops and average yields given in Table 15-2 resulted.
Source: Computed from Table 15-2.

pounds of nitrogen fertilizer is used per capita; in the less developed countries, 6.2 pounds; in the centrally-planned countries, 19.6 pounds; and for the world, 17.6 pounds. The United States uses 78.3 pounds of nitrogen per capita; the Soviet Union, 41.2 pounds. In the less developed countries like India and Nigeria, less than one pound per person is used.

Poor quality land, low yielding varieties, poor cultural and management practices result in low yields. In Table 15-2 cereal crop yields are compared. In Table 15-4 the comparison is expressed on a per capita basis. All the crop acres times the average yield of cereal crops for each nation were used to compare the adequacy of food production. Remember that nations produce many food items other than cereals and also use many acres for such nonfood production as cotton and tobacco. But computed per capita cereal output gives an index of food adequacy for comparisons among nations.

If all crop acres were planted to cereal crops, the world could produce 1,557 pounds per capita. The developed countries could produce more than twice the world average. The less developed countries, could produce only two thirds of the world average.

Using a four nation comparison, the United States could produce nearly twice as much per capita as the Soviet Union and ten times that of India and Nigeria.

The scarcity of the world land resource is a great problem. There are about 33 billion acres of land, but only about 11 percent, 3.5 billion acres, can be used for crops and much less than that, about 2.5 billion acres, are actually planted to food crops. Man has only about 7.5 percent of the land surface to use for crop production. Irrigating deserts and draining wet lands adds to the land used for crops, but land taken from farm production for residences, transportation, and factories just about offsets the gain.

THE LABOR RESOURCE

For most nations, but particularly for those with the least land, labor on farms is an abundant resource. In the nations where labor is most abundant, the use of more labor would add little to output. *The marginal productivity of labor in farm production in those nations is near zero.* Under such conditions wages are extremely low. Except for peak planting and harvesting times, the labor resource is unemployed or at best underemployed. In less developed countries the demand for industrial labor is inadequate to provide off-farm employment for the unemployed farm labor resource. Those moving from rural to urban areas usually do not have the technical skills needed by the industry; thus there are unemployment and unfilled jobs simultaneously.

Increased employment in the farm sector could be achieved if certain capital inputs were available, for example, better seeds, fertilizer, irrigation, and insecticides. However, labor saving capital (tractors and machinery) would substitute for labor and intensify employment problems in rural communities until industrialization provided new jobs.

High labor input is usually associated with low labor productivity. Table 15-1 shows the inverse relationship between concentration of labor in farming and economic well-being. The higher the portion of people in farming, the lower the per capita output. Food and Agriculture Organization data further illustrate that (Table 15-5). The most developed continents, North America, Europe, and Oceania have lowest percentages of their population in farming.

THE CAPITAL RESOURCE

Except in a few nations, capital investment consists of handmade hoes, sickles, and axes, and home produced seed and manure. Mechanic-

Table 15-5. Agricultural Population as a Percentage of Total Population, 1970.

Continent	Percent
North America	4
Europe	19
Oceania	22
U.S.S.R.	32
South America	39
Asia	64
Africa	69
World	51

Source: Food and Agriculture Organization of the United Nations, Production Yearbook, 1972.

ally powered equipment, chemicals, and other capital are extensively used only in North America, Europe, Oceania, the Soviet Union, and a few other locations. Credit and knowledge of its use are unknown among most farmers. In nations such as the less developed ones, where per capita income is less than a hundred dollars, capital formation is nearly impossible. It is not possible to save current production for later use in production in very poor societies. Occasionally in years of low yields, seeds saved for next year's crops must be eaten to ward off hunger. Even as incomes improve, the need for consumption expenditures are so pressing that it is difficult to save much for capital investments from the increased income. Improving per capita incomes enough to permit savings is impeded by the rapid population growth. With a two percent population growth, national income must increase at least two percent just to maintain per capita incomes.

Under such conditions it is nearly hopeless for the individual farmers to save for investments that would improve productivity. Often the government, through its taxing power, attempts to raise capital for investment in agriculture. But where economic well-being is low, the tax potential is also low and demands on the limited public revenues are great. Roads, electrical plants, irrigation, schools, fertilizer plants, research, communication systems, and many, many more public services are critically needed for development. Available capital is so thinly spread among all those needs that it cannot effectively stimulate economic growth.

To supplement the internally raised capital, less developed countries have sought loans and grants from the more developed countries. The United States and other nations during the 1950s, 1960s, and 1970s have provided billions of dollars of investment capital for agriculture in the less developed countries. The external sources of capital, were intended to serve as a pump priming activity that would get the economy growing enough to generate its own investment capital.

TECHNOLOGY AND MANAGEMENT

The productivity of land, labor, and capital depends on levels of technology and managerial skills in a nation.

Technology we have defined as applying knowledge to improve production. To be adopted, technology must reduce unit costs of production. A new variety of higher yielding grain increases output relative to resources used, thus increasing productivity. One of the keys to growth in the developed nations has been the availability and adoption of technology on farms. The successful use of technology, particularly in U.S. agriculture, has provided a model for less developed nations. Technology appeared to be the immediate solution to their developmental problems. In Harry Truman's 1949 inaugural address, he committed the United States to providing technical assistance when under point four of his address, he said,

"I believe that we should make available to peace-loving peoples the benefits of our store of technical knowledge in order to help them realize their aspirations for a better life."

We are now in our third decade of providing technical assistance to the less developed countries. The results are below expectations; technology is more difficult to share than was envisioned. Under point four programs, and its successors—now the United States Agency for International Development (AID)—thousands of Americans have traveled to, and lived in, less developed countries to teach agricultural knowledge. Thousands of students, farmers, agribusinessmen, and teachers from the less developed countries have visited the United States and other developed countries to observe and study agricultural practices. In many nations technical assistance has helped greatly to stimulate growth. In others it has had little impact.

Technology, we have learned, has certain characteristics that may explain why sharing it has not been easy or always successful.

First, technology is location specific. For example, a wheat variety does best under certain soil and climatic conditions. A variety developed for Ohio will not do equally well in North Dakota. Cultural practices developed for one area are not necessarily suited to other areas; for example, stubble mulch cultivation of the Great Plains is unnecessary in Illinois. Locations' importance soon was observed in Land Grant experiment station work.

Thus must states have several substations and experimental fields distributed throughout the state. Agriculturalists soon found location important in attempting to share technology with other nations. Technology was not an easily exported item. As shown earlier, most countries with less developed agriculture are in warm climates. Most agricultural technology was for temperate climates. New technology was needed for the less developed areas. The methods of developing technology have more universal application than technology itself.

Second, technology is cumulative. As it is passed from generation to generation, a base for new technology is established. The broader and deeper the cumulative base, the easier it is to develop and to use new technology. Thus far it appears that technology accumulates at an increasing rate. The fastest rate of technological advance seems to be in nations already technologically advanced.

Third, there is a time lag between the time of discovery and adoption on farms. Among farmers accustomed to using technology, the time lag is shorter than among farmers not accustomed to using new technology. Brandner and Kearl, in studying adoption of new grain varieties in Kansas, compared adoption rates between hybrid corn and sorghum.[1] They found the time between release and nearly universal planting of hybrid corn varieties, during the 1930s and 1940s when farmers had no experience with hybrids, to be much longer than for grain sorghum during the 1950s, after their successful experience with corn. If that holds for the less developed countries, farmers must have successful experiences with innovations before they become rapid adopters of technology.

Fourth, there is a significant difference in the rate of diffusion of technology within nations. Factors affecting the rate of diffusion include: the receptivity of the society, level of education of the people, efficiency of the communication system, how well the technology considered meshes with the culture of those considering it, and the level of capital available to finance technology.

In technology lies the hope for agricultural development, but past experience suggests that results will not be immediate.

POPULATION GROWTH

Overcoming world hunger is not just a matter of producing more food. The world's farmers are annually increasing their output. It is output per person that is crucial; total food production must increase more rapidly than total population if we are to be a better fed world. In this section we look at world population growth.

In economics people are both the ultimate input or resource and the ultimate users of the products produced. People provide labor and management in the production process. Improving the efficiency of human production was considered in the sections on labor and technology. In this section the emphasis is on feeding the world's people, three and a half billion of them in 1975.

In Tables 15-2 and 15-3 we presented data on the distribution of the three and a half billion people among geographical areas. More than two and a half billion are in the less developed countries, including China. In 1900 world population was one and a half billion people. Population then was increasing one percent a year. The annual increase now exceeds two percent. Each year the number of people increases by about seventy-five million. Only in the twentieth century have we had to deal with such rapid increases. It required 1,600 years for the population to double after A.D. 1. Today population doubles every thirty to forty years. By 2000 A.D. six billion people are expected, by 2040, twelve billion, by 2080, twenty-four billion, unless birth rates decline. The rapid increase results not so much from change in birth rates, as from improved living conditions. Infant mortality has been greatly reduced, so more babies reach maturity and reproduce. Medical advances have greatly extended the average age of people so that all of us are here for more years. Medical technology has reduced the death rate, but has not found widely accepted and practiced methods to reduce birth rates.

A consequence of the rapidly growing population is that farmers must double their output of food before the end of this century just to maintain present, often inadequate, diets.

FOOD PRODUCTION TRENDS

The Food and Agriculture Organization of the United Nations (FAO) has estimated that a four percent annual growth rate in food production is needed to meet increased demands due to population growth and increasing incomes. From 1961 to 1972 the less developed countries' average annual increase in agricultural production was 2.7 percent, just equal the annual average population increase so there was no improvement of diet in the less developed countries. The bad crop year, 1972-73, worsened their food situation. The developed nations had fairly adequate diets in 1961. Their average annual increase in agricultural output was 2.0 percent and their average annual population growth was 1.2 percent, thus their already good food situation improved. Worldwide the average annual increase in agricultural output exceeded population growth 0.6 percent.

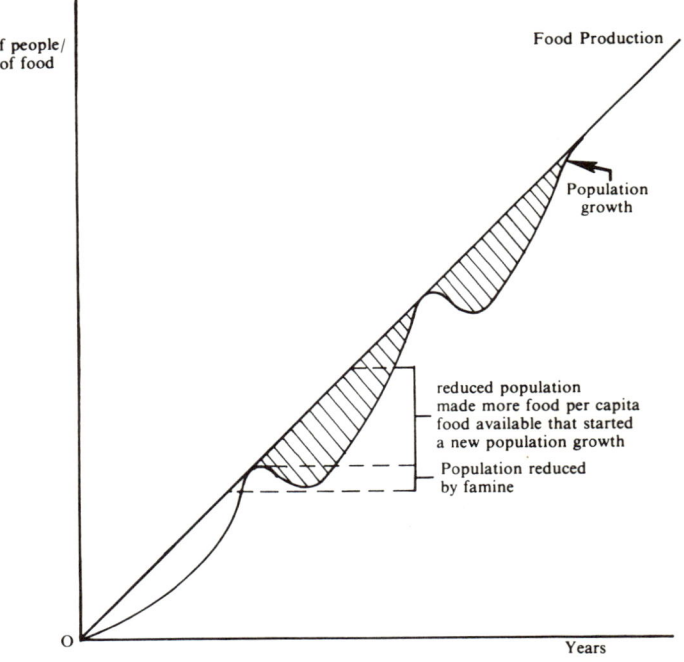

Figure 15-1. Malthus's Theory of Population Growth.

Table 15-6. Average Annual Increases in Agricultural Production and Population.

Geographical Regions	Production, Average Annual Increase (1961-72) Percent	Population, Average Annual Increase (1961-72) Percent
Developed Countries		
North America	2.2	1.2
Western Europe	1.8	.9
Oceania	2.4	1.9
Region	2.0	1.2
Less Developed Countries		
Africa	2.6	2.5
Latin America	2.7	3.0
Near East	3.3	3.0
Far East	2.6	2.6
Region	2.7	2.7
Eastern Europe and U.S.S.R.	3.4	1.0
China and other Asian centrally planned countries	2.9	1.8
World	2.6	2.0
Selected Countries		
U.S.A.	1.8	1.2
U.S.S.R.	2.7	1.1
India	2.1	2.5
Nigeria	.4	3.0

Source: Food and Agriculture Organization of the United Nations, Production Yearbook, 1972.

In 1975 the Malthusian spector seems to be upon us again. Malthus, an eighteenth century English economist, observed that food production increases arithmetically, 1, 2, 3, 4, 5, 6, while population increases geometrically, 2, 4, 8, 16. He believed the only limiting factor to population growth would be famine, disease, and wars. He could not foresee the twentieth century effect of technology on food production or the effect of birth control methods on population growth. Many agriculturalists in the twentieth century discarded Malthus's theory of population, illustrated in Figure 15-1, as unnecessarily alarmist. In recent years such evidence as that in Table 15-6 has renewed interest in the ideas of Malthus and today, as evidenced at the 1974 Rome food conference, there is growing pessimism about our ability to feed ourselves adequately.

After nearly three decades of concentrated effort to increase food production more rapidly than population growth, we find disappointingly little progress in improving per capita food output. Perhaps mankind's greatest problem of this century is to solve the pressure of population against food.

MAN'S ALTERNATIVES

If we do not accept that man must live with the Malthusian prophecy of chronic human starvation, then we have two alternative approaches to solving the world food problem: more food, fewer people, or some combination of the two. To achieve those objectives, the less developed countries in the last two decades have undertaken programs, with technical and financial assistance from the developed countries, to improve agricultural productivity and to slow population growth. Success in either could increase food production more rapidly than population, and permit diets to improve, see Figure 15-2.

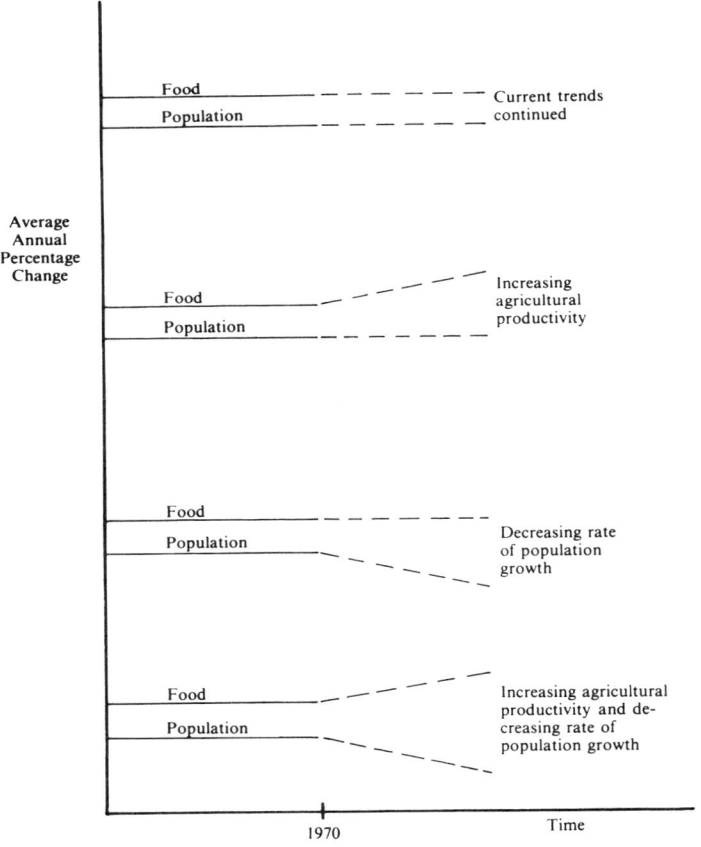

Figure 15-2. Strategies to Improve the Food-Population Relationship.

POPULATION POLICIES

Centuries-old customs place a high value on large families. Begetting and bearing children has been a test of womanhood or manhood. A large number of children in an agricultural society improved the economic well-being of the family, as they provided a large family labor force. Family ties were strong, so children took care of their parents and grandparents. Large families were the only "social security" program available. Until recently, high infant and child mortality made many births vital to survival of the family, clan, and community. The well-being of the elderly depended on having surviving children. Large families were so socially, morally, and economically valuable that societies developed beliefs and values that encouraged many births. The USSR in 1975 still encouraged births by special recognition of mothers of ten or more children.

Under such conditions advocating birth control practices, recommending a reversal of deeply-held attitudes, could not be well received or accepted. Thus improving diets by reducing population growth rates appears to be a long term program. Even if birth control measures were accepted immediately it would require at least a generation for any really effective reduction in the increasing number of people. Under zero growth rate in births, total population would continue to increase for years because people live longer and because so many people of child bearing age would replace themselves 1:1 under a zero growth rate.

While we have been able to do little to reduce birth rates in the countries least well fed, great strides have been made in reducing death rates. Higher survival rates accelerate total population growth.

Although the short run improvement in diets through population policies will be small, the long run hope of a well fed world seems to rest on acceptance of family planning.

FOOD POLICIES

Increasing food supplies in the less developed countries holds greater promise for short run dietary improvement than do population policies. The potential for increased quantities of food by applying technology to producing, storing, and processing food, is great for the short run. But achieving that potential, as discussed in the section on technology, will not be easy. Yet the real hope during the waiting period for population policies to be effective and to be accepted lies in increased food production, both in less developed countries, and in developed countries for export to them.

In the less developed countries, food production can be increased by:

1. Applying technology, such as new varieties, improved breeds, and improved cultural and management practices to farming
2. Using capital, such as fertilizer, irrigation, insecticides, substitution of mechanical power for animal power, disease control
3. Bringing more land into cultivation, such as draining wet land, irrigating dry lands, settling virgin areas, and developing cropping practices that permit continuous cropping on tropical soils

Increasing food production often depends on off-farm developments. We usually call it improving the infra structure. *Infra structure refers to the social capital invested to support economic growth.* Social capital investment most needed for agricultural development includes transportation facilities, marketing organizations, processing facilities, storage facilities, research institutions, schools, communication systems, and financial institutions. Without those institutional improvements preceding and accompanying new technology and capital in farming, there is little improvement.

Much food produced is lost before it is consumed. Lack of preservation and storage techniques and facilities results in a large percentage of food being lost to spoilage, insects, and rodents.

Countries with food shortages may be able to augment what they produce by increasing food imports. Usually imports are minor compared to domestic production. To be able to import, a nation must export to earn international currencies to pay for imports. Most less developed countries' financial situations restrict food imports. In cases of famines and other emergencies, some food is provided in form of aid and grants by nations with food reserves. Such supplies are short term and do little to solve long term food shortages.

Long run increases in food supplies, it seems, must come from increased production within the nation itself. For that reason the United States has emphasized technical assistance to the less developed countries rather than food give-away programs. Assistance that increases food production has long-run effects; food gifts are gone after they are eaten.

TRADE IN AGRICULTURAL PRODUCTS

With a world divided between food deficit and food excess, it seems international trade could be used to alleviate world food problems. Northern America, Western Europe, Oceania, and a few other nations have food enough to be able to export. Most other nations need to import to meet their peoples' basic diet needs. Before the 1950s most food exports were from the less developed countries to the developed countries. With the very rapid population increases in the less developed countries and increased grain production in the developed nations, the flow of grain has reversed. Figure 15-3 shows the diet-deficit regions of the earth. Most of them are in the tropical and subtropical climatic zones.

RESTRAINTS TO IMPORTING

As discussed in Chapter 4, need is only part of demand. To import food a food-deficit nation must have the ability to pay for it. To import food, a nation must have two levels of ability to pay. First, the nation must have enough exports of some type to earn foreign currency to pay for the food purchases. Second, individuals in the nation must have the ability to purchase the imported foods. Most of the less developed countries have few exports, so have limited ability to import. Individual incomes are

WORLD AGRICULTURE 179

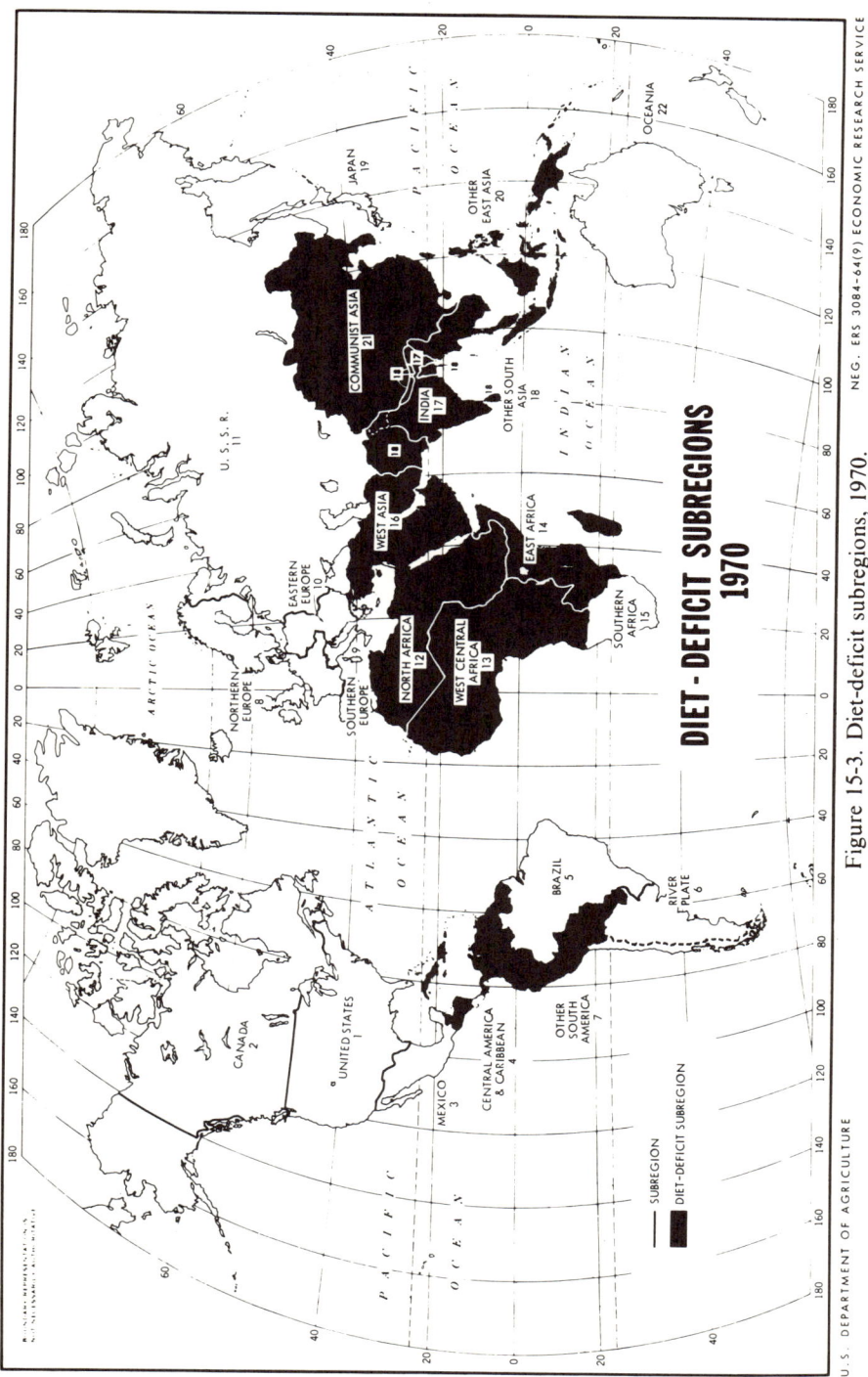

Figure 15-3. Diet-deficit subregions, 1970.

usually also low, so hungry families are unable to purchase imported foods.

The United States and other developed countries recognizing the limited purchasing power of less developed countries have made concessional sales of food to them. Concessional sales occur when the exporting country assists the importing country in making imports. The United States has, by accepting currencies of the importing nations, through U.S. subsidies and grants, provided large quantities of food exports to developing nations.

Even concessional sales and gifts do not mean the food ends up in the stomachs of hungry people. Shipping food to a less developed country is costly and the port where it arrives may be far from those needing the food most. The recipient nation may lack storage and transportation facilities to handle the imports. Then much may be lost to spoilage, insects, and rodents. Another restraint is the effect of cultural and social heritage on the eating habits of people. What is good food in one country may be unacceptable in another. High quality gluten wheat has little value to a people accustomed to rice diets. One nation's excess production may go uneaten in a deficit nation if its use and preparation for eating are unknown or if it cannot be prepared to resemble dishes they are accustomed to eating.

Competing with food for foreign currency are many other import needs. The importing nations must choose among food, such other agricultural imports as fertilizer, tools, equipment, and the nonagricultural imports. Choosing to import food may mean not importing industrial inputs (heavy equipment for factories, road building equipment) needed to stimulate long term development.

FOOD FOR THE FUTURE

Assuring that mankind has adequate food will require the best efforts of all people in the decades ahead. Agriculturalists vary from optimism to deep pessimism on the prospects for success. Most agree there is potential technology to increase the food supply and to decrease the population growth rate to assure adequate food. Nearly all also agree it will be a slow and difficult task to apply the technology to the food-population problem. It will require major research and extension programs to develop and apply technology to that problem. It appears to be man's greatest problem, and certainly one with sufficient challenge to fulfill the greatest ambitions of young men and women studying agriculture to serve fellow human beings.

SUGGESTED READINGS

Brown, Lester R. *Man, Land and Food*, Foreign Agricultural Economic Report No. 11. United States Department of Agriculture, November, 1963.

Eicher, Carl and Witt, Lawrence. *Agriculture in Economic Development*. McGraw-Hill Book Company, 1964.

Hardin, Clifford M., ed. *Overcoming World Hunger*. Prentice-Hall, Inc., Englewood Cliffs, New Jersey, 1969.

Mellor, John W. *The Economics of Agricultural Development.* Cornell University Press, Ithaca, New York, 1966.

President's Science Advisory Committee. *The World Food Problem*, Report of the Panel on the World Food Supply, Vol. I and II. The White House, May, 1967.

ENDNOTE

1. Brandner, Lowell and Kearl, Bryant, *Evaluation for Congruence as a Factor in Adoption Rate of Innovation,* Rural Sociology, Vol. 29, No. 3, Sept., 1963.

Part VII

AGRICULTURAL PROBLEMS AND POLICIES

RURAL WELFARE   16

The people of the United States have been particularly successful in meeting their economic needs. The seemingly inexhaustible rich land of the western frontier for a century offered the poor an opportunity to start anew. The federal land distribution program, at the expense of the American Indian, was an effective public welfare program. (Welfare here refers to economic well-being and not to social welfare programs.) When the public lands were fully settled, we lost forever the chance for the poor to acquire free land and to leave their poverty behind. In the twentieth century we have had to seek new ways to meet the needs of the poor. In this chapter we evaluate the economic condition of our rural communities.

How well farmers and the communities where they live are doing is a major concern today. Farming is the largest sector of the economy characterized by pure competition, that is, many small units each with little influence on prices. An individual farmer's impact on his economic well-being depends on his efficient use of resources as well as on many forces beyond his control. The well-being of nonfarmers living in the rural communities furnishing goods and services to farmers is tied to the well-being of farmers as is the farmers' well-being tied to strong rural agribusiness. Rural America's economic status has been strongly affected by structural changes in agriculture. In this chapter we consider some of the structural changes—changes in population, employment opportunities, income, health facilities, education, housing, and local public services.

QUALITY OF LIFE

The welfare of people cannot be determined by income and wealth information only. Although both contribute to personal and community welfare and both improve the quality of life, today we are aware that many other factors contribute. Clean air and water, quiet nights, leisure for social and cultural pursuits, quality education, comfortable housing, meaningful friendships, and good health all are parts of that good life. Each of us has our own optional combination. Many of the above factors' contribution to the quality of life are difficult to measure; and therefore, difficult to verify. Several factors for which there is information are reviewed in the following pages. For detailed statistical information see "The Economic and Social Condition of Rural America in the 1970's," a report prepared by the Economic Development Division, Economic Research Service U.S.D.A. for the Committee on Government Operations, U.S. Senate, U.S. Government Printing Office, May, 1971.

CHANGES IN RURAL POPULATION

Population shifts, although not directly a measure of rural welfare, profoundly affect rural residents. The migration of rural people to urban centers has concentrated our population in metropolitan areas while depleting rural communities. Within the rural areas people have moved from farms to towns and from the smallest towns to the larger towns. The result is a rural America that is predominately nonfarm and an urban America whose population is concentrated in an area from Boston to Washington, in Florida, south of the Great Lakes, and in California. In recent years the growth of the largest cities has slowed, and there is evidence that a revitalization of some small towns is occurring.

Although rural America has had a population of about fifty million since 1920, the portion on farms has declined. In 1920, sixty percent of all rural people lived on farms, now only about twenty percent do. Migration from farms to towns and cities and from small towns to metropolitan centers was most rapid after the Great Depression of the 1930s through World War II. See Figure 16-1 for a summary of the net out-migration from farms, 1920-72.

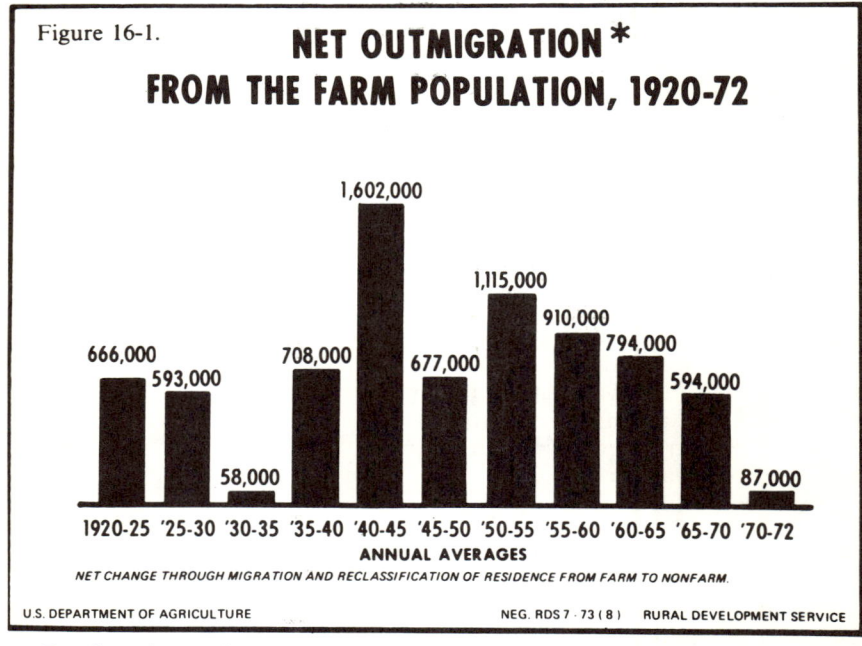

Figure 16-1. NET OUTMIGRATION* FROM THE FARM POPULATION, 1920-72

Declines in business activities in rural communities accompanied the out-migration. Closed and deteriorating buildings on main street have been the result. Both private and public services formerly available in the closest town may no longer be available there. Or, if available, only at a quality below the standard of metropolitan areas. To get the service wanted at the quality wanted often means driving to a distant city. As soon as local support declines, the local service declines even further. As rural residents move their economic support—banking, buying groceries, equipment maintenance—from their local communities, the unity and cohesiveness characteristic of rural communities are lost.

The loss of population and the decline of economic activity within a community have had strong impact against providing public services by local governments. A study of local government services in Kansas by Erickson, Biere, and Sjo found that[1]:

1. Seventy-four of 105 countries lost population during the 1960's
2. Total state and local government expenditures rose from $755 million in 1963 to $1,439 million in 1971
3. Per capita expenditures for public services rose at a rate double the inflation rate.

The local jurisdictions are confronted with providing public services—school, hospitals, fire protection, police, roads, water, waste disposal—to a community with a declining population and tax base when costs of providing public services are rising rapidly.

Rural areas are particularly hard hit in providing education to their youth. The community not only is confronted with the rising cost of education, but the loss of educated young persons to urban communities where they become productive workers. The economic benefit from the education goes to the urban community rather than to the rural community that bore the cost of the education. Out-migration takes a triple bite from the rural taxpayer's pocketbook. First, he pays most of the bills, in Kansas 72 percent for his community's schools. Second, the tax base is reduced by the out-migration, leaving the remaining citizen a higher per capita cost. Third, his investment to increase the productivity of the community's youth is lost when the young person leaves his home community[2].

From 1950 to 1970 Kansas had a net out-migration of 158,000 persons, most of whom were educated in rural communities. The average cost per person for education was $8,029. The twenty year loss to Kansas was $1.5 billion dollars or an annual investment loss of 75 million dollars. That has happened in many rural states. It is indirect subsidization of urban development by rural citizens.

EMPLOYMENT OPPORTUNITIES

The reason for the rapid out-migration by rural youth has been to seek employment opportunities. Technological advances in farming were mostly labor saving; consequently, labor needs on farms declined. With surplus farm labor, the youth from farms sought off-farm employment. The industrialization of the United States resulted in an ever-growing need for more laborers to man the urban factories and businesses. Since industrialization in the cities occurred simultaneously with the growing surplus of farm labor, farm youth left the rural communities. This mass rural-to-urban movement further reduced economic activities in rural communities and thus reduced employment opportunities there even more.

Although annual out-migration from rural communities has declined, there are still strong incentives (employment opportunities) for rural youth to move to metropolitan centers. In the 1960s employment in cities of fewer than 50,000 population increased 17 percent or 3.4 million new jobs. In cities of more than 50,000 population, jobs increased by 27 percent or 12.3 million.

In recent years there has been some movement of manufacturing to smaller communities. For example, the rate of growth of jobs in manufacturing in smaller towns during the 1960s was greater than in large cities. However, in most other lines of economic activity not only are total jobs increasing more rapidly, but the rate of increase has also accelerated in urban centers. At the same time farm employment opportunities have continued to decline. In 1970 there were 355,000 fewer persons employed on farms than in 1968.

Unemployment in agriculture remains high. In 1970 7.5 percent of the farm labor force was unemployed compared with 5.2 percent of the nonfarm labor force. Underemployment, having a job but not one that fully uses the laborer's full potential, is a serious problem on farms. Underemployment occurs most often because the farm is too small in land and capital to fully utilize the skills and time of those working on the farm. Even with high unemployment and underemployment, average productivity of farm workers is high and is increasing more rapidly than for nonfarm workers. In 1970 the index of output per man-hour was 113 on farms, but 105 for all workers.

EDUCATION

Rural education is not equal to urban education. United States Department of Agriculture figures show persons past 25 living in urban centers completed an average of 11.1 years of education, while rural persons completed 9.5 years on the average (Figure 16-2). The most rural states, North Dakota, Mississippi, West Virginia, and South Dakota, have per pupil average expenditures below the national average. A larger portion of the lower rural expenditure goes for such out-of-classroom expenditures as transportation. The lower quality and fewer years of education mean rural youth are at a disadvantage in the labor market. Poorly prepared for employment, they are at a further disadvantage because they must seek work in urban centers where they find social and cultural values strange to them.

INCOME

The growing urban and declining rural economic activity has little affected the rural-urban income disparity. For the last forty years, although rural incomes have risen faster than urban incomes, rural incomes remain well behind. Comparing metropolitan counties to nonmetropolitan coun-

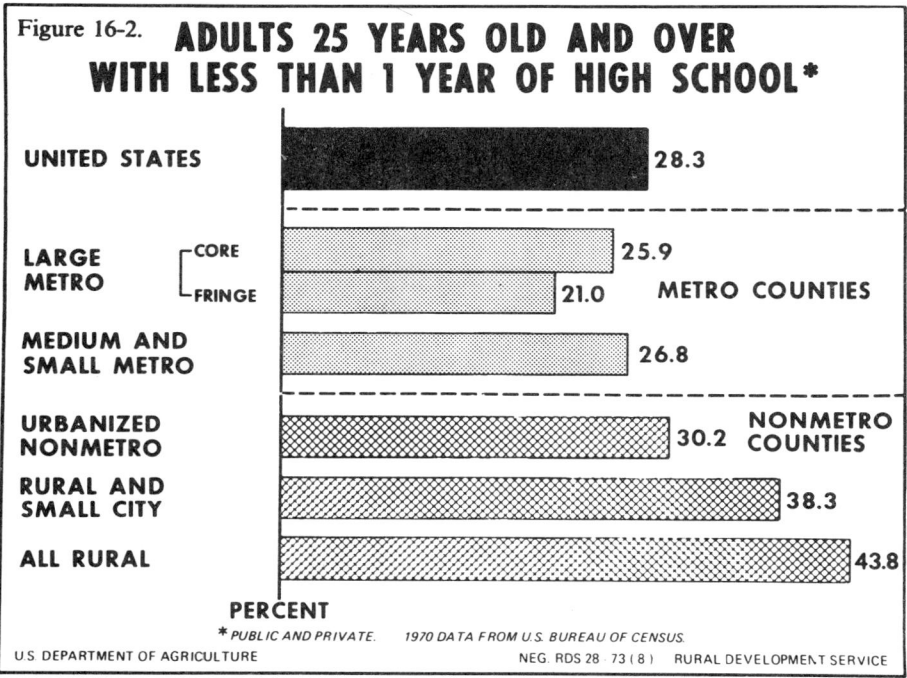

Figure 16-2. ADULTS 25 YEARS OLD AND OVER WITH LESS THAN 1 YEAR OF HIGH SCHOOL*

ties, we find metropolitan per capita annual personal income about $1,000 ahead. That gap remained almost constant for several decades. A farm family has a per capita income of about 81 percent of the national average, $3,153 compared with $3,876 (1972). In 1972, 3.6 percent of all farm families had family incomes of less than $1,000; 7.6 percent, less than $2,000; 12.2 percent, less than $3,000; 26.1 percent, less than $5,000; and 57.0 percent less than $10,000. The average farm family depended heavily on nonfarm sources of income, for example, wages earned off the farm, wife's wages, rent, interest. In 1972, 49 percent of the average farm family's income was from nonfarm sources. The smaller the family income, the greater the portion from nonfarm sources.

Poverty, usually associated with city slums, is a more serious rural problem. In 1970 a nonfarm family of four had a poverty threshold of $3,968 and a farm family $3,385. Using those measures of poverty, 18.6 percent of all farm families were below the poverty level compared with 12.2 percent of all families. In cities of more than 50,000, 9.5 percent of all families were below the poverty level. Of rural families, both farm and nonfarm, 17.1 percent were below the poverty threshold. Even though nearly twice the number of people live in large cities as in rural areas, the number of poor in each is nearly equal.

Rural poverty is most severe among American Indians, blacks of the southeast, the cut-over areas of the Great Lakes, and in Appalachia. The seriousness of rural poverty is often overlooked because, unlike urban poor, rural poor are scattered over large geographical areas and often interspersed among higher income families. The drabness of the ghetto is replaced with the freshness of open country. A run-down mountain cabin is picturesque while an urban slum apartment is distasteful to most of us, but both are low quality housing.

Another problem is variability of income from year to year for a particular farmer. Farm income records show that a farm may often have a 100 or 200 percent increase or decrease from one year to the next. This can be confirmed by comparing the August 11, 1973, price of live beef, $55.90 per hundred weight, to the December 15, 1973, price of $38.25.

HEALTH FACILITIES

The availability of health facilities can be judged by health personnel. Most rural areas have general practitioners available but few, if any, specialists. Most are within a reasonable distance of a hospital, but it may lack quality. The low incomes of rural residents often prevent them from seeking medical assistance.

Rural counties of the United States have 6.8 doctors per 10,000 population, whereas metropolitan areas have 14.3. The rural counties have less than half the nurses per 10,000 population as do urban counties. There are only about one third the number of dentists per 10,000 population in rural counties as in urban ones. Similarly there are many fewer pharmacists in rural areas. But rural counties are most deficient in medical specialists. The most urban counties have 13.7 specialists per 10,000 population; the most rural counties have 0.8.

Rural Americans, because their income is lower, cannot afford the same quantity and quality of medical services as urban Americans. The result is fewer visits per year to doctors and dentists. Rural people also are less likely to have health insurance protection. Of people more than 25 years old in 1968, 86.4 percent of the most urban people had hospital insurance, 70.8 percent of the farm population had such protection.

HOUSING

Comfortable housing for all our people has been a national objective. Quality of housing depends directly on income; therefore, as incomes have risen, so has the adequacy of housing. Geographical areas with the lowest personal incomes have the highest portion of sub-standard housing. Because rural areas have lower average per capita incomes, inadequate housing is concentrated in rural areas. In 1970 there were 1.8 million sub-standard housing units in the rural areas compared with 2.6 million in the urban areas. The rural areas with 30 percent of the population have nearly half the sub-standard housing units.

PUBLIC SERVICES

The ease of acquiring goods and services of quality, whether it be through private or public sectors, is a measure of the welfare of people.

So far in this chapter we have considered several services from the private sector and education from the public sector. We must also deal with the problems of local governments in providing police, fire, roads, waste disposal, and many other services our citizens have come to expect through their government.

Many local governments are being squeezed between increasing demands for public services and declining populations. In our most rural states, state and local expenditures have been increasing more rapidly than population. The increasing demand for services arises from the desire of rural people to upgrade existing services and to add new ones. Our rural people are no longer satisfied with fewer and poorer services than the nonrural have. As demand for services has increased in rural communities, population has decreased. Often the new services wanted are started by a new government organization, for example, soil conservation, water, waste disposal, fire districts. Except for school districts, which were greatly reduced in number through consolidation, the number of local government units have been increasing. The result has been overlapping jurisdictions and fragmentation for citizens wanting to use public services. For the public policy maker, the legislator, or government administrator, the additional agencies to perform new services create problems in effective and efficient management.

Per capita expenditures are often used as a rough measure of the quality and quantity of public services. A comprehensive survey of the 105 counties and 238 incorporated cities of Kansas revealed that per capita expenditures for all their public services have been increasing about seven percent annually since 1960. The increase has been most rapid in the largest growing cities. That should indicate an improvement in public services. Small towns have increasing public expenditures, but also declining populations, which means that part of the increasing per capita expense arises from new expenditures, but part is from spreading total expenditures among fewer people.

Providing public services has become a serious economic and social problem for rural communities. Already confronted with declining adequacy of services, the communities become less attractive as places to live and to establish businesses. That leads to further declines in population and a smaller tax base. Maintaining existing services can be accomplished only with higher taxes. That, in turn, discourages new people from moving to the community and present residents from remaining there.

The economic survival of, and the quality of life in, rural communities depends on alleviating problems associated with public services. Alternatives being tried and considered include:

1. *Consolidating local governments.* The best known example has been school districts. Other possibilities to consolidate include special districts—water, waste disposal, conservation, hospital, mental health—perhaps all under county jurisdiction, consolidating townships, counties, and towns, and then perhaps consolidating counties.

2. *Consolidating functions.* Existing governmental units may jointly offer a particular service. Counties are now sharing mental health centers. Cities and counties are sharing buildings and have joint police and fire departments. Some states are considering a county unit system of government where all local government services are consolidated within the county government. Many other opportunities for cooperative effort among local governments are possible.
3. *Revitalizing communities.* Inherent in our traditions is a strong desire for economic growth. Healthy communities have increasing population, new businesses, and new employment opportunities. Many rural communities have tried, through public subscriptions, bond issues, tax incentives and other ways, to make their communities more attractive places to live and to locate businesses.
4. *Improving the efficiency of local government management.* Most local governments were established when the services they provided were few. Their accounting procedures, usually prescribed by law, provide primarily that the public be informed how expenditures were made. The prescribed budgeting, accounting, and financial systems often limit what public managers can do to improve operational efficiency.

Many local governmental units are so small and so poorly financed that it is difficult, if not impossible, to hire personnel with the needed managerial skills. Or if the position is an elected one, it is not possible to attract well qualified candidates to seek the job.

Local communities are looking for ways to apply present day business management methods to local governments and ways to get well qualified administrative personnel. An example is two counties, each too small to hire a full time health officer, that hire one jointly. Another example is several small units making pooled purchases to get discounts that large agencies and businesses are accustomed to.

There is no easy or magic way for rural communities to provide public services effectively. Nor is it easy to reverse the economic downward trend of many rural communities. How effectively communities provide public services largely determines the level of welfare in our rural communities.

SUGGESTED READINGS

Brinkman, George. *The Development of Rural America.* The University Press of Kansas, 1974.

The National Advisory Commission on Food and Fiber. *Food and Fiber for the Future.* United States Printing Office, Washington, D.C., 1967, Pages 115-128 and 197-217.

Tweeten, Luther G. *Rural Poverty: Incidence, Causes, and Cures.* Oklahoma Agricultural Experiment Station, P-590, Stillwater, Oklahoma, 1968.

United States Senate Committee on Government Operations. *The Economic and Social Condition of Rural America in the 1970's.* Prepared by the Economic Development Division, Economic Research Service, United States Department of Agriculture United States Government Printing Office, Washington, D.C., 1971.

ENDNOTES

1. Erickson, Donald; Biere, Arlo; and Sjo, John, *City and County Public-Service Expenditures, 1960-70*, Kansas Agricultural Experiment Station Bulletin 578, Manhattan, Kansas, 1974.
2. Sjo, John; Trapp, James; and Munson, Robert, *State Costs and Benefits from Education*, Kansas Agricultural Experiment Station Bulletin 561, Manhattan, Kansas, 1972.

THE ECONOMIC CONTROL OF AGRICULTURE 17

Throughout this text we have emphasized the changing economic structure of agriculture. The shifting of the processing, storing, and supply from farms to nonfarm agribusinesses and the resulting rural-to-urban migration have been basic factors causing the changes. In the complex interdependent agriculture of today, it is still undetermined where the control of our largest industry will eventually rest—with farmers, with large conglomerates, or with government. In 1972 and 1973 a committee of land grant university agriculturalists from the twelve North Central Public Policy Education Committee studied the problem. Their findings are the basis of this chapter.

WHAT IS MEANT BY ECONOMIC CONTROL

Ultimate control rests with the decision makers and with those who get the financial benefits derived from the decisions. We can identify the individuals and organizations in whom control rests if we know who owns or controls the resources used in agriculture and who makes the key decisions regarding producing, selling, and buying agricultural products.

The debate over bargaining power has focused on the control-of-agriculture issue. Farm leaders have sought to gain more bargaining power for farmers by taking the power from agribusiness firms. Often farmers have sought legislation to aid their quest for bargining power. An example is the Capper-Volstead Act of 1922 authorizing cooperatives as a type of business organization. Farmers' concern for bargaining power or control of farming is not a recent concern.

The economic issue at stake in the contest for control is who will own the agricultural resources and how the income from agriculture will be divided among owners of the resources.

THE BASIS FOR THE PROBLEM

If you do not recall the different market structures, return to Chapter 11 for review. The farmer sells in a nearly competitive market where there are so many small individual sellers that each cannot affect prices. The buyers of farm products are few and large enough firms to influence prices of the products they buy, the products farmers sell. That is the basis for the saying, "individually, farmers are price takers on the selling market." As a group, however, the producers of a farm product can influence prices and exercise some monopoly control in the market. Another way to look at it is to consider the price elasticity of demand for the products sold. Demand is perfectly elastic for the individual farmer. He can sell any amount in a given market at the stated price, but none at a higher price. Confronted with those two conditions, farmers find they have little or no market bargaining power in their selling markets.

Analyses of farm supply market soon show the farmers buying their equipment, fuel, and supplies lacking competitive conditions; although they often haggle over price they usually cannot greatly influence prices of tractors, gasoline, and fertilizer. Firms selling those inputs can influence the price at which they sell to farmers. As in their selling activities, farmers find that they have very little individual market bargaining power in their buying activities.

Market margins, the spread between the price received by farmers and what the consumer pays, are usually wide and are cited as evidence of the lack of farmers' market power. The portion of the consumer's dollar going to the farmer may or may not be evidence of how much or how little control farmers have over the distribution of income among the owners of the factors of production. Marketing costs are discussed further in Chapter 18.

WHAT HAS BEEN HAPPENING IN MARKET DECISIONS?

"Industrialization of our food and fiber system appears to be a major force that is shifting future control of agriculture from the farm".[1]

As agriculture has become industrialized, production and selling farm products often can be done only under contracts specifying quantity, quality standards, and delivery dates. That is particularly true in broiler, egg, turkey, and vegetable production and in cattle feedlot operations.

As food processing and retailing became concentrated in an ever-decreasing number of plants and stores, often in vertically integrated operations, key market decision making has shifted to their managers.

Farm supplying similarly has been concentrated in a small number of large firms. They may integrate and include farm operations under their managements. Feed processors entering broiler production is an example. That type of operation shifts decision making away from the farmers.

WHAT HAS BEEN HAPPENING TO
CONTROL OF AGRICULTURAL RESOURCES?

As the processing of farm products and supplying of inputs shifted to nonfarm agribusiness, control of resources began to shift from farms to the new nonfarm firms.

LAND

Processing and supply firms occupy land, so there has been minor shifting of land control to them. Nonfarm individuals have acquired land holdings to lease to farmers, but that trend has not resulted in any large shift in control of land to non-farmers.

The federal government, through supply-control programs (restrictions on plantings) and conservation programs, restrict farmers' freedom to use land. Local and state governments, through land use restrictions, have shifted some control of land to their jurisdictions.

LABOR

Only a few decades ago a majority of the labor force was on farms. Now less than ten percent is. Hired laborers on farms have always been a small portion of the farm workers; most were, and continue to be members of the farm family.

Rural-to-urban migration certainly has shifted labor from the farm to the city, but that shift has not noticeably affected the farmers; control of labor on the farms. Opportunity of off-farm employment of sons and daughters has had some effect on working conditions for family members. With off-farm opportunities, more favorable farm conditions must be offered to induce youth to remain on farms.

In labor intensive farm operations for example, vegetable and fruit growing, broiler operations, commercial feedlots—much of the labor input is hired. Only recently have farm laborers unionized to increase their bargaining power on wages and working conditions. Similarly, agribusiness employees are unionized. Agricultural firms, either farm or agribusiness, that hire labor may share control of that labor with a union.

Modern agricultural employers must share control of labor with state and federal governments. Minimum wage standards, safety standards, work hours and conditions, social security benefits, and unemployment compensation are examples of government control over hired labor.

CAPITAL

Large capital investments in either farming or agribusiness restricts decision making, particularly the decision of whether to begin an agricultural business. There is more than a bit of truth in the saying that the only way to enter farming is to inherit, marry, or be given a farm.

For those in farming, with a limited amount of capital, decision making is severely limited. A decision to expand the cowherd may never be carried out if the decision maker has neither the cash nor credit to purchase the additional cows. If he can borrow the capital, he may be able to carry out his decision. But the loan agreement may give the lender a voice in the management of the entire cowherd operation.

No accurate estimate of nonfarm public corporations' capital investments in farming is possible. Specific examples are known, but as discussed in Chapter 14, the total is probably still small.

MANAGEMENT

The basic management unit in farming continues to be the family and is usually a joint responsibility with labor. In large operations, management, labor, and ownership functions rest with different individuals. In such cases hired managers may be used.

Management functions of family farms often are shared with a number of experts. Farmers hire technical management services related to taxes, soil fertilization, marketing, resource use, and other management factors. A farmer's own management capability may restrict his decision making. He may be able to handle only a certain size operation which may be below the size necessary to provide an adequate family income.

WHAT HAS HAPPENED TO FARMERS' ABILITY TO USE POLITICAL POWER TO ACHIEVE ECONOMIC GOALS

A look at the distribution of population between rural and urban tells us much about farmers' ability to use political power to achieve their economic goals. In 1850 a majority of the population was farm; in 1900, 40 percent; in 1920, 30 percent; in 1940, 23 percent; and in 1974, about 4.5 percent. Even in the most rural states more people live in towns than on farms. For two reasons, however, there was a lag between the loss of a majority of the population and the loss of political influence. First, a great portion of the nonfarm population lived in small rural towns whose interests were nearly identical with those of farmers. Even in the large cities many families were first generation migrants from farms and retained strong farm loyalties. Secondly, congressional and legislative districts had been established before the big rural-to-urban migration to assure representation of all geographical regions. Often an elected official from a rural district might represent only a few hundred people, while those from urban districts represented several hundred thousand. The rural population, as a consequence, was disproportionately represented in state legislatures and Congress.

The loss of farm political power occurred gradually, but by 1950 farmer interests no longer were vital to control of the legislative bodies. Urban people were further away from farm ties and no longer had strong rural sympathies. After the 1963 Supreme Court "one person one vote" ruling legislative reapportionment was required. Legislative districts were required to have nearly equal numbers of people so that each representative would represent about the same number of constituents. Urban representation was increased. Rural representation was decreased.

Simultaneously, the emerging agribusiness firms, wiser to political organizations and ways than farmers, began to exert influence on agricultural legislation and policies. For an interesting and controversial exposition on the results of the shift of political power from the family farm to agribusiness and large nonfamily farm firms, read Jim Hightower's *Hard Tomatoes, Hard Times, A Report of the Agribusiness Accountability Project on the Failure of America's Land Grant College Complex*, Schenkman Publishing Company, Cambridge, Massachusetts, 1972.

WHAT ALTERNATIVES FOR FARMERS

A first alternative is to retain what is left of the dispersed open market system and introduce legislation to broaden it and to assure a return to the open market system. Under that alternative the management choices would remain with operating farmers. They would be free to sell and buy in the market when and how they saw best. That alternative would come closest to keeping farming much as it is today.

A second alternative is a system of corporate, integrated firms. In such a system the number of firms controlling farm production would be small. Much of the farming would be done directly by large firms, which would probably also handle processing, storage, and perhaps even retailing of food. Such large firms might tend to become complete food systems, integrated both horizontally and vertically. The large firms would operate under imperfect competition. Many adjustments in resource ownership would accompany this alternative. Today's commercial farmers would be replaced. There would be few or perhaps no small independent family farms. Forces in action today have already caused much movement in that direction. Examples are found in fruit and vegetable production, commercial feedlots, sugar production, and milk production.

A third alternative is a system with farmers retaining control of agriculture through tightly organized cooperatives. The cooperatives would market all farm production, and buy at least part of the farm inputs, control the market system, and serve as a bargaining agent for its members. To do that effectively farm members would assign rights to control and allocate production to the cooperatives. Farmers would retain ownership of land, operate independent businesses, and provide much of their own labor. Individual farmers would face more restrictions, self-imposed through the cooperative, than they do now. Certainly there would be fewer resource control adjustments than under a corporate system. Farmers, particularly in milk production, have had extensive experience with cooperative action along the lines listed.

A fourth alternative is a government administered agriculture. Under such a system society as a whole, through the legislative process, would replace private decision making by farmers. In the price support-production control programs, we have had experience with government restriction of individual decision making. Such a system could be partial, leaving most of the decision making and control of resources with individual operators. Or it could be more complete, even to the point of government ownership of resources and control of most decisions.

A fifth alternative would be a mixed system. Today we have some of each of the alternative systems—an open diverse market, corporate operations, cooperative action, and government control. The mixed system requires positive action and a reversal of the trend toward concentration of production in very large firms to assure its survival. Decision-making control and resource ownership, as they exist today, would be an objective of a mixed system.

IN SUMMARY

United States agriculture is in transition. The economic control of this, our largest, industry can remain largely in the hands of many independent firms, be taken over by a few large firms, come under government control. Public decisions during this period of structural changes can determine who will control agriculture for generations ahead.

SUGGESTED READINGS

Doll, John P., Rhodes, V. James, West, Jerry G. *Economics of Agricultural Production, Markets, and Policy.* Richard D. Irwin, Inc., 1968, Chapters 18-22.

Hathaway, Dale E. *Government and Agriculture, Public Policy in a Democratic Society.* The Macmillan Company, 1963.

McCune, Wesley. *Who's Behind our Farm Policy?* Frederich A. Praeger, 1956.

North Central Public Policy Education Committee. *Who Will Control U.S. Agriculture?* A series of 6 leaflets 32-1, 32-2, 32-3, 32-4, 32-5, and 32-6. University of Illinois, Urbana, Illinois, 1973.

Tweeten, Luther. *Foundations of Farm Policy.* University of Nebraska Press, 1971.

ENDNOTE

1. Sundquist, W. B. and Guither, H. D., "The Current Situation and the Issues," in *No. 1. Who Will Control United States Agriculture.* North Central Regional Extension Publications, University of Illinois.

AGRICULTURE TODAY—FARM INCOME, PRICES, MARKETS, ENERGY, INTERNATIONAL TRADE, AND TAXES

18

All economic issues considered in this chapter have one thing in common; either directly or indirectly they are related to farm income goals. None of the issues—prices, markets, energy, trade, or taxes—remains the most pressing one over the years for all farmers. Each farmer has different problems that are most pressing. Then each year has its most pressing problem. In Chapter 18 we look at several problems and situations important to agriculture today.

PRICES AND INCOME

Farmers individually and as a whole have been confronted with the twofold problem of low and unstable incomes. The farm subsector of agriculture is made up ot two groups of farmers who share that basic problem—farmers who are underpaid but not always poor and those who are poor but not always underpaid.[1] The nearly 600,000 farmers selling more than $20,000 worth of farm products each are the farmers who have had low returns from their land, labor, and capital, but because of their size, are not necessarily poor. In other words they sell enough to have reasonable net incomes and to support families, but the income gives a low re-

Table 18-1. A Farmer's Twelve-year Farm Income Record, Kansas, 1962-1973.

Year	Crop Acres	Gross Farm Income	Total Expenses	Net Farm Income
1962	842	$32,017	$20,569	$11,448
1963	842	35,680	21,113	14,567
1964	842	38,102	23,737	14,365
1965	842	47,887	23,298	24,589
1966	842	39,622	19,793	19,829
1967	1015	41,220	25,328	15,892
1968	1015	43,937	29,812	14,125
1969	1015	40,587	23,646	16,941
1970	1015	45,617	26,116	19,501
1971	1015	59,728	31,937	27,791
1972	1015	65,908	33,638	32,270
1973	1015	139,167	39,506	99,661

Source: Kansas Farm Management Association, Department of Agricultural Economics, Kansas State University.

turn to the resources and fluctuates widely from year to year. Table 18-1 illustrates the wide variation in one farmer's income.

Another 2,738,000 farmers sell less than $20,000 worth of farm products each. Among them are the rural poor, but they are not necessarily underpaid. Their net incomes are low. Some are in poverty—not because their returns to resources used are low, but because they have so few resources to use. Too little land and capital to use results in a low output. In Chapter 16 we dealt with the extent and seriousness of low farm incomes. Here we will deal with the reasons for low and unstable farm incomes.

In discussing farm income problems we must keep in mind that some farmers have low and variable returns on their investments; others have low and variable incomes. Different solutions are required to solve the problems of each group. Our agricultural policies do not always recognize that. Since the 1930s we have largely sought to solve farm income problems through prices. The reason for that is clear—prices directly affect incomes. We can see that by looking at the way we figure net farm income:

```
    Units of production           300 acres harvested
  X Yield                          30 busheld per acre
  -----------------------          -----------------------
  = Total production            9,000 bushels
  X Price                        $3.00 per bushel
  -----------------------          -----------------------
  = Gross farm income       $27,000.00 gross farm income
  - Operating expenses      $21,000.00 operating expenses
  -----------------------          -----------------------
  = Net farm income          $ 6,000.00 net farm income
```

If the price of wheat were $6.00, income would be affected as follows:

```
                    300 acres harvested
                     30 bushels per acre
                  -----------------------
                  9,000 bushels
                  $6.00 per bushel
                  -----------------------
             $54,000.00 gross farm income
             $21,000.00 operating expenses
                  -----------------------
             $33,000.00 net farm income
```

Net farm income was raised from $6,000 to $33,000. Clearly a higher price means a higher income. But as is often the case, what appears to be so clear and simple needs to be examined carefully.

First, factors other than prices affect net farm incomes—units of production, yields, and operating expenses. Let us examine the influence of units of production on income by comparing farms of different sizes. Assume that we have three wheat farms, each with the acreage shown below:

AGRICULTURE TODAY 203

	Farm A	Farm B	Farm C
Acres harvested	3,000	300	30
Yield (bushels)	30	30	30
Total production (bushels)	90,000	9,000	900
Operating expenses	$210,000.00	$21,000.00	$2,100.00

The difference between $3.00 and $6.00 wheat would affect net farm incomes as follows:

	Farm A		Farm B		Farm C	
Bushels	90,000	90,000	9,000	9,000	900	900
Price	$3	$6	$3	$6	$3	$6
Gross farm income	$270,000	$540,000	$27,000	$54,000	$2,700	$5,400
Operating expenses	$210,000	$210,000	$21,000	$21,000	$2,100	$2,100
Net farm income	$ 60,000	$330,000	$ 6,000	$33,000	$ 600	$3,300

Higher prices meant higher net farm income for all three size farms. But even a $3 a bushel increase did not eliminate the low income situation of the smallest farm. Certainly $3,300 is preferred to $600, but the income spread between the big farm and the small one increased as price increased.

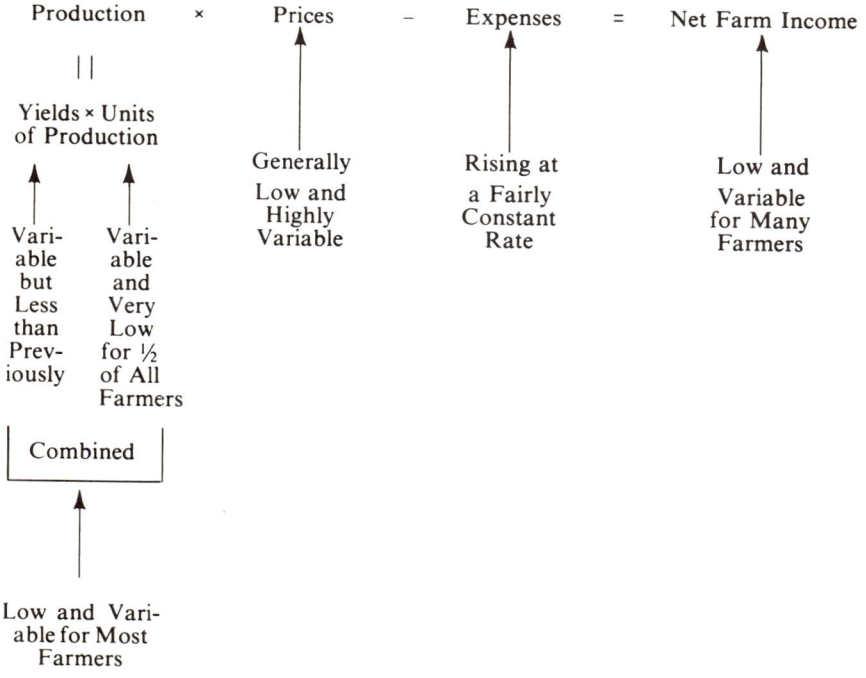

Figure 18-1. Factors Affecting Net Farm Income.

The number of farm families with low incomes is greater than we often realize; 1973 was a good farm income year, but 43.6 percent of all farms in the United States were like our smallest farm—sold less than $5,000 of farm products. They need more than high prices to solve their low income problem. They need more resources.

Another factor affecting incomes is yields. Low yields mean low income even if prices are high. On an individual farm yields vary widely from year to year, but with improved varieties and cultural practices low yield years occur less frequently than in past decades.

The third factor that may affect net farm incomes as greatly as prices is farm costs. Over the years the cost of production has continuously risen and often much faster than prices for farm products. Also per unit costs are often inversely related to output. If small farms have higher per unit costs

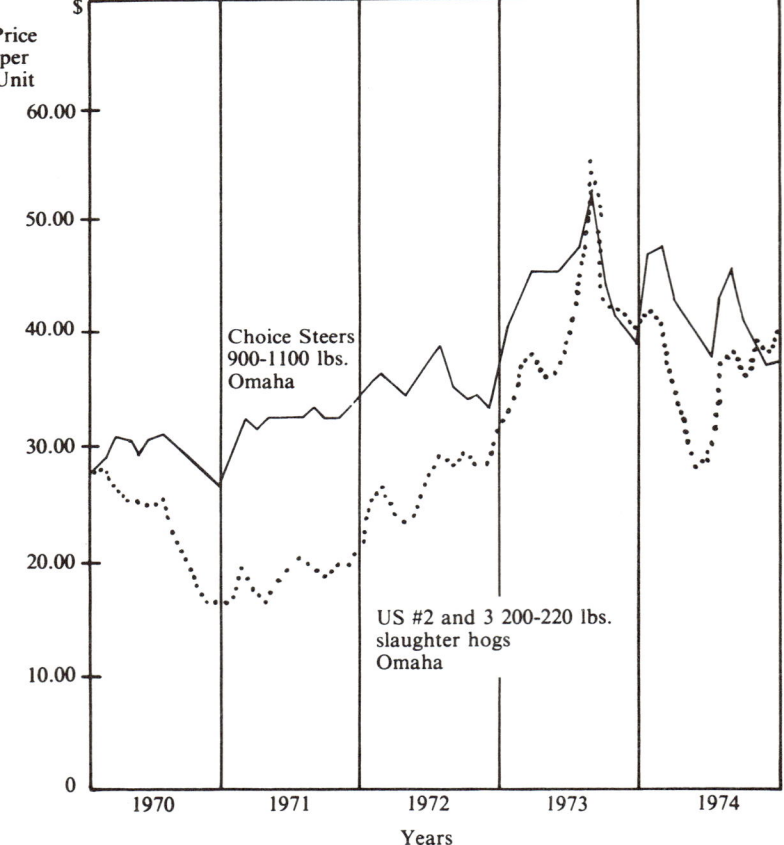

Figure 18-2. Monthly Average Prices for Slaughter Steers and Hogs, 1970 to 1974.

Source: USDA Consumer and Marketing Service, Livestock Division.

than a big one, then small farmers' incomes are adversely affected by low levels of output and higher per unit costs.

Farm prices, as important as they are, do not alone determine net farm incomes. Therefore, farm income problems cannot be solved through prices alone. In Figure 18-1, using the net income formula, we have summarized our discussion of farm incomes.

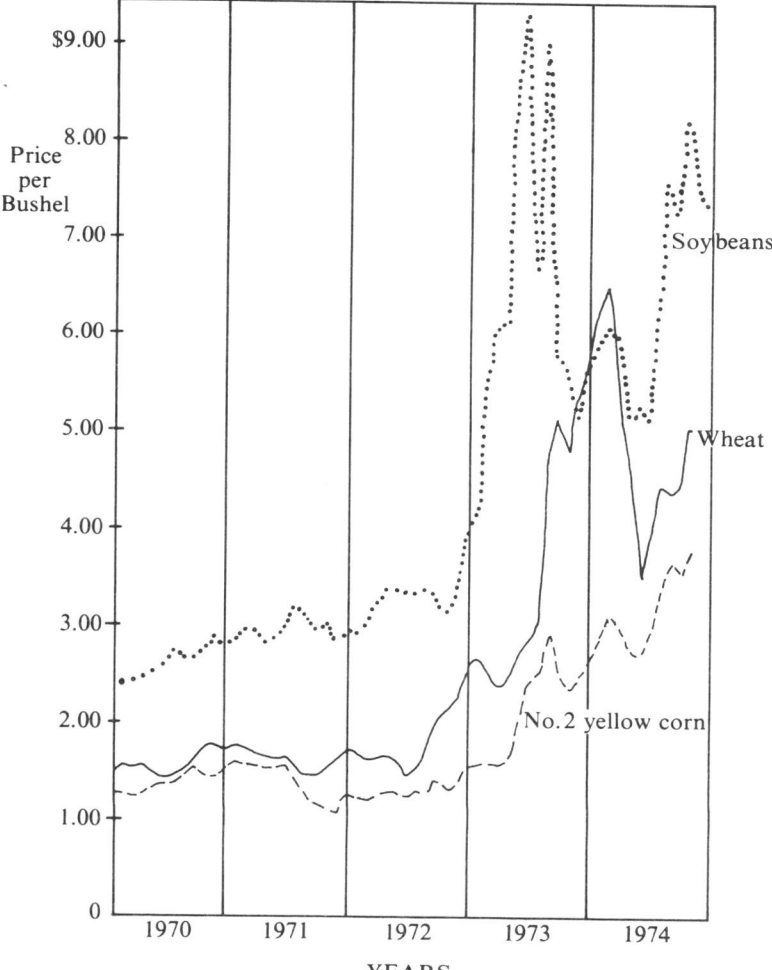

Figure 18-3. Monthly Average Prices for Selected Crops, 1970-74.
Source: Wheat Situation, Feed Situation, and Agricultural Prices.

VARIATION IN FARM PRICES

Decision making for farmers is made particularly difficult because of the uncertainty of farm prices which fluctuate widely both day-to-day and from year-to-year. Such rapid and great price movements, as shown in Figures 18-2 and 18-3, along with natural conditions, have made farm planning difficult. The years 1973 and 1974 had particularly great price uncertainty. Grain prices doubled during 1973 and then dropped in early 1974 to rise again the latter part of 1974. Livestock prices have also fluctuated but not so widely as have grain prices.

The wide price fluctuations are a major contributor to the income variability shown in Table 18-1. Price stability would do much to solve farm income instability. However, instability due to yield variations would still remain.

MARKETING COSTS

An issue, always with us but with varying intensities, is the difference between farm prices and food retail prices. The consumer, particularly when prices rise, complains against high food prices, often blaming farmers for the high cost of living. Farmers, often receiving less than 35 percent of consumer dollars spent for food, feel that middlemen are to blame. The middleman passes the blame to the farmer for higher raw material prices, to labor for higher wages, and to bankers for higher interest costs. Farmers often express the view that eliminating the middleman would give them a bigger share of the consumer's dollar and thus higher incomes.

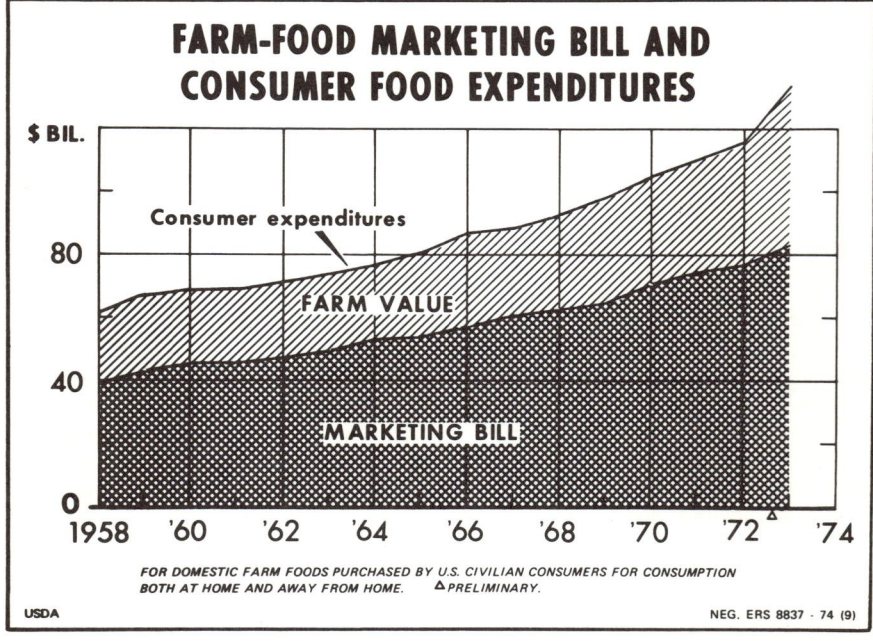

Figure 18-4. The Farm-Food Marketing Bill and Consumer Food Expenditures.

AGRICULTURE TODAY 207

FOOD MARKETING BILL

The difference between what consumers pay and what farmers receive is referred to as the *food marketing bill* or the *marketing margin*. Annually the United States Department of Agriculture reports the food marketing bill. In Figure 18-4 the farm value, the marketing bill, and consumers' expenditure for food are given. In 1973 the farmer received a larger portion, 38 percent, of the consumer expenditures for food than in previous years. The reason was that in 1973 farm prices rose more rapidly than prices in general.

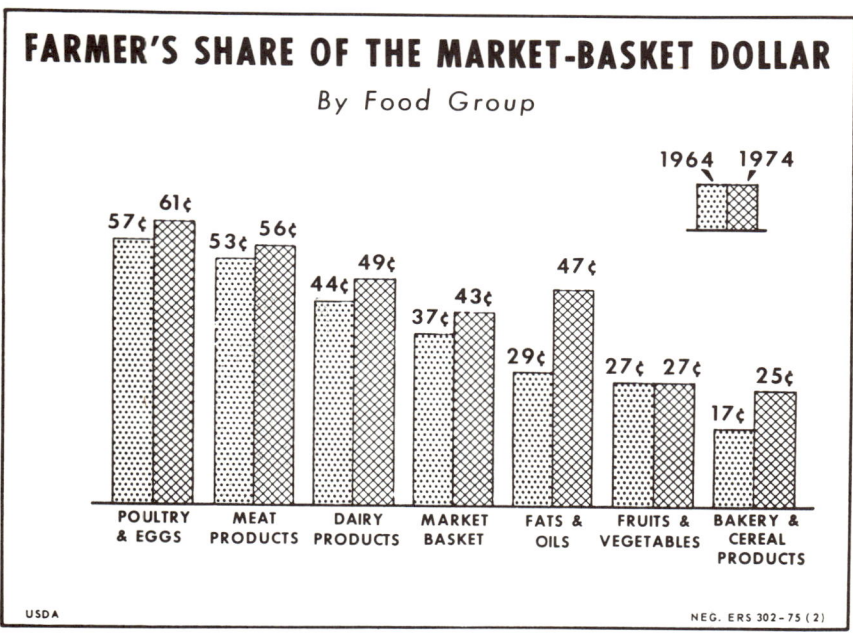

Figure 18-5. The Farmer's Share of the Market-Basket Dollar by Food Groups, 1963 and 1973.

In Figure 18-5 farmers' shares of the consumers' dollars spent on food are compared by food groups. The more processing, the lower the farmers' share. The utility added to an egg after it leaves a farm is small. Almost no form utility is added. The middleman largely provides an exchange function and adds time and place utility. The utility added to wheat in a loaf of bread is much greater. The wheat is made into flour, the flour baked into bread, the bread is packaged, and delivered fresh. The consumer is buying all those services as well as the wheat that went into bread. Not many consumers today buy wheat, make flour, and bake bread. If they would, the wheat farmer, like the egg farmer, would receive a larger share of the consumer's dollar, and consumers would eliminate some middleman costs.

The size or the portion of consumer expenditure of the marketing bill does not measure the efficiency of the marketing system. The fact that farmers receive 64 cents of each dollar spent for eggs compared with 22 cents for bakery and cereal products does not mean that egg marketing is more efficient than grain marketing. To measure efficiency, output and utility added must be compared with inputs used. Efficiency of the market is determined by the per unit cost of services added.

Nor does the size or portion of consumer expenditure going into marketing indicate profitability of farm production or of marketing firms. A big marketing bill does not necessarily mean excessive profits to the marketing middlemen. To determine net returns, a careful analysis of costs and returns is necessary. Similarly products such as eggs with the lowest marketing bill have not necessarily been the most profitable line of farm production. In 1974 food grains, with the highest marketing bill, were among the most profitable farm enterprises.

From the farmer's viewpoint, particularly in years of low income, seeing fifty or more cents of each consumer's dollar spent for food going to middlemen appears to be an injustice. We hear cries to eliminate the middleman. We hear demands for a redistribution of the consumer's dollar—a bigger portion to the farmer.

If we look carefully at the situation we will see that the middlemen are continuing the production process begun on the farm. Each participant in the production process adds utility to the product. Today's consumers have demonstrated they are willing to pay for the utility added by the middleman, and it is unlikely we will ever see middlemen eliminated. The issue is then reduced into two parts. First, who will perform the middlemen functions? Second, how will the consumer's expenditure be divided among the participants in the whole production and marketing process.

Farmers originally performed most of the production and processing function on their farms. A return to that situation would give them a larger share of the consumer's dollar, but might not increase their net incomes. For example, a cattle feeder who undertakes to butcher his cattle, process the meat, and retail it to consumers would have to divert some of his capital and labor from feeding to processing. That is an enterprise combination problem. In Chapter 9 we showed that diverting resources from one enterprise to another will increase profits only if the marginal returns are higher in the new enterprise. For a farmer to increase his income by processing meat, a dollar of resource put into processing must return more than that dollar would return in feeding. Most farmers have found they have an advantage when they specialize in producing the raw product, so do not enter processing. At times farmers have joined cooperative associations to process and market farm products as a group. If their cooperative can process and market profitably, farmers participating can increase both the portion of the consumer expenditure going to them and their incomes. Note the middlemen and their functions remain with the farmers taking over the role.

Secondly, strength of participants in the production, processing, and marketing organization will affect the distribution of the consumer's expenditure among owners of the resources used. Farmers traditionally have lacked *bargaining power*. Because they produce and sell in a competitive market, individual farmers have had little influence on the price received. Cooperative marketing has been used to give farmers bargaining power, that is, to increase their ability to influence the price they receive.

ARE MARKETING COSTS TOO HIGH

Most studies have shown that, except for some products, middleman profits are not excessive. But if profits are high, new middleman firms enter, and profits are reduced. Consumers, through buying, cast votes for the processing and marketing services wanted. In affluent societies consumers have voted for built-in-maid and food preparation service provided by the middlemen. Consumers have been willing to pay the price to get four pork chops with the fat trimmed in a clear wrapped package. Few today will buy a side of pork and process it at home. It seems that as long as we remain affluent, consumers will demand middleman services, and the controversy over how the consumer's dollar is divided among all the participants in processing and marketing will remain.

THE FUTURES MARKET

Many processors, such as millers, need a continuous supply of raw material to keep their plants in year around operation. Or a cattle feeder wants to be assured he will have replacement stock available for each feeding period. Originally the farm commodity cash markets provided no way the miller or the feeder could contract inputs for future delivery. Individuals seeing the advantage of guaranteed delivery at a certain future date begin to make contracts with individual suppliers to accomplish that objective. For example, a cattle feeder, knowing in May he will need 200 steers in October to fill his lot, would contact a rancher in May to see if he could furnish 200 steers in October. The ranchers may have said yes, but wished a guarantee the feeder would actually take the steers in October. To assure fulfillment to each other they worked up a contract that specified such things as quantity, size, health condition, price, method of payment, date of delivery, and other similar details. Each signed the contract. That was a cash contract for forward delivery of a specified commodity.

Now let us say the feeder saw in August it would be to his advantage not to feed the steers. Perhaps he had a poor feed crop. In discussions with other feeders he finds one who wants feeder calves in October. He told the second feeder about his purchase contract. Eventually the second feeder asked if he could buy the contract or the right to the forward delivery of the steers. They agree upon the terms of transferring legal rights to the contract. Or the rancher, seeing he may have difficulty in delivering the steers, could have arranged a transfer of his contract to another rancher who could deliver the steers. Many farm products are produced under contract to a processor. A fruit grower may contract for the delivery of his fruit to a cannery months before it ripens. The contract specifies the terms of delivery. Contracts for forward delivery spread the risk. The seller is assured of the terms by selling earlier. The buyer is similarly assured of a supply. Those contracts for forward delivery or acceptance were negotiated and fulfilled directly between individuals. Such *cash contracts* for the future were the forerunners of today's futures markets.

We have a long history of such individual contracting for forward delivery. Even in colonial times such agreements were drawn. But there were problems with such contracts. There was no established market. Someone wanting to buy had to find someone wanting to sell. Without a market organization there were no established future prices. Each party to the contract had to negotiate the price for each contract. Also there were no established rules and procedures for determining the terms of the contracts. Disputes between buyers and sellers could be settled only in the courts.

To facilitate future buying and selling of commodities, *commodity exchanges* were opened in the mid-nineteenth century. Over the years the number of futures markets and the number of commodities handled have greatly increased. Both farm and nonfarm commodities are traded in the futures markets. Among the farm products traded are most grains, potatoes, onions, broilers, eggs, wool, carcass beef, boneless beef, skinned hams, frozen pork bellies, live hogs, live slaughter cattle, and live feeder cattle.

THE FUTURES MARKET

A futures market is a specially organized market, often called a commodity exchange or a board of trade, where contracts for future sales or purchases are traded. The exchange provides for swift and standardized methods of trading in contracts. The exchange establishes the rules for trading and terms of the contracts. Most contracts will specify the commodity, the quantity, the quality, the price, the time of delivery, and the place of delivery. The exchange specifies who may trade, time and place trading may occur, and the rules and regulations of actual trading.

The principal purpose of the futures market is to provide a way to spread risk. The example of the feeder arranging a contract to guarantee the 200 steers reduced his risk. He was assured of delivery of a specified type of animal at a specified time. It also reduced the price risk. That way he knew in May the October price of the steers. The rancher who raised the steers derived the same risk-reducing benefits.

FUTURES TRADING

Only members of an exchange may trade at that exchange. To trade, the members are physically there. All nonmembers must trade through a member by placing an order to buy (or sell) a contract. The member then finds another member who has an order to do just the opposite, sell (or buy) a contract. The contract specifies the terms of the trade.

In futures trading, as contrasted to cash trading, no exchange of the actual commodity occurs when the contract is traded. The contract on the part of the buyer is a promise to accept delivery of the commodity on the delivery date. On the part of the seller, it is a promise to deliver the commodity on a future specified date. Actual delivery of the commodity occurs only if the contract is held to delivery. In practice contracts are seldom held until the delivery date. A contract to buy is cancelled by an equal contract to sell. A contract to buy is termed being long on the market; one to sell is being short on the market. The longs must be just equal to the shorts. Futures trading depends on offsetting transactions to fulfill contractual obligations. Less than one percent of all trades are actually delivered.

A. L. Frederick, Extension Economist at Kansas State University, helped to develop the following example to show how futures trading works.

Because futures contracts are standardized, they have one essential feature different from other contracts. The contractual obligation may be fulfilled by taking an offsetting position in the futures market. That is in contrast with other types of contracts that can be fulfilled only by exchanging ownership of the commodity.

For example, once an individual has purchased a promise to deliver (which is really all that a futures contract is) he may sell his promise to someone else. That takes him out of the market before actual delivery time. If he had originally sold a promise to deliver, he could buy it back at any time before the contract expiration date.

Futures trading has come to rely increasingly on offsetting transactions as a means of fulfilling contract obligations. Since offsetting trades are so important, let's look at them more closely. The diagram below shows three individuals who are trading in soybeans.

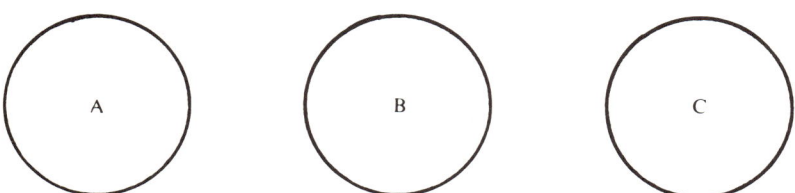

Individual A, whom we will assume to be a soybean producer, decides that he would like to transfer the price risk before he harvests his beans. He would like to set his price at today's level, but the crop is still growing and cannot be disposed of on the cash market. He, therefore sells a promise to deliver so many bushels of beans to individual B. B holds the promise for some time, several days to several months, and then sells A's promise to deliver to individual C. If B sells at a higher price than he originally paid, he makes a profit. If the price has declined, he experiences a loss. In either case, A is still entitled to the original purchase price and neither gains, nor loses, from any subsequent price fluctuation. B's net position in the futures market is now zero, and he need not take part in the delivery process. A and B do not seek each other out in the trading process. All sales and purchases are made through broker representatives by a process similar to a public auction. All willing buyers would have an equal chance to bid on A's contract.

We have seen how one individual operates of the 99 percent who never take part in actual delivery. Now, let's look at the delivery mechanism. Here we have our same individuals, A, B, and C but we add one more and a clearing house. A has sold a promise to deliver to B, who, in turn, sold it to C, leaving B with no net outstanding obligation. C held A's promise to deliver for a period of time, either making a profit or loss depending on the price fluctuation, and finally sold it to individual D. C thus bought a promise to deliver, but resold it, so his net position in the market is zero. C joined the 99 percent of the traders who never take part in the delivery process. Many individuals like B and C could be shown, but only two are included here to keep the example simple.

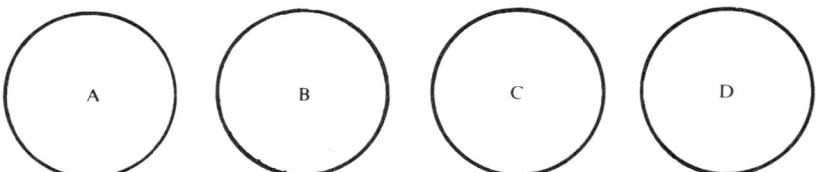

Now, let's assume the contract expiration date has arrived. A still has a promise to deliver outstanding. He has not repurchased it because he has decided to become part of the one percent who fulfill their contractual obligation by actually making delivery. He gives notice to the commodity clearing house and transports the beans to a contract-designated warehouse. The clearing house then gives notice of delivery to individual D, who is still holding the promise to deliver. D comes to the appropriate warehouse and picks up the beans. D and A never had any direct contact with each other; their dealings were entirely through the clearing house. In fact, none of the people involved ever knew who was on the other side of their contracts. The market is impersonal in that respect.

HEDGING

A function of the futures market is to reduce price risk. That is accomplished by a market operation called *hedging*. *Hedging is protecting oneself against price changes by making a transaction in the futures market that offsets a cash market transaction.* A hedger is trying to protect against an unfavorable price change in the commodity he is producing, processing, or storing. Hedging is possible only when a commodity is traded in both the cash and futures market. If traded in both markets the commodity will have both cash and a futures price. The two prices will differ by approximately the cost of holding the commodity (storage, insurance, interest, etc.) for the time period. Figure 18-6 illustrates this. The shaded area between the two prices is the cost of holding wheat for that time period. As we move from January to July the cost of holding decreases, and the cash and futures prices come closer together. In July, the delivery date for July futures contracts, we would expect the cash and futures price to be the same. Because there are imperfections in our knowledge of market conditions, such a perfect relationship does not always exist. Both prices may fluctuate from the expected relationship if conditions exist that affect the cash market differently from the way they affect the futures market. With grain price uncertainty, hedging can be used to reduce risk by setting the price at harvest time, setting the price of grain stored for future delivery, and fixing the cost of feed grain without taking immediate delivery.

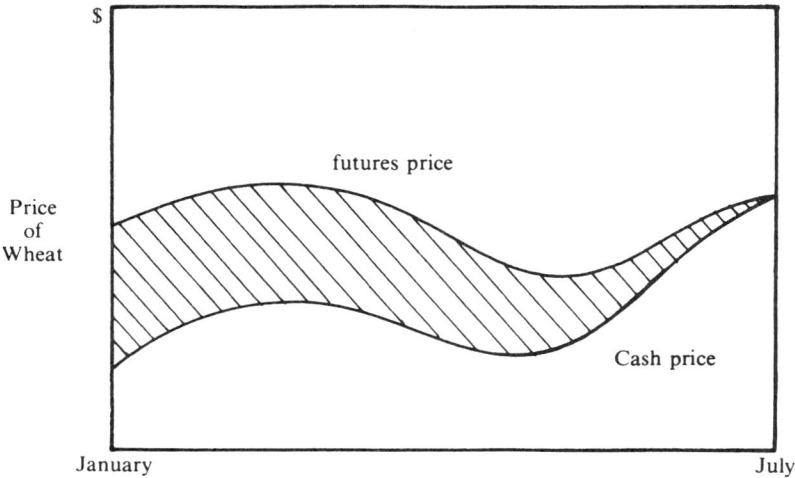

Figure 18-6. Futures and Cash Prices of Wheat Compared.

Using a cattle feeder wishing to establish his cost of feed grain at the beginning of the feeding period, we can show how hedging works. This cattle feeder needs more grain than he produced and wishes to buy the additional feed at the lowest risk. To protect himself against price increases before the cash purchases, he decides to hedge his expected cash purchase of corn. He makes the following transactions: December 1 he buys 5,000 bushels of corn on the July futures at $1.60 for July delivery. The December cash price of corn is $1.40. June 1 he buys 5,000 bushels of corn on the cash market at $2.20. He sells his futures contract at $2.40. The result of his hedging:

Cash market transactions		Futures market transactions	
Dec. cash price	$1.40	Dec. July futures price	$1.60
June cash price	2.20	June July futures price	2.40
Net loss by waiting	.80	Net gain	.80

If that price situation had existed in the two markets, the feeder increased his cost by 80 cents a bushel by waiting until June to buy. However, by hedging through buying a futures contract in December at $1.60 and selling it in June for $2.40, he cleared 80 cents a bushel on the futures market. He successfully protected himself from the big price increase in corn by hedging. Our example shows that the loss in the cash market was exactly offset by the gain in the futures market. Had cash prices increased relatively more than futures prices, he would have had a net cost of corn higher than the $1.40 December price, but less than the June $2.20, so he still would have gained by hedging. However, if prices had fallen in both markets, he would not have gained.

Our example was against a price rise. By selling in the futures market, one could protect against a price fall.

SPECULATION

How was it possible for our livestock feeder to buy a futures contract in December and sell it again in June? He could do that because in December someone was willing to sell a corn contract for July delivery at $1.60. That someone may have bought a July contract earlier for $1.50 and was willing to take a 10 cent gain. In June someone was willing to buy the contract at $2.40 because he expected prices to rise before the delivery date. That may have been another farm producer wishing to protect himself from price decreases. Usually it is not another farm hedger who makes the other half of the transaction. Some people try to make their living by taking advantage of price changes. They are known as speculators. The speculators are the risk underwriters of hedging. Without people willing to speculate on price changes, there could be no hedging. A speculator expecting price increases should buy futures contracts, then sell them later at a higher price; if he expects lower prices he should sell futures contracts, then buy them back at the lower price. A successful speculator can benefit either from price increases or decreases.

The whole concept of futures prices, hedging, and speculation is a complex one, and we have only introduced the subject in these paragraphs.

ENERGY

Farming is one of the biggest users of nonrenewable energy of all sectors of the economy. That may seem surprising, but because there are so many small units, each using such a small part of the total, we do not think of the magnitude of all put together. Nonrenewable energy used by farmers includes gasoline, diesel fuel, natural gas, manufactured gas, and electricity. Other sources of energy used by farmers are animal and human energy, both renewable. The most overlooked source of energy is the sun, which provides the energy for plant photosynthesis.

Farmers' great dependence on nonrenewable energy has resulted from the mechanization of their operations. As mechanically and electrically powered equipment was substituted for animal and human power, the farmers' dependence upon petroleum and electricity increased. Gasoline and diesel fuel were at one time so abundant and cheaply produced that farmers could economically make the substitution. Acres saved from producing hay and grain for horses and mules more than paid for the fuel. Those acres became available for food production and were partly the reason for the abundance of food through the 1930s, 1940s, 1950s and 1960s. In the 1950s and 1960s farmers began to use large amounts of chemical fertilizers. One of the principal sources of nitrogen fertilizer was natural gas processed into anhydrous ammonia.

No other nation became so dependent upon petrochemicals on farms as the United States. In no other place, until just recently, were petrochemicals in such abundant supply and so inexpensive that they could be used without much thought of how much their use added to cost of production.

Gradually energy consumption in the United States exceeded domestic production, and it became necessary to import oil. Abundant South American and Middle East production had been largely from United States owned companies. Until the 1960s we were net exporters of energy. Ninety-six percent of our energy needs were met from the fossil fuels—coal, oil, and natural gas.

In the years of abundance the United States, with less than ten percent of the world's population, consumed about fifty percent of the oil produced. We should have been able to see that we would soon be faced with an energy problem because we had become such heavy consumers, so dependent upon foreign supplies, so dependent upon one type of energy, and so accustomed to low priced energy. Even though energy experts had been expressing concerns, the energy crisis of 1973 came as a jolt to the nation. Agriculture, one of the major users of energy to produce, process, store, and transport goods, was particularly hard hit. Farmers were unaccustomed to fuel and fertilizer shortages. The sudden increase in fuel and fertilizer prices increased farm costs of production. Tables 18-2, 18-3, and 18-4 give use, price, and expenditure information on farm fuels and fertilizer use.

Table 18-2. U.S. Farm Consumption of Gasoline, Diesel Fuel, and Anhydrous Ammonia, 1970 to 1974.

Year	Gasoline (billion gals.)	Diesel Fuel (billion gals.)	Anhydrous Ammonia (million tons)
1970	4.0	1.9	3.5
1971	4.0	2.1	4.0
1972	4.0	2.2	3.6
1973	4.0	2.5	3.3
1974	4.1	2.7	N.A.

Source: 1974 Handbook of Agricultural Charts, U.S.D.A.

Table 18-3. Prices Paid by U.S. Farmers for Fuel and Fertilizer, 1970 to 1975.

Year	Gasoline ($ per gallon)	Diesel Fuel ($ per gallon)	Anhydrous Ammonia ($ per ton)
1970	.30	.18	75.00
1971	.31	.19	79.00
1972	.31	.19	80.00
1973	.33	.21	88.00
1974	.48	.36	183.00

Source: Agricultural Statistics, U.S.D.A.
1974 Handbook of Agricultural Charts, U.S.D.A.
Agricultural Prices, U.S.D.A.

Table 18-4. U.S. Farmer Expenditures for Fuel and Fertilizer as Percentages of Total Expenditures, 1970 to 1974.

Year	Total Farm Production Expenditures (million $)	Gasoline Expenditures (million $)	Percent of total	Diesel Fuel Expenditures (million $)	Percent of total	Anhydrous Ammonia Expenditures (million $)	Percent of total
1970	44,100	1,200	2.7	342	.8	263	.6
1971	47,200	1,240	2.6	399	.8	316	.7
1972	51,900	1,240	2.4	418	.8	288	.6
1973	64,400	1,320	2.0	525	.8	290	.5
1974		1,930		972		604	

Source: Farm Income Situation, U.S.D.A., July, 1974.

ENERGY AND FOOD

The calories used to produce, process, transport, and store proteins and calories in the form of food are energy costs. A primitive society uses fewer calories than it produces. Gathering seeds, nuts, roots, and hunting animals, requires very little besides human energy. Such primitive production methods are very energy-efficient.

Modern agricultural production requires nearly ten calories of energy to produce a single calorie of food. We are subsidizing today's food output from the millions and millions of years' natural storage of the petrochemicals. Figure 18-7 compares the energy subsidies for various types of food production and shows a 60-year (1910-70) trend for the United States energy subsidy of food.

In the United States food system energy is used at every step from the farm to the consumer's table. Steinhart and Steinhart reported that of the total energy used in the food system, about 40 percent was in the agribusiness sub-sector, 25 percent on the farms, and 35 percent in home preparation[2]. Energy use since 1940 has increased threefold in agribusiness and home preparation and fourfold on the farms.

Farmers, by increasing their energy use four times since 1940, have made significant changes in the mix of energy used as shown by these data:

	Percent of energy used	
	1940	1970
Direct use of fuel	56.3	44.1
Electricity	.6	12.1
Fertilizer	10.0	17.9
Irrigation	14.6	6.6
Manufacture of farm equipment	18.5	19.3
	100.0	100.0

The quantity used in each category except irrigation increased. The use of electrical power and fertilizer increased more rapidly than the other categories of energy. Pimentel[3] in 1973 reported on energy inputs to produce an acre of corn. Table 18-5 clearly demonstrates heavy energy input

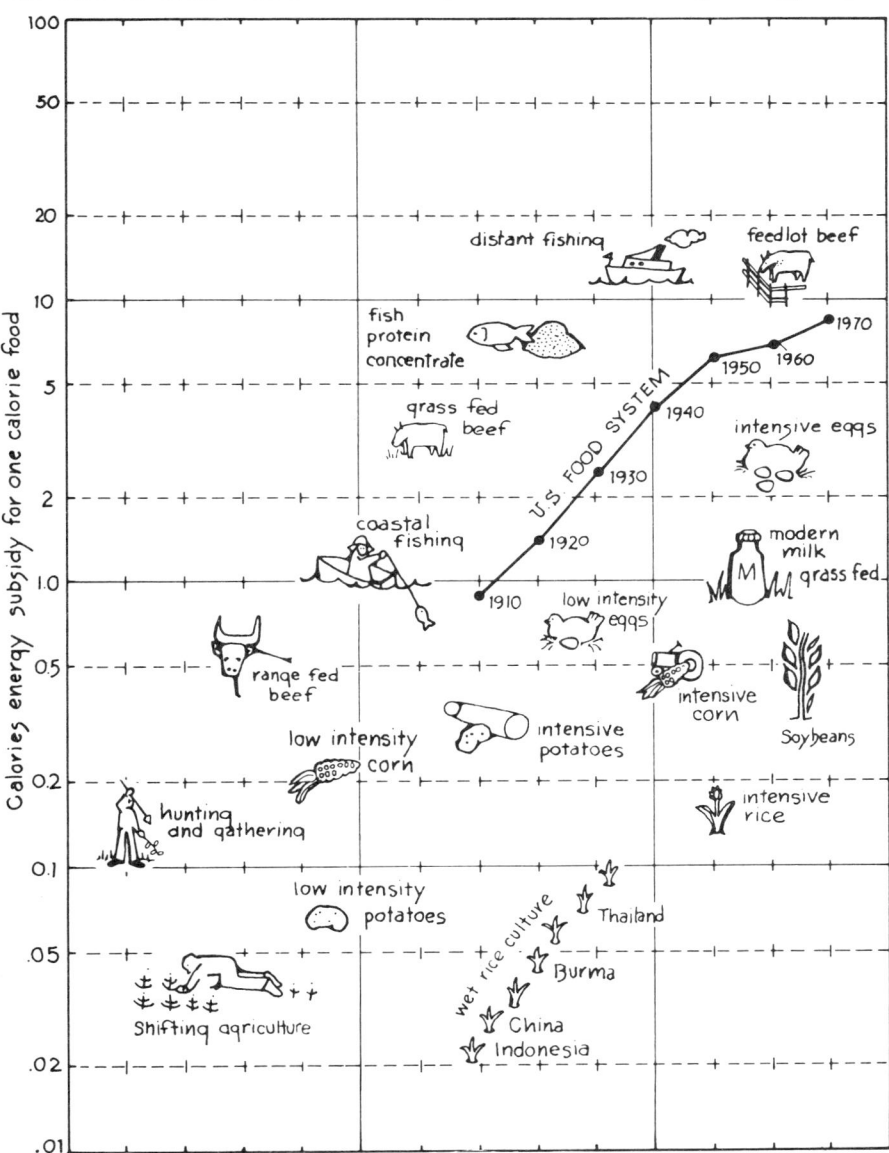

Figure 18-7. Comparison of energy subsidy for types of food production and history of United States energy subsidy of food.

From ENERGY, SOURCES, USE, AND ROLE IN HUMAN AFFAIRS by Carol E. Steinhart and John S. Steinhart. © 1974 by Wadsworth Publishing Company, Inc., Belmont, California 94002. Reprinted by permission of the publisher, Duxbury Press.

through nitrogen fertilizer from 1945 to 1970. The other rapidly increasing category was electricity. During the 25 years energy-use efficiency declined. Corn yields increased 2.38 times, but energy used to produce it increased 3.1 times. In 1945 one calorie of input produced 3.7 calories of corn; in 1970, one produced 2.8.

Table 18-5. Percent of Total Energy Inputs by Categories to Produce an Acre of Corn, 1945 and 1970.[1]

	Percent of Total Energy Used	
	1945	1970
Labor	1.4	.2
Machinery	19.4	14.5
Gasoline	58.7	27.5
Nitrogen	6.4	32.5
Phosphorus	1.1	1.6
Potassium	.5	2.2
Seed	3.7	2.3
Irrigation	2.0	1.2
Insecticides	0	.4
Herbicides	0	.4
Drying	1.1	4.1
Electricity	3.5	10.7
Transportation	2.2	2.4
Total	100.0	100.0
Energy yield ÷ Energy input	3.7	2.8

[1]This table is based on average United States data. One or more of the energy inputs may not be used in some areas.
Source: Pimental, David, "Energy Crisis and Crop Production," in *Energy and Agriculture: Research Implications, Seminar Proceedings*, edited by Lloyd Fischer and Arlo Biere, North Central Regional Strategy Committee on Natural Resource Development, 1973.

It is clear that had we measured farm efficiency by total energy rather than labor input, the conclusions of Chapter 2 would have been very different. Rather than saying productivity had increased we would have said productivity of United States farming had decreased. As energy becomes scarce and costly we, of course, will have to seek ways to improve that input-output ratio. Energy use could become a measure of farm efficiency rather than labor use. It should also be clear that farmers, particularly in such lines of production with high energy requirements as feedlot operations and intensive crop production, will have a new management problem in controlling energy costs. Energy conservation is not only a national problem, but an individual producer one. The survival of individual businesses may depend on how well an operator handles energy use when both its use and its price are increasing rapidly.

INTERNATIONAL TRADE

Foreign trade in farm products is essential to the economic well-being of farmers and consumers in the United States. It is estimated the crop production of one of each five U.S. acres is exported. Aggregate demand for farm products consists of two parts: domestic and export. A change in the amount exported significantly affects farm prices and incomes, as we shall see when we look at the big export sales of 1973. The consumer benefits from foreign trade by increasing the range of choices available and through cheaper prices. Among farm products imported and not produced in the United States are coffee, tea, bananas, cocoa, and many spices. Among the main farm products imported that are supplementary to domestic production are beef, pork, and sugar. Importation increases domestic supply, thus reducing the price for producers and to consumers. We will explore that idea further after looking at the significance of foreign agricultural trade.

THE IMPORTANCE OF FOREIGN TRADE TO UNITED STATES AGRICULTURE

The United States has the largest volume of foreign trade in agricultural products of any nation. We are the biggest exporter and the second largest importer of agricultural products. The volume of United States trade is given in Table 18-6. The exports of agricultural products has increased nearly fourfold since 1960. The biggest increase was in 1973 when large grain sales were made to the Soviet Union and People's Republic of China. Imports of agricultural products, although increasing, are doing so at a slower rate than total imports. Note that in every year agricultural exports exceed imports, meaning that agriculture helps finance the import of other items such as iron ore, copper, industrial products, and oil.

Table 18-6. Foreign Trade in Agricultural Products, 1960-74.

Year	Exports (in million dollars)			Imports (in million dollars)		
	Total	Agriculture	Percent of Total	Total	Agriculture	Percent of Total
1960	20,375	4,832	24	15,014	3,824	25
1965	27,135	6,229	23	21,283	4,087	19
1970	42,590	7,259	17	39,756	5,700	15
1971	43,492	7,693	18	45,516	5,823	13
1972	48,876	9,401	19	55,282	6,467	12
1973	69,121	17,676	26	68,656	8,383	12

Source: United States Foreign Agricultural Trade Statistical Report, Calendar Year 1973, U.S.D.A.

The principal export products are wheat, corn, cotton, tobacco, and soybeans (Tables 18-7 and 18-8). Foreign trade is more vital to the producers of those products than to many other producers. On a volume basis for those five commodities we see the same rapid increase in exports. The exports of wheat and corn more than doubled during the three years. The very heavy exports were possible because of large stocks carried over in the United States from previous years. As shown in Table 18-9, the domestic stocks in wheat and corn have been greatly lowered by the heavy exports.

Table 18-7. Leading U.S. Agricultural Exports, 1971 to 1973.

Product	Value of Exports 1971	(in millions of dollars). 1972	1973
Wheat	1,005	1,366	4,042
Soybeans	1,326	1,508	2,757
Corn	741	1,234	2,825
Cotton	583	503	929
Tobacco	496	672	714

Source: United States Foreign Agricultural Trade Statistical Report, 1973.

Table 18.8. Leading U.S. Agricultural Exports, 1971 to 1973.

Product	1971 Production	Export	Percent Exported	1972[a] Production	Export	Percent Exported	1973[a] Production	Export	Percent Exported
Wheat (mil. bu.)	1,618	596	36.8	1,545	783	50.7	1,711	1,374	80.3
Soybeans (mil. bu.)	1,176	424	36.1	1,283	441	34.4	1,567	486	31.0
Corn (mil. bu.)	5,641	506	9.0	5,553	880	15.8	5,643	1,305	23.1
Cotton (mil. bales)	10.5	4.1	39.0	13.6	3.1	22.8	12.9	5.4	41.9
Tobacco (mil. lbs.)	1,705	504	29.6	1,751	635	36.3	1,743	639	36.7

[a] The high portion exported was possible by depleting stocks carried over.

Source: Agricultural Statistics, 1973. United States Foreign Agricultural Trade Statistical Report, Calendar year 1973, Crop Production.

Table 18-9. Domestic Stocks, April 1, 1971 to 1974.

Product	Million Bushels			
	1971	1972	1973	1974
Wheat	683	669	566	364
Corn	3,380	3,340	4,469	2,858

Source: Grain Stocks, U.S.D.A., 1974.

The heavy export demand has increased the aggregate demand (domestic plus foreign) for food and feed grains. The result has been substantial increases in prices of the commodities, as shown in Table 18.10. A decrease in foreign demand could have a similar reverse effect.

Table 18-10. Commodity Prices, Average, for the United States, 1971 to 1974.

Product	Average Annual Price			
	1971[a]	1972[a]	1973[a]	1974[a]
Wheat (bu.)	$1.34	$1.77	$4.20	$4.87
Corn (bu.)	1.08	1.29	2.18	3.32
Soybeans (bu.)	3.03	4.13	5.14	7.44

[a] 1971 and 1972 are annual averages. 1973 and 1974 are November 15 averages.
Source: Agricultural Statistics, 1973.
Agricultural Prices, November, 1974.

The principal foreign markets for agricultural products have been Japan, The Netherlands, West Germany, Canada, Italy, and the United Kingdom. In 1973 not only did those nations make substantial increases in their imports of United States agricultural commodities, but two communist nations entered the market in a big way. The Soviet Union bought nearly one billion dollars worth of farm products, primarily grain. Similarly, People's Republic of China made big grain purchases in the United States, nearly 500 million dollars worth (Table 18-11).

Table 18-11. Principal Markets for United States Agricultural Products, 1971 to 1973.

Country	Value of U.S. Agricultural Exports, in Millions of Dollars		
	1971	1972	1973
Japan	1,215	1,163	2,997
The Netherlands	550	616	1,241
West Germany	590	607	1,181
Canada	785	805	1,034
U.S.S.R.	12	136	916
Italy	247	306	674
United Kingdom	472	430	616
Peoples Rep. of China	—	61	575

Source: Agricultural Statistics, 1973.
United States Foreign Agricultural Trade Statistical Report, Calendar Year 1973.

The data presented clearly show how important foreign trade is to United States farmers and how changes in foreign trade can influence the domestic market. In the next section we see why international trade arises.

WHY NATIONS TRADE

Trade, whether it is between two neighbors on adjacent farms or between individuals living in the United States and Brazil, takes place because of differences in individual ability to produce goods. Each has unique resources and abilities that permit him to do a better job on one type of production than another. If there were no trade, each of us would have to produce everything. Trade permits each to specialize in producing what he can produce best. Through specialization the group, a family, tribe, or nation, can produce more goods than if each were self-sufficient; output is thus increased because of differences in the productive capacities of natural resources and skills among individuals.

The most obvious natural influence on production is temperature. Bananas grow in Illinois only in a greenhouse at very high cost. Wheat does not grow well in the tropics. Grain sorghum can be grown under drier conditions than corn. Some plants can tolerate greater soil acidity than others. Cattle and sheep do best where there are large quantities of roughage. Swine and poultry do best where there is grain. Thus we find that geographical areas begin to specialize in certain types of production: the Great Plains in wheat and sorghum, the Corn Belt in corn and soybeans, the South in cotton, Florida in citrus fruits.

Differences in human skills as a result of training, education, tradition, experience, or temperament, also lead to specialization. Some of us seem to do carpentry best, others mechanical work, others animal care, others accounting, and so forth.

When an individual or a group produces a product, the resources used cannot produce anything else. Producing a high cost good means giving up a low cost good. For example, an Iowa farmer planting a field of cotton cannot plant that field to corn. The Iowa farmer gives up a high yielding crop to produce a low yielding crop. He would do better to produce corn, let an east Texas farmer produce the cotton, and then trade. Not only will both farmers fare better, but we all will because with specialization we will have a greater combined output of corn and cotton than if each produced both.

COMPARATIVE ADVANTAGE

In our previous examples we have shown how it pays to specialize in production and enter into trade when individuals or areas have an advantage in producing a particular product. But even when an individual or area appears to be at a disadvantage in producing all products, it will pay to specialize. For example, Iowa has higher yields for both wheat and corn than has North Dakota. Iowa has an absolute advantage for producing both. Yet we can observe that North Dakota has tended to specialize in wheat and Iowa in corn. Why?

That is explained by the economic *principles of comparative advantage*. Since we are explaining why foreign trade occurs, we will use an example between two nations. However, keep in mind that it also explains why individuals within a nation specialize in production, then trade among themselves with everyone gaining.

Let us take Japan, our best market for farm products, and the United States as our example, with just two products, soybeans and transistor radios. Both nations can produce both, but at different costs. If we assume that the United States produces both more cheaply than Japan, it would at first appear that there would be little incentive for Japan to produce either. In that case the United States has an absolute advantage in producing both radios and soybeans. If the United States can produce soybeans more efficiently than radios, it would have a comparative advantage in producing soybeans over transistor radios. Japan would have an absolute disadvantage for producing both, but there is a comparative advantage for transistor radios over soybeans in Japan.

In Table 18-12 we illustrate the principle of comparative advantage. The United States can produce both soybeans and radios at a lower cost than Japan. In soybean production the United States is twice as efficient as Japan. In radio production, the United States is but one and one-half times more efficient. The United States is, relative to Japan, more efficient in producing soybeans, so the United States will use its resources to produce soybeans and leave radio production to Japan. This is an extension of the equi-cost concept (product-product) discussed in Chapter 9. Each nation will try to use its resources where they will return most. This leads to specialization and foreign trade.

Table 18-12. Comparison of Assumed Cost of Producing Soybeans and Transistor Radios in the United States and Japan.

	Per Unit Cost of Production	
	Soybeans	Radios
United States	$2.00	$10.00
Japan	4.00	15.00

Of course our example is too simple. Nations, like individuals, are not motivated only by economic maximization. Political and cultural conditions often outweigh economic considerations in production decisions. Also, there are costs involved in foreign trade itself—transportation, inspection, commissions—that may offset the lower production costs. However, if nations wish to optimize their economic well-being, they will use resources where the returns are greatest—that is, follow the principle of comparative advantage.

RESTRAINT OF FOREIGN TRADE

Although we can show that trade between individuals and between nations results in improved economic well-being, there are many pressures to restrict foreign trade. Why? The "common sense" conclusion is that imports of goods we can and do produce are bad. The producer of watches wants watch imports restricted, oil producers want oil imports restricted, and livestock producers want livestock product imports restricted. Great pressure is brought on Congress to impose trade restrictions.

Arguments used to support the case for restricting foreign trade include:

1. To maintain self sufficiency. Fear that future wars will cut off the supply of commodities vital to the country cause nations to maintain production of some products at very high costs.
2. To guarantee a strong national defense. That argument has often been used to protect the United States precision instrument industry.
3. To protect labor from cheap foreign labor.
4. To keep the United States dollar at home.
5. To protect infant industries.
6. To reduce domestic unemployment.
7. To yield revenue.
8. To retaliate against trade restrictions of other nations.

The first two arguments go beyond economics and are largely political arguments. Self-sufficiency and a strong national defense through trade restrictions can be achieved only at increased costs of production and higher prices to the consumers. At some point the economic cost outweighs the benefits to be gained. Also, the argument can be stretched to cover products not closely related to either objective. For example, just after World War II the list of products vital to national defense as passed by Congress included blue cheese.

The other six arguments for restraint of trade are more nearly economic ones. It is easy to find one or more apparently valid reasons to restrict trade.

Keep in mind the reason producers in any nation need protection is because they are trying to produce a product for which someone else has the comparative advantage. Using restrictive trade measures against another nation not only hurts that nation, but also the one imposing the restrictions. Anything that keeps producers from producing goods in which they have a comparative advantage reduces economic well-being. Restriction of trade in watches makes all consumers pay a higher price for watches. The real income of all purchasers of watches is reduced by the price increase. Only the owners of the watch-producing firms gain. Their gain comes as a transfer of income from all who pay the higher prices. Whether it is the manufacturers of watches, refiners of oil, textile manufacturers, or beef cattle producers, the result is always the same, the producer of the product may gain temporarily, but everyone else loses from restricting trade.

TAXES

Throughout recorded history man has been taxed to support government and to finance public services. Among the first functions of government were to establish order (raise and maintain police forces and armies), provide roads, establish a system of protecting property rights, and provide schools. An effective tax is one that is easily collected, related to the citizen's ability to pay, and related to the benefits received by the citizen. In frontier America, land was the principal wealth held by citizens. It was a wealth not easily concealed. The citizen's income and ability to pay taxes was closely related to the amount of land owned. Many of the public services were related to protecting and enhancing the value of land so a tax against land directly benefitted the payer. Most of the public services were provided by state and local governments. The property tax became their principal source of revenue and has continued to be so.

The federal government at first relied largely upon import and excise taxes as sources of revenue. As the federal government assumed a greater role in providing public services, those sources became inadequate. Personal and corporate income taxes were adopted to provide most of the federal revenue.

State governments in this century have also sought new ways to raise public revenue. They have used the income, sales, gasoline, tobacco, and alcoholic beverage taxes as their principal sources of public financing.

Local governments have continued to rely primarily on property taxes. As the portion of personal property in the form of intangibles increased (stocks and bonds, which are easily concealed from taxing authorities), several states have shifted away from personal property taxes for local government. That has shifted the tax burden for counties, townships, school districts, and towns to real estate.

Agriculture is subject to all those taxes. Farmers and agribusinessmen pay federal income taxes—personal and corporate—if their business is incorporated. State income taxes are levied and collected very similarly to the way federal income taxes are. Today a few cities and counties have adopted local income taxes. Among farmers, as well as among tax experts, income taxes have been accepted as one of the best methods of taxation. If progressive, the tax rate increases as income increases so it is related to ability to pay. Also the individual against whom the tax is levied has to pay it. He is usually unable to shift the tax to someone else.

Local government (in rural America usually the school district and the county) is the closest to the people. County and school district operations are mostly financed from property taxes, the tax most familiar to farmers. It is collected and spent locally. They know what they are getting from their property tax dollar. When farmers complain about taxes, they usually have property taxes in mind.

THE PROPERTY TAX

The property tax is the most important source of local government revenue. Nearly all local government revenue comes from property taxes, although its portion of the total has declined over the years, from 51 percent in 1902 to 17 percent in 1970. Local governments have collected a smaller share of the total taxes over the years as shown in Table 18-13.

Table 18-13. Percent of Tax Collections by Level of Government, 1902, 1942, and 1970.

Year	Level of Government			Total
	Federal	State	Local	
1902	38 percent	11 percent	51 percent	100 percent
1942	59	19	22	100
1970	63	20	17	100

Source: Financing State and Local Government in Kansas, 1972 Edition, Kansas Cooperative Extension Service.

The property tax is not used by the federal government and only slightly by the states. The 1970 source of taxes by level of government is shown in Table 18-14.

Table 18-14. The Source of Taxes by Level of Government, 1970.

Source of tax	Level of Government		
	Federal	State	Local
Individual income	62 percent	19 percent	4 percent
Corporate income	23	8	—
Sales and Gross receipts	13	57	8
Property	—	2	85
Other	2	14	3

Source: Financing State and Local Government in Kansas, 1972 Edition, Kansas Cooperative Extension Service.

The Department of Agriculture reports that state and local governments levied $2.77 billion taxes against farm real estate in the United States in 1972. That was 4.1 percent above 1971 and the thirtieth consecutive year farm real estate taxes had increased. The average United States levy in 1972 was $2.74 per acre. The per acre tax has risen continuously since the 1930s. However, farm real estate taxes have recently risen less rapidly than the value of the real estate. The tax per $100 real estate value has remained nearly constant since 1950. In recent years real estate taxes have been about four percent of gross farm income for the whole United States.

Property taxes are important to farmers. They affect the amount of disposable income left to farm families. They determine the quantity and quality of local public services.

In studying the property tax, tax experts have found certain characteristics of this tax. One of the characteristics is the difficulty to shift the *incidence* of the farm real estate tax. *Incidence* refers to where the tax burden finally rests; who finally pays the tax. Often the individual or business initially responsible for paying the tax can shift a part or all of it to someone else. For example, a tax on crude oil will be treated as an added cost of producing gasoline and will be added to the price of gasoline. Consumers who continue to buy the same quantity of gasoline after the price increase pay the full tax. The producer of the gasoline serves only as the tax collector. However, if the consumer buys less gasoline after the price increases, the producer loses revenue and pays at least a part of the tax. Similarly a tax on real estate, when it is rental property, may be passed on as higher rent. However, in farming, much of the real estate is owned by the farmer himself. In the competitive market, he has little influence upon the price of his products, so the incidence of the farm real estate tax remains with the farmer.

The real estate tax is based on the value of the land, not on the income earned from the land. In years of low incomes farm real estate taxes remain at the established level. Several consecutive low income years make the real estate tax particularly burdensome. During the Great Depression real estate was often auctioned to pay back taxes.

In the rural counties much of the real estate is held by farmers; yet a majority of the citizens may be nonfarm wage and salary earners. Their average income may exceed that of the farmers. They share in the public services based on the real estate taxes, very little of which they pay. Farmers in such instances believe they bear too heavy a tax burden.

Despite such complaints the real estate tax remains the basis for financing local governments.

SUGGESTED READINGS

Clark, Fred E., and Clark, Carrie P. *Principles of Marketing*, 3rd Edition. The Macmillan Company, 1947, Chapters 6, 17, and 20.

Fischer, Lloyd, and Biere, Arlo, Editors. *Energy Use in the U.S. Food System*, in Energy and Agriculture: Research Implications, Seminar Proceedings. North Central Regional Strategy Committee on Natural Resource Development, University of Nebraska, 1973.

Hathaway, Dale E. *Government and Agriculture: Public Policy in a Democratic Society*. The Macmillan Company, 1963.

Kohls, Richard L., and Downey, W. David. *Marketing of Agricultural Products*, 4th Edition. The Macmillan Company, 1972, Chapters 3, 7, and 21.

McCoy, John H. *Livestock and Meat Marketing*. The AVI Publishing Company, Ind., 1972, Chapters 10 and 15.

Steinhart, Carol E. and Steinhart, John S. *Energy, Sources, Use, and Role in Human Affairs*. Wadsworth Publishing Co., 1974.

United States Department of Agriculture. *Contours of Change, The Yearbook of Agriculture*, 1970, pages 243 to 320.

ENDNOTES

1. Hathaway, Dale E., *Government and Agriculture: Public Policy in a Democratic Society*. The Macmillan Company, 1963, Chapters 4, 5, and 6.
2. Steinhart, Carol E. and Steinhart, John S., *Energy, Sources, Use and Role in Human Affairs*. Wadsworth Publishing Company, Inc., 1974.
3. Pimentel, David, *"Energy Crisis and Crop Production,"* in *Energy and Agriculture: Research Implications, Seminar Proceedings*, edited by Lloyd Fischer and Arlo Biere, North Central Regional Strategy Committee on Natural Resources Development, 1973.

INDEX

Agribusiness, 9
  processing and distribution, 15
  supplying, 16
Agricultural economics, 4
  related to other areas of knowledge, 5
Agricultural industrialization, 196
Agricultural Marketing Act, 155
Agriculture
  agribusiness, 9
  changing structure of, 13
  defined, 9, 10
  farm, 9
  public service, 16
  resources of the world, 166
  role in economic growth, 164
  structure, 11, 12
Applied economics, 4
Assumptions, 7
  use of, 57, 58
Average physical product
  defined, 53, 55

Bargaining power, 195, 196, 209
Board of trade, 210
Business organization
  business trust, 156
  cooperative corporation, 154
  corporation, 153
  holding company, 156
  incorporated, 149
  joint stock company, 156
  joint venture partnership, 156
  limited partnership, 152
  limited partnership association, 158
  ordinary corporation, 153
  partnership, 152
  sole proprietorship, 151
  tax option corporation, 154
  types, 149, 150
  unincorporated, 149
Business trust, 156

Capper-Volstead Act, 155
Capital, 54, 170, 197
Cash contract for future delivery, 209
Cash cost, 77
Commercialization of farms, 18
Commodity exchange, 210
Comparative advantage, 222, 223

Competition in the market
  monopolistic competition, 129, 131
  monopoly, 129, 130
  oligopoly, 129, 130
  perfect competition, 129, 130
Consumer preference, 23
Consumer sovereignty, 23
Cooperative Marketing Act, 155
Constant substitutibility of factors, 19
Consumption economics, 6
Control of agricultural resources, 196
  capital, 197
  land, 196
  labor, 197
  management, 197
Corporation, 153
  cooperative, 154
  farm, 157
  family, 153
  ordinary, 153
  tax option, 154
Costs, 79
  cash, 77
  computation of, 78
  effect of technology on, 83
  effect of time on, 84
  fixed, 77
  marginal, 78
  noncash, 77
  opportunity, 77
  public services, 85
  variable, 78

Demand, 33
  change in, 36
  factors causing change in, 36
  for agricultural products, 46
  income elasticity of, 38, 39, 40, 41
  law of, 34, 35
  market, 37
  price elasticity of, 41, 42, 43, 44
  schedule, 33
Diminishing marginal rate of factor substitution, 90
Diminishing marginal utility, 25, 26
Diminishing returns, 57
  law of, 57
Diseconomies of scale, 85

Economic control of agriculture, 195
   basis for problem, 195
   farmer alternatives, 198
Economic growth, 164
   capital resource in, 170
   labor resource in, 170
   land resource in, 166
   management in, 171, 172
   role of agriculture, 164, 165
   technology in, 171, 172
Economics, 3
   agricultural, 4
   applied, 5
   a social science, 3
   a study of human behavior, 4
   consumption, 6
   defined, 4
   macro, 6
   micro, 6
   normative, 6, 7
   positive, 6, 7
   production, 6
Economies of scale, 84
Economizing, 3
Education, 188
Effect of a change in input prices on factor-factor combination, 98, 99, 100
Elastic demand, 38, 39, 40, 41, 42, 43
Elasticity
   elastic demand, 38, 39, 40, 41, 42, 43, 44, 45
   income elasticity of demand, 38, 39, 40, 41
   inelastic demand, 42, 43, 44, 45
   price elasticity of demand, 41, 42, 43, 44
   price elasticity of supply, 119, 120
   unit elasticity of demand, 42, 43, 44, 45
Energy, 214
   required for food production, 217
   required to produce corn, 218
Equi-marginal returns, 105
Expansion path
   factor-factor, 101
   product-product, 112
Exports, agricultural, 220

Factor-factor, 87
Factors of production
   capital, 53
   labor, 53
   land, 53
   management, 54
Factor substitution, 87
Family farm, 17
Farm
   commercial, 18
   corporation, 157
   defined, 9
   family, 17
   number of, 14
   number of people on, 14
   prices, 204
   size of, 14
Farm input flow in the market, 126, 127
Farm product flow in the market, 124, 125, 126
Farmers' share of the market-basket, 207
Fixed costs, 77
Fixed resource, 56
Food expenditures, 206
Food marketing bill, 207
Food production trends, 174, 175
   food deficits, 179
   increasing production, 177
Futures market, 209
Future trading, 210

Health facilities, 190
Hedging, 212
Holding company, 156
Horizontal integration, 19
Housing, 190

Imperfect substitutibility of factors, 92
Imports, agricultural, 220
Incidence of tax, 226
Income
   effect of a price change, 36
   elasticity of demand, 38
   factors affecting, 203
   farm, 201, 202
   rural, 188
Incorporated business, 149
Increasing marginal rate of product substitution, 107
Indifference curves, 28, 29
Indivisibility of inputs, 72
Industrialization of farming, 18
Inelastic demand, 43, 44, 45, 46
Inferior goods, 40
Integration
   horizontal, 19
   vertical, 18
International trade, 219
   agricultural exports, 220
   agricultural imports, 220
   arguments for restraint of, 224
   comparative advantage, 222, 223
   effect on prices, 221
   importance of, 219
   in agricultural products, 219
   markets for U.S. products, 221
   restraint of, 223
   why nations trade, 222
Iso-cost line, 90
Iso-product curve, 88
Iso-revenue line, 105

Joint stock company, 156
Joint venture partnership, 156

Labor, 54, 166, 197
Labor productivity, 14
Land, 53, 166, 196
Law of demand, 34, 35
Law of diminishing returns, 57
Law of supply, 115
Least cost combination, 87
Limited partnership, 152
Limited partnership association, 158

Macroeconomics, 6
Malthus theory, 174, 175
Management, 54, 143
    agribusiness, 145, 147
    contrasted to labor, 144
    effect on resource productivity, 144
    farm, 145, 146
    functions, 145
    return to, 148
    role in economic activity, 143
    role in economic growth, 171
Marginal, 24
Marginal cost, 78
Marginal physical product, 56-60
Marginal rate of factor substitution, 88, 89
Marginal rate of product substitution, 106
Marginal utility, 24, 25
Market, 124
    competition, 128
    costs, 206
    demand, 37
    efficiency, 128
    margin, 196, 207
    structure, 128, 129
    supply, 117
Microeconomics, 6
Middlemen, 208
Monopolistic competition, 129, 131
Monopoly, 129, 130
Multiple expectations, 72

Necessary conditions, 70
Noneconomic goals, 74, 75
Normative economics, 6, 7

Oligopoly, 129, 130
Opportunity costs, 77, 105

Partnership, 152
Perfect competition, 129, 130
Perfect complementarity of factors, 92
Point of inflection, 65
Political power, 198
    farmers use, 198

Population
    changes in U.S., 186
    Malthus, 174
    outmigration from farms, 186
    policies, 177
    rural, 186
    world growth, 173
Positive economics, 6, 7
Price, 123, 201
    determination
        under monopolistic competition, 139
        under monopoly, 137
        under oligopoly, 138
        under perfect competition, 133
    effect of change in, 134, 135, 136
    elasticity of demand, 38, 39, 40, 41, 42
    elasticity of supply, 119, 120
    farm, 204, 205
    taker, 129
Product, 28
Product-product, 103
Product-product relationships, 107
    competitive, 107, 108
    complementary, 107, 108
    supplementary, 107, 108
Production economics, 6
Production function, 56
Production possibility curve, 104, 105
Productivity
    constant, 59, 60
    decreasing, 59, 60
    increasing, 59, 60
Profit maximization
    costs, 81, 82
    factor-factor, 93
    factor-product, 65, 66, 67, 68, 69
    product-product, 109, 110, 111, 112
Property tax, 225
Public services, 190

Quality of life, 185

Resource, 28
Rural
    education, 188
    employment, 187
    health facilities, 190
    housing, 190
    income, 188
    population, 186
    public services, 190
    quality of life, 185
    welfare, 185

Sole proprietorship, 151
Stages of production, 63, 64, 66, 70
Structure of agriculture, 11, 12
Speculation, 214

Substitution effect of a price change, 37, 38
Sufficient condition, 70
Superior goods, 41
Supply, 115
    change in, 118
    elasticity of, 119, 120
    law of, 115
    market, 117
    schedule, 115, 116, 117
Supply schedule, 115, 116, 117

Taxes, 224
    incidence of tax, 226
    property tax, 225
    sources of tax, 226
Theory, 5, 6

Unincorporated business, 149
Unit elasticity of demand, 42, 43, 44, 45
Urbanization, 19
Utility, 24
    diminishing marginal, 24, 25
    marginal, 25, 26

Variable costs, 77
Variable resource, 53
Vertical integration, 18

Welfare, 185
World agriculture, 163

Yield maximization, 74